Prophecy Papers

Biblical Prophecy

[Blank Page]

Prophecy Papers

Biblical Prophecy

by

Walter R. Dolen

President of the Becoming-One Church

Copyright © 1989, 2000, 2018 by Walter R. Dolen

This **2018 Expanded Edition** supercedes all previous editions

ISBN: 9781619180499

Portions of the *Prophecy Papers* were first written in 1971-72 and published in 1977 under the title: *The Becoming-One Papers.* An enlarged version appeared in 1989 and again in 1993. The text in this expanded edition is the same as the 2000 year version except an appendix has been added of charts that were included from our website (www.becoming-one.org).

July, 2024 Printing
with clarification for pr198-199
Book cover photos by the author Walter R. Dolen

The *Prophecy Papers* is part of the *BeComing-One Papers*
1993 Cumulative Edition
and subsequent editions

Trade Paper (Year 2000):
ISBN 1-877981-36-2 or 978-1-877981-36-4

Paper (Year 1989):
ISBN: 9781877981012

BeComing-One Publications

https://becoming-one.org/books.htm

PR: Table of Contents

Prophecy Papers. . . . .

PR: Table of Contents. . . . .

PR1: Seed Paper. . . . . PR 1:1 | Pg 13
    Promises and Prophecies. . . . . PR 1:1 | Pg 13
        Concerning Mankind and Israel. . . . . PR 1:1 | Pg 13
    Physical Promises to Israel. . . . . PR 1:2 | Pg 14
        Abraham. . . . . PR 1:2 | Pg 14
        Isaac. . . . . PR 1:3 | Pg 15
        Jacob (Israel). . . . . PR 1:4 | Pg 16
        Jacob's Name Changed. . . . . PR 1:4 | Pg 16
        Joseph, Ephraim and Manasseh. . . . . PR 1:5 | Pg 17
            Judah. . . . . PR 1:5 | Pg 17
        Fulfillment of Physical Promises. . . . . PR 1:6 | Pg 18
        Moses & Joshua. . . . . PR 1:6 | Pg 18
        Judges. . . . . PR 1:6 | Pg 18
        Samuel, "Make us a King". . . . . PR 1:6 | Pg 18
        Saul. . . . . PR 1:7 | Pg 19
        David. . . . . PR 1:7 | Pg 19
        Solomon. . . . . PR 1:8 | Pg 20
        Jeroboam. . . . . PR 1:9 | Pg 21
        Israel and Judah Split. . . . . PR 1:10 | Pg 22
        Israel Scattered. . . . . PR 1:10 | Pg 22
        Judah Scattered. . . . . PR 1:11 | Pg 23
        Promises That Did and Did Not Come True. . . . . PR 1:11 | Pg 23
    Spiritual Promises of God. . . . . PR 1:13 | Pg 25
        Seed. . . . . PR 1:13 | Pg 25
        Promises To The *Seed*. . . . . PR 1:13 | Pg 25
        Other Promises. . . . . PR 1:15 | Pg 27
        Judah and the Scepter. . . . . PR 1:16 | Pg 28
        Promises to David. . . . . PR 1:16 | Pg 28
        Conditions. . . . . PR 1:17 | Pg 29
        Branch. . . . . PR 1:18 | Pg 30
        Christ: The Branch, The King, The Savior. . . . . PR 1:19 | Pg 31
        Christ versus Satan; David versus Saul. . . . . PR 1:19 | Pg 31
        Spiritual Seed of Abraham. . . . . PR 1:20 | Pg 32
        Spiritual Jews. . . . . PR 1:20 | Pg 32
        Spiritual Virgins. . . . . PR 1:20 | Pg 32
        Christ The Mediator. . . . . PR 1:20 | Pg 32
        Summarize: Jews and Israelites = Christians. . . . . PR 1:21 | Pg 33
    Notes for PR1. . . . . PR 1:22 | Pg 34
        Three Orders/Divisions. . . . . PR 1:22 | Pg 34
        Ur of the Chaldeans. . . . . PR 1:22 | Pg 34
        Ur of Abraham located near Haran in Mesopotamia. . . PR 1:23 | Pg 35
        Ur of the Chaldeans by the river Chebar. . . . . PR 1:23 | Pg 35

- Land of Abraham's Nativity was the real Ur of the Chaldeans .... PR 1:24 | Pg 36
  - Ebla Tablets' Proof............................. PR 1:25 | Pg 37
  - Ur was in the Territory of Haran................ PR 1:26 | Pg 38
  - Chaldeans Language Confusion.................... PR 1:26 | Pg 38
  - Babylonians and the Hittites.................... PR 1:27 | Pg 39
    - Summarize..................................... PR 1:27 | Pg 39

PR2: Beast-System Paper.................................. PR 2:1 | Pg 41
- System of the Beast................................ PR 2:1 | Pg 41
- Four Beasts.. PR 2:2 | Pg 42
- Four Beasts = Four Kingdoms........................ PR 2:2 | Pg 42
- Seven Heads.. PR 2:3 | Pg 43
- Seventh Head With Ten Horns........................ PR 2:3 | Pg 43
- Ten Horns = Ten Kingdoms or Nations................ PR 2:4 | Pg 44
  - Ten crowns...................................... PR 2:4 | Pg 44
- Ten to Seven....................................... PR 2:4 | Pg 44
    - Eighth Head?.................................. PR 2:5 | Pg 45
- First End-of-the-age Beast......................... PR 2:6 | Pg 46
- Second End-of-the-age Beast........................ PR 2:6 | Pg 46
  - Image of the Beast.............................. PR 2:6 | Pg 46
- 1260 Days: the Last Days Before Christ Rules....... PR 2:6 | Pg 46
- Four Beasts or Kingdoms............................ PR 2:7 | Pg 47
- Nebuchadnezzar Until The Stone..................... PR 2:8 | Pg 48
- Fourth Beast....................................... PR 2:9 | Pg 49
- Identity of the First Three Beasts................. PR 2:9 | Pg 49
  - Image... PR 2:9 | Pg 49
  - Tree.. PR 2:9 | Pg 49
  - Four Beasts..................................... PR 2:9 | Pg 49
  - Seven-Head, Ten-Horn Beast...................... PR 2:9 | Pg 49
  - Ram, Goat....................................... PR 2:9 | Pg 49
  - Greek Culture................................... PR 2:11 | Pg 51
- Babylon — The First Beast.......................... PR 2:11 | Pg 51
- Media-Persia — The Second Beast.................... PR 2:11 | Pg 51
- Greece With Four heads — Third Beast............... PR 2:11 | Pg 51
- Six Heads = Babylon, Media-Persia, And Greece...... PR 2:12 | Pg 52
- Who Or What Is The Seventh Head?................... PR 2:12 | Pg 52
- Mean and Base Horn................................. PR 2:12 | Pg 52
- Unity Power.. PR 2:13 | Pg 53
- Kings of the North and South....................... PR 2:14 | Pg 54
- Identity of the Fourth Beast....................... PR 2:14 | Pg 54
- Identified by the Number of Nations Unified........ PR 2:15 | Pg 55
- When Is The Beast Set Up?.......................... PR 2:15 | Pg 55
- Daily Sacrifice.................................... PR 2:15 | Pg 55
  - Abomination of Desolation....................... PR 2:16 | Pg 56
- 1290 Days.. PR 2:17 | Pg 57
- 2300 Evenings and Mornings Sacrifices or 1150 Days .... PR 2:18 | Pg 58
- 1335th Day... PR 2:18 | Pg 58

PR3: Beast-Man Paper.................................... PR 3:1 | Pg 61

Individual Beast.................................... PR 3:1 | Pg 61
    System of the Beast versus Beast-man......... PR 3:1 | Pg 61
Last False-Christ................................... PR 3:1 | Pg 61
    Abomination of Desolation.................. PR 3:1 | Pg 61
Little Horn... PR 3:2 | Pg 62
Man with the Number Six Hundred Sixty Six – 666.... PR 3:2 | Pg 62
Beast-man = Last Antichrist = Last False-Prophet = Little Horn = Man of Sin = Abomination of Desolation = Man with the Number 666
.... PR 3:3 | Pg 63
    Metonymical Names for the Same Person..... PR 3:3 | Pg 63
    Antichrist................................ PR 3:4 | Pg 64
    69 Weeks.................................. PR 3:5 | Pg 65
Mark of the Beast.................................. PR 3:6 | Pg 66
    Monetary System........................... PR 3:6 | Pg 66
Beast and Church in the 1260 Days.................. PR 3:6 | Pg 66
Tree of Daniel..................................... PR 3:8 | Pg 68
    Kingdom of the Enemy...................... PR 3:8 | Pg 68
Band of Iron and Brass............................. PR 3:8 | Pg 68
Who or What Is the Stump?.......................... PR 3:9 | Pg 69
Kingdom of Satan................................... PR 3:9 | Pg 69

PR4: God's Wrath, What is it?.......................... PR 4:1 | Pg 71
    Definition of God's Wrath..................... PR 4:1 | Pg 71
    Does this mean that God has purposely made the Bible difficult?
.... PR 4:2 | Pg 72
    Love Is................................... PR 4:2 | Pg 72
    Christ Comes to *Save* Mankind................. PR 4:3 | Pg 73
    Righteous Judgment........................... PR 4:3 | Pg 73
    How Will God Repay Their Deeds?.............. PR 4:4 | Pg 74
        What is God's Wrath?...................... PR 4:5 | Pg 75
    Spiritual Influence.......................... PR 4:6 | Pg 76
        Wine...................................... PR 4:6 | Pg 76
    Pride.. PR 4:7 | Pg 77
    Destruction Comes From God Himself?.......... PR 4:8 | Pg 78
    Anger of the Lord............................ PR 4:9 | Pg 79

PR5: Last War and God's Wrath.......................... PR 5:1 | Pg 81
    Faulty Translations.......................... PR 5:1 | Pg 81
    Aorist Verbs & Other Timeless Verbs.......... PR 5:1 | Pg 81
    Simultaneous Events.......................... PR 5:2 | Pg 82
    Day of the Lord.............................. PR 5:3 | Pg 83
    Here Some, There Some........................ PR 5:4 | Pg 84
    Higher Meaning............................... PR 5:4 | Pg 84
    Great City................................... PR 5:5 | Pg 85
    Metonymical Names For The Antitypical Beast, Or The Kingdom of Satan....................................... PR 5:6 | Pg 86
    Seventy Years And Seventy Weeks.............. PR 5:7 | Pg 87
    Wine Cup..................................... PR 5:7 | Pg 87
    Cyrus.. PR 5:7 | Pg 87
    Antitypical Seventy Years.................... PR 5:8 | Pg 88
        483 Years or 69 weeks..................... PR 5:9 | Pg 89

7 Years Cut in Half.	PR 5:10	Pg 90
Two Witnesses In Their 1260 Days.	PR 5:10	Pg 90
To Review.	PR 5:11	Pg 91
Old Wars as Pattern of the Last War.	PR 5:12	Pg 92
All Nations Destroyed.	PR 5:12	Pg 92
Pattern of the Last War Throughout Bible.	PR 5:13	Pg 93
Day of Trouble.	PR 5:13	Pg 93
Wicked and Evil Ones.	PR 5:13	Pg 93
All Evil and War Destroyed.	PR 5:13	Pg 93
How Long Will The War Last?.	PR 5:13	Pg 93
Wrath: All At Once..	PR 5:14	Pg 94
Greater Detail.	PR 5:15	Pg 95
Angel and Angels of Revelation.	PR 5:15	Pg 95
Things We Should Understand.	PR 5:16	Pg 96
God's Throne.	PR 5:16	Pg 96
Seals, Trumpets Plagues, and 1260 Days.	PR 5:17	Pg 97
Wrath All at Once..	PR 5:18	Pg 98
No War Or Evil Will Be Around After The Kingdom of God Takes Over:.	PR 5:18	Pg 98
	PR 5:18	Pg 98
Summarize.	PR 5:19	Pg 99
Similarities of the Seals, Trumpets, and Vials.	PR 5:20	Pg 100
Seals.	PR 5:20	Pg 100
First Seal.	PR 5:20	Pg 100
Four Horses.	PR 5:20	Pg 100
God's Power Over the World's Kingdoms.	PR 5:21	Pg 101
Four Winds; Four Horses.	PR 5:22	Pg 102
Four Horns of Brazen Altar.	PR 5:22	Pg 102
First Seal..	PR 5:22	Pg 102
Second Seal.	PR 5:22	Pg 102
Third Seal.	PR 5:22	Pg 102
Fourth Seal.	PR 5:23	Pg 103
Fifth Seal.	PR 5:23	Pg 103
Sixth Seal.	PR 5:23	Pg 103
Seventh Seal.	PR 5:24	Pg 104
Trumpets..	PR 5:24	Pg 104
First Trumpet.	PR 5:25	Pg 105
Second Trumpet.	PR 5:25	Pg 105
Third Trumpet.	PR 5:26	Pg 106
Fourth Trumpet..	PR 5:26	Pg 106
Fifth Trumpet.	PR 5:27	Pg 107
Sixth Trumpet.	PR 5:28	Pg 108
Seventh Trumpet.	PR 5:30	Pg 110
Vials.	PR 5:30	Pg 110
What Is Important.	PR 5:31	Pg 111
Notes for PR5.	PR 5:32	Pg 112
Church In Symbolism.	PR 5:32	Pg 112
PR6: God's Wrath: An Outline.	PR 6:1	Pg 115
Outline Review.	PR 6:1	Pg 115

PR7: End of the Age.................................... PR 7:1 | Pg 123
   End of the Old Age; Beginning of the New Age...... PR 7:1 | Pg 123
   Father Only Knows the Date?..................... PR 7:1 | Pg 123
   We Will Know the Date......................... PR 7:1 | Pg 123
   Principles of Biblical Study..................... PR 7:1 | Pg 123
   Christ Given All The Power..................... PR 7:2 | Pg 124
      Christians to Receive Power............... PR 7:2 | Pg 124
      Christians to Receive Knowledge.......... PR 7:2 | Pg 124
   Church Knows Hidden Secrets.................... PR 7:3 | Pg 125
     Notice the scriptures about the Church knowing the hidden secrets
     .... PR 7:3 | Pg 125
   Spirit Reveals Hidden Wisdom and Knowledge...... PR 7:4 | Pg 126
      Spirit Reveals........................... PR 7:4 | Pg 126
      Times known............................. PR 7:4 | Pg 126
      Daniel's Vision.......................... PR 7:4 | Pg 126
   Mistakes of Others' Interpretation.................. PR 7:5 | Pg 127
   If we won't know what day the Lord comes back, why watch?
   .... PR 7:6 | Pg 128
   Correct the Translation......................... PR 7:6 | Pg 128
   As in Noah's Day so at the Coming of the Lord...... PR 7:7 | Pg 129
   Wicked Servant Will Not Know the Time........... PR 7:7 | Pg 129
   Christians Not Asleep......................... PR 7:8 | Pg 130
      Christians not Asleep.................... PR 7:8 | Pg 130
   All Must Watch.............................. PR 7:8 | Pg 130
   Times of the Gentiles.......................... PR 7:9 | Pg 131
   End of the Times on a Feast Day.................. PR 7:9 | Pg 131
   Festivals of Israel Pre-Figured the Real Events...... PR 7:10 | Pg 132
   Which Year?................................ PR 7:11 | Pg 133

PR8: Two Witnesses.................................. PR 8:1 | Pg 135
   Elijah will come............................. PR 8:1 | Pg 135
   Two Olive Trees / Two Witnesses.................. PR 8:2 | Pg 136
   Purpose of the Two........................... PR 8:2 | Pg 136
   Anointed Ones.............................. PR 8:3 | Pg 137
   Power of the Two............................ PR 8:3 | Pg 137
   Rain..................................... PR 8:3 | Pg 137
   Elijah is One of the Witnesses.................... PR 8:4 | Pg 138
   Who Is the Other Witness?...................... PR 8:4 | Pg 138
   Two at Christ's Ascension...................... PR 8:4 | Pg 138
   Two at Transfiguration........................ PR 8:5 | Pg 139
   Scripture Together........................... PR 8:5 | Pg 139
   Moses and Elijah............................ PR 8:5 | Pg 139
   Further Proof............................... PR 8:6 | Pg 140
   The Two Witnesses Are Coming In The Spirit Or Antitypical Sense of
     Moses And Elijah........................ PR 8:7 | Pg 141
   Notes for PR8.............................. PR 8:8 | Pg 142
   30 Years................................... PR 8:8 | Pg 142

PR9: Seven Churches of Revelation..................... PR 9:1 | Pg 143
   Days at Hand When Book Fully Opened........... PR 9:1 | Pg 143

Book to All the Churches in Christ.	PR 9:1	Pg 143
Book Speaks to the End Time and Thereafter.	PR 9:1	Pg 143
Chapters Two and Three Speak of the Condition of Today's Church	PR 9:2	Pg 144

PR10: Great Falling Away . . . . PR 10:1 | Pg 147
    Antitypical Ezekiel. . . . . PR 10:2 | Pg 148
    Great Falling Away.. . . . . PR 10:2 | Pg 148
    390 & 40 Days . . . . PR 10:3 | Pg 149
    Forty Days /Forty Years. . . . . PR 10:3 | Pg 149
    One-Third. . . . . PR 10:4 | Pg 150
    Tithe of God's People.. . . . . PR 10:4 | Pg 150
    Antitypical John. . . . . PR 10:5 | Pg 151
    Two-thirds of Mankind Cut Off. . . . . PR 10:5 | Pg 151
    Copy of 1977 Copyrighted Prediction pertaining to the 7,000 of the 70,000 found on next page:. . . . . PR 10:6 | Pg 152

PR11: Information on the Beast and his Name . . . . PR 11:1 | Pg 155
    How important is a name? . . . . PR 11:1 | Pg 155
    Christ came in his Father's Name. . . . . PR 11:1 | Pg 155
    Last Antichrist comes in his Father's Name. . . . . PR 11:2 | Pg 156
    Beast as Superhuman?. . . . . PR 11:2 | Pg 156
    Deadly Wound. . . . . PR 11:3 | Pg 157
    There is a "deadly wound" to the *system* of the Beast: . . . . PR 11:3 | Pg 157
    There must also be a "deadly wound" for the Beast-man. . . . . PR 11:4 | Pg 158
        Superhuman: To Summarize . . . . PR 11:4 | Pg 158
  How to Calculate the Number of the Beast . . . . PR 11:4 | Pg 158
    Calculate from Hebrew or Greek or Both?
. . . . PR 11:4 | Pg 158
    Things to know when Calculating the Number of the Beast
. . . . PR 11:5 | Pg 159
    Use your own mind and study the following tables:
. . . . PR 11:6 | Pg 160
More on calculating the number of the Beast. . . . . PR 11:14 | Pg 168
Method at Least 18 Centuries Old. . . . . PR 11:16 | Pg 170
    Evidence of Alphabetic-Number Systems goes Back to BC
. . . . PR 11:16 | Pg 170
        Hebrew's system can be traced back to at least 2nd Century BC
. . . . PR 11:16 | Pg 170
        Greek's system can be traced back to about the 8th century BC
. . . . PR 11:17 | Pg 171
    No English system exists. . . . . PR 11:17 | Pg 171
  Antichrist exists in the last 3 ½ Years. . . . . PR 11:18 | Pg 172
    Not Seven Years. . . . . PR 11:18 | Pg 172

Index. . . . . Page 181

Appendix (Beast of Revelation and Daniel; Characteristics of the Individual Beast; Christ's End Time Chart; End Time Dates) . . . . Page 186

Acknowledgment

I wish to thank and acknowledge my God, the Great Power, who made/makes all things possible. Second, I thank and acknowledge my wife Shirley Clare for her patience and for her help reading and editing the grammar of this work. Third, I thank all Believers for their work and dedication, for without them (and the Spirit) we would be in the dark. Fourth, I thank all scholars who wrote Biblical helps (concordances, interlinear Bibles, grammars, computer programs, creation v. evolution works, etc.) and critiques of doctrine, for they made my work easier. Fifth, I thank all scholars of serious works (philosophy, science, etc) for their work for no one person can think through all opinions pertaining to the truth: we need to compare our knowledge with others in order to ascertain the real truth. Lastly, I thank all who gave me constructive criticism.

Walter R. Dolen
March, 2011

Documentation

When you see, "The God, all in all" (1 Cor 15:28), it means that this is a quote from the New Testament letter called First Corinthians, chapter 15, verse 28. If you see "2 Cor" it would mean the *second* letter of the Corinthians. If you see "2 Cor 11:4" it would mean we quoted from the second letter of the Corinthians, the 11th chapter, and the 4th verse. But sometimes you will see a documentation such as "(1 Pet 2:4)" after a sentence that has no quotes. This kind of documentation is used in order to *support* the previous sentence or sentences, or to *point out other similar or related views* of the previous sentence or sentences, or to *add new light* to the previous sentence or sentences.

When you see reference to "**PR7**" it means more information can be found in *Prophecy Papers*, **Part 7**.

When you see reference to "**pr2**" this means more information can be found in the *Prophecy Papers*, **paragraph 2**.

NM	= *New Mind Papers*
GP	= *God Papers*
PR	= *Prophecy Papers*
CP	= *Chronology Papers*
cf or cf.	= confer or compare
p. or pp.	= page or pages
w/	= with

> "I am the BeComingOne [יהוה]; that is my name! See the former things have taken place, and new things I declare; before they spring into being I announce them to you."
> [Isaiah 42:9]

PR1: Seed Paper

Physical Promises to Israel
Spiritual Promises to Israel
Ur of the Chaldeans

Promises and Prophecies

Concerning Mankind and Israel

pr1» In the first book of the Bible God gave the patriarchs of Israel (Abraham, Isaac, & Jacob) certain promises that He would perform through their children. We will examine these promises in two ways — physically and Spiritually, for these promises are dual. Each promise given to the patriarchs has a typical and an antitypical fulfillment for the Bible is dual in meaning. The Bible has its physical and Spiritual fulfillment. It is the physical that prefigures the Spiritual.

pr2» Among other things, in examining the scriptures on the promises given to the patriarchs we will be able to ascertain where the Real Israel is today. We will deal with the physical promises first, then in part two we will cover the Spiritual promises. Both the physical and Spiritual promises are important and must be understood correctly.

Physical Promises to Israel

Abraham

pr3» God called Abram, whose name was later changed to Abraham, in the land of Ur of the Chaldees (Acts 7:2-4). God asked Abram to go out of his land and from his nativity "unto a land that I will show you."

[Gen 12:1; Abram or Abraham was born in the "Ur of the Chaldeans" in northwestern Mesopotamia in today's northern Syria and southeastern Turkey. See Notes, "Ur of the Chaldeans"]

pr4» And God said: "I will make you a great nation, and I will bless you, and make your name great; and you shall be a blessing: and I will bless them that bless you, and curse them that curse you: and in you shall *all* families of the earth be blessed" (Gen 12:2-3). Abram departed Ur and went to Haran. When Abram's father died he departed Haran: "So Abram departed ... And Abram passed through the land unto the place of Sichem, unto the plain of Moreh. And the Canaanite was then in the land. And the LORD appeared unto Abram, and said, Unto your SEED will I give this land."(Gen 12:4, 6-7)

pr5» Therefore, the first promises to Abraham (Abram) were:

- of him God would make a *great nation* (Gen 12:2)
- in him would *all* the families of the earth be blessed (Gen 12:3)
- his seed (offspring) would inherit the land of Canaan (Gen 12:6-7)

pr6» Next Abraham (Abram) was promised that his seed would have this land in the Middle East (Canaan) for a distance as far as he could see to the north, south, east, and west (Gen 13:14-15). He said his seed would obtain the land for an agelasting period, not "for ever" as it is mistranslated in most Bibles (See "Age Paper" [NM 7]). Therefore for an age of unknown length Abraham's seed (offspring) would have this land of the Middle East.

pr7» At this same time God promised, "I will make your SEED as the dust of the earth: so that if a man can number the dust of the earth, then shall your seed also be numbered"(Gen 13:16). Therefore the offspring of Abraham would be a great number of people. This promise of a great number of offspring is reiterated in Genesis 15:5; 22:17; 26:4; etc. (as the stars of heaven), and in Genesis 22:17; 32:12 (as the sand of the sea). And in Genesis 24:60 it says the number of offspring would be thousands of myriads (KJV, "millions"). Hence we see Abraham's children would become a *great* nation that would have a great population, and that all families (nations) of the earth would be blessed therein: "in thee shall all families of the earth be blessed" (Gen 12:3).

pr8» When God changed Abram's name ("exalted father") to Abraham ("father of a multitude") He said, "my covenant is with you, and you shall be a father of many nations ... and I will make you exceeding fruitful, and I will make nations of you, and kings shall come out of you" (Gen 17:4,6). Therefore Abraham's offspring would be rich (fruitful) and kings would come out of them.

pr9» Also note in Genesis 17:8 that the possession of the Middle East is for an *AGE* (KJV, "everlasting"), *not* everlasting. As it turned out they only did possess this land for a certain age although this promise is a dual one and later we will explain this better.

pr10» Next as a *token* of this covenant between God and Abraham, "Every man child among you shall be circumcised" (Gen 17:10-11). This was an *AGE*lasting covenant, not "everlasting" as it is mistranslated (Gen 17:13). As it turned out this *token* of the covenant did only last for an age, for physical circumcision was cut off as a requirement when Spiritual circumcision was installed through Christ (Col 2:11-12; Acts 15:5-29).

Isaac

pr11» Next we see this covenant between Abraham and God was passed on to the son of Sarah — Isaac (Gen 17:19,21). It is through Isaac that the SEED of Abraham would be called (Gen 21:12).

pr12» After Abraham obeyed God to the point of attempting to sacrifice his son Isaac (Gen 22:1-14), God again reiterated the promises to Abraham (Gen 22:16-18):

- to multiply his SEED as the stars of heaven;
- that in his SEED the nations would be blessed;
- and that his SEED would possess the cities (KJV, "gates" as in "city gates"; see Septuagint and cf. Deut 12:21; Mic 1:9 of his enemies.)

pr13» Later God again promised the same thing, but this time directly to Isaac, "I will make your seed [offspring] to multiply as the stars of heaven, and will give unto your seed all these countries [or lands or cities of his enemies — the Canaanites]; and in your seed shall *all* the nations of the earth be blessed; Because that Abraham obeyed my voice, and kept my charge, my commandments, my statutes, and my laws" (Gen 26:5). Notice the reason Abraham's seed was given these promises is because Abraham followed the directions of God. Again God appeared to Isaac and said, "I am with you, and will bless you, and multiply your seed for my servant Abraham's sake" (Gen 26:24). Abraham's faith was proven through his deeds (Rom 4:13-16; James 2:17-24, see "Proof Paper" [NM 10]). Therefore what God promised to Abraham was passed on to Isaac.

Jacob (Israel)

pr14» Isaac's blessing in turn was passed on to Jacob. Isaac's wife Rebekah had twins — Esau and Jacob (Gen 25:21-26). Now Esau was the first born of the twins, thus the rights of Isaac was passed on to Esau. But Jacob got Esau to sell his birthright to him (Gen 25:29-33). So the rights that went with being first born was passed on to Jacob. Thus, Jacob was the seed of Isaac in whom God would bestow his promises.

pr15» Further, Jacob took the blessing Isaac wanted to give Esau — his first born — whose right it was to have these blessings. Yet Esau sold his birthright and God told Rebekah that her younger child (Jacob) would become the greater nation than the elder (Esau), and that Esau would serve Jacob (Gen 25:23). Genesis 27:1-36 shows how Jacob took the blessing away from Esau. Genesis 27:27-29 pictures the blessing given to Jacob in the form of a prophecy, "Therefore God give you of the dew of heaven [good weather], and fatness of the earth [good land], and plenty of corn and wine [good crops]: let people serve you and nations bow down to you [thus other nations would serve Jacob's prophesied nation in one way or another]...."

pr16» Again God promises Jacob what he promised to Abraham and Isaac, "your seed shall be as the dust of the earth, and you shall spread abroad to the west, and to the east, and to the north, and to the south; and in you and in your seed shall *ALL* the families of the earth be blessed" (Gen 28:14). Hence, the *whole* world would benefit from Jacob's SEED (cf. Acts 3:25). To the four corners of the earth Jacob's SEED would physically bless the world.

Jacob's Name Changed

pr17» "And God appeared unto Jacob again ... and God said unto him, your name is Jacob: Your name shall not be called any more Jacob ['supplanter'] but Israel ['ruling with God'] shall be your name: and he called his name Israel. And God said unto him, I am God Almighty: be fruitful and multiply; a nation and a company of nations shall be of you, and kings shall come out of your loins; and the land which I gave Abraham and Isaac, to you I will give it, and to your seed after you I give the land" (Gen 35:9-12). This confirms again that the promises of Abraham was passed on to Jacob whose name was changed to Israel. Thus every time one sees Jacob or Israel in the prophecies he knows it speaks of the same nation or nations who grew up out of Jacob. A list of Jacob's children to whom the promises were passed on is in Genesis 35:23-26. Some of the blessings that were passed on to these children are noted in Genesis 49:1-28.

Joseph, Ephraim and Manasseh

pr18» Joseph, one of the sons of Israel (Jacob), was sold by his brothers and was brought into Egypt. Joseph became a great leader under the Pharaoh. Jacob moved over into Egypt because there was a famine in the earth, and Joseph in Egypt promised Jacob his father and his sons food and land in Egypt (Gen 45:17-20). In Egypt "Jacob [Israel] said unto Joseph, God Almighty appeared unto me at Luz in the land of Canaan, and blessed me, and said unto me, 'Behold, I will make you fruitful, and multiply you, and I will make of you a multitude of people; and will give this land to your seed after you, for an agelasting [KJV. 'ever-lasting'] possession. And now your [Joseph's] sons, *Ephraim* and *Manasseh*, which were born to you in the land of Egypt before I came unto you into Egypt, *ARE MINE*; as Reuben and Simeon, they [Ephraim and Manasseh] shall be MINE. And your issue [children], which you begettest after them [Ephraim and Manasseh], shall be yours..." (Gen 48:3-6).

pr19» Notice that Jacob called Joseph's two children, *Ephraim* and *Manasseh*, his — he adopted them as his own children (V.5). BUT the rest of Joseph's children are Joseph's children (V.6).

pr20» Next Jacob blessed Ephraim and Manasseh, "and let my name [Israel or Jacob] be named on them and the name of my fathers Abraham and Isaac; and let them grow up into a multitude [a great population] in the midst of the earth" (Gen 48:16). Notice that ABRAHAM and ISAAC names would be on Ephraim and Manasseh. Further Jacob qualified this blessing by saying that *Manasseh* would become "a people, and he also shall be great . . " (Gen 48:19). But he added "truly his younger brother [EPHRAIM] shall be greater than he, and his seed shall become a multitude of nations" (Gen 48:19). This is a very important qualification of God's promises.

pr21» God had promised to make of Abraham's offspring a great nation (Gen 12:2; 18:18; 35:11) *AND* a company or multitude or congregation of nations (Gen 17:4; 35:11; 48:4). Now this promise is qualified: *Manasseh* is to become a great nation ('people'); and Ephraim is to become a company or multitude of nationS.

pr22» Further notice something about Jacob's blessing, "And he blessed them [Joseph's sons — Manasseh and Ephraim] that day, saying In you [Manasseh and Ephraim] shall Israel be blessed..." (Gen 48:20; see *Septuagint*). So Israel will be blessed through Joseph's sons.

pr23» **Judah**. Let's notice a few more promises made to the children of Israel. Judah, one of Jacob's sons was promised that "the scepter [the right of rulership] shall not depart from Judah ... until Shiloh [CHRIST, see *Young's Analytical Concordance*] come" (Gen 49:10). And, "Now the sons of Reuben the first-born of Israel [Jacob], (for he was the first-born; but, forasmuch as he defiled his father's bed, his birthright was given unto the sons of Joseph the son of Israel ... for Judah prevailed above his brethren, and of him the chief ruler; but the birthright was Joseph's)" (1 Chron 5:1-2). So we see the chief ruler would come from Judah, and that the birthright was given to Joseph's sons — Ephraim and Manasseh. And we see the scepter, or the right of rulership in Israel, would not depart from Judah until Christ comes.

Now let's show the *physical* fulfillments of these promises of God to the children of Abraham, Isaac, and Jacob — the children of Israel.

Fulfillment of Physical Promises

pr24» After Jacob had brought his family into Egypt because of the lack of food elsewhere, Israel (his children) grew into a nation of about two or three million people (cf Num.1:46; notice that this number included only men, not their wives and children).

Moses & Joshua

pr25» Moses brought Israel out of Egypt. God gave his commandments of the covenant to Moses who passed it on to the children of Israel. Moses was leading Israel into the promised land of Canaan. It took 40 years for Israel to enter the land of Canaan. Moses did not bring Israel into this land but Joshua did. God showed the land to Moses before he died of old age, and God "buried him in a valley in the land of Moab ... But no man knows of his sepulcher unto this day" (Deut 34:6, 1-7). The movement of Israel into the promised land under Moses and Joshua is shown in the books of Exodus, Leviticus, Numbers, Deuteronomy, and Joshua. Moses appointed judges to judge Israel (Exo 18:13-27; Deut 1:9-18; 16:18-20).

Judges

pr26» After the death of Joshua, judges were set up to rule the people under the chief judge — God (Judges 2:16; 3:9-10). The whole theme of the book of Judges is that, "every man did that which was right in his *own* eyes" (Jud 17:6; 21:25), not in the eyes of God. In other words the people did as *they* pleased, not what God pleased. "In those days there was no king in Israel every man did that which was right in his own eyes" (Judges 21:25). But, "there is a way that seems right unto a man; but the end thereof are the ways of death" (Prov.16:25). The people of Israel were following the ways of death during the time the judges ruled Israel.

Samuel, "Make us a King"

pr27» Samuel was a judge in Israel "and it came to pass, when Samuel was old, that he made his sons judges over Israel.... And his sons walked not in the ways [of God], but turned aside after money, and took bribes, and perverted judgement. Then all the elders of Israel gathered themselves together, and came to Samuel unto Ramah, and said unto him, Behold, you are old, and your sons walk not in the ways [of God]: now *make us a king to judge us like all the nations*" (1 Sam 8:1, 3-5). Thus the elders of Israel were asking Samuel, the head judge, to make them a king to rule Israel.

pr28» Samuel was greatly displeased by the elders request, "and Samuel prayed unto the LORD. And the LORD said unto Samuel, Listen unto the voice of the people in all that they say unto you: for they have not rejected you, but they have rejected me, that I should not reign over them" (1 Sam 8:6-7).

pr29» God told Samuel to listen to the people and make them a human king. It was God they rejected not Samuel. God was the king of Israel up to this time. Notice that when Solomon sat on the throne of David he actually was sitting on God's throne (cf 1 Chron 29:23; 2 Chron 9:8). God was considered king up to this time when the elders of Israel asked Samuel to make them a human king.

pr30» After Samuel was told to let the people have their way, God asked Samuel to also warn the people of the effects of having a human king instead of God as king. For such a king would take their sons for soldiers and civil servants, and would levy great taxes and generally oppress the people (1 Sam 8:9-18).

pr31» "Nevertheless the people refused to obey the voice of Samuel; and they said, Nay; but we will have a king over us; that we also may be like the nations; and that our king may judge us, and go out before us, and fight our battles ... And the LORD said to Samuel, Listen unto their voice, and make them a king..." (1 Sam 8:19-22).

Saul

pr32» Saul was anointed Israel's first king (1 Sam.10:1). Saul was a Benjamite and physically impressive (1 Sam 9:1-2). But Saul did not follow in the ways of God, thus Saul was rejected by God (1 Sam 13:1-14; 15:1-26; 16:1). Samuel was sent to Saul, "And Samuel said to Saul, You have done foolishly; you have not kept the commandment of the LORD thy God, which He commanded you; for now would the LORD have established the kingdom upon Israel, for agelasting. But now your kingdom shall not continue: the LORD has sought him a man after his own heart, and the LORD has commanded him to be captain over His people, because you have not kept that which the LORD commanded you" (1 Sam 13:13-14).

David

pr33» The man God appointed to take Saul's place as king was David. (1 Sam 16:1, 13 & 2 Sam 2:4, 5:3) Although Saul was physically impressive he was a bad leader, for "he feared the people, and obeyed their voice: instead of God's" (1 Sam 15:24). "The LORD said unto Samuel, Look not on his [Saul's] countenance, or on the height of his stature; because I have refused him: for the LORD sees not as a man sees; for man looks on the outward appearance, but the LORD looks on the heart" (1 Sam 16:7). Although David made mistakes when he was made king after Saul died, he had the right attitude in his mind (2 Sam chap. 11 & 12). When David's mistakes were pointed out to him he would acknowledge them and turn away from them (2 Sam 12:9-13). Read of David's attitude in Psalm's 51. The Bible projects to us, by using the physical David as an example (1 Cor 10:11), the heart or attitude that God wants in everyone (note: 1 Kings 11:4,6). And that attitude is one of admitting mistakes and correcting these mistakes when ascertained. Read all the scripture on David to see this attitude in action (also note: Job 33:27-28; Prov 28:13; Luke 15:21-24; 1 John 1:9).

pr34» David was anointed king over Judah after Saul's death (2 Sam 2:4), then later he was anointed king over Israel (2 Sam 5:3). In all he reigned over Judah 7 and 1/2 years, and 33 years over Israel and Judah together (2 Sam 5:5). Notice that here the Bible deals with Judah and Israel *separately*.

Solomon

pr35» The next king over Israel was David's son — Solomon, "then Solomon sat *on the throne of the* LORD as king instead of David his father, and prospered, and all Israel obeyed him.... And the LORD magnified Solomon exceedingly in the sight of all Israel, and bestowed upon him such royal majesty as had not been on any king before him in Israel" (1 Chron. 29:23,25). So Solomon actually sat on the throne of God in the nation of Israel and had great wealth.

pr36» To see what happened next in Israel's history let's quote directly from the Bible:

- "King Solomon was a lover of women, and besides Pharaoh's daughter he married many foreign women, Moabite, Ammonite, Edomite, Sidonian, and Hittite, from the nations with whom the LORD had forbidden the Israelites to intermarry, 'because,' he said, 'they will entice you to serve their gods.' But Solomon was devoted to them and loved them dearly. He had seven hundred wives, who were princesses, and three hundred concubines, and they turned his heart from the truth. When he grew old, his wives turned his heart to follow other gods, and he did not remain wholly loyal to the LORD his God as his father David had been. He followed Ashtoreth, goddess of the Sidonians, and Milcom, the loathsome god of the Ammonites. Thus Solomon did what was wrong in the eyes of the LORD and was not loyal to the LORD like his father David. He built a hill-shrine for Chemosh, the loathsome god of Moab, on the height to the east of Jerusalem, and for Molech, the loathsome god of the Ammonites. Thus he did for the gods to which all his foreign wives burnt offerings and made sacrifices.

- The L ORD was angry with Solomon because his heart had turned away from the L ORD the God of Israel, who had appeared to him twice and had strictly commanded him not to follow other gods; but he disobeyed the L ORD's command. The L ORD therefore said to Solomon, '**Because you have done this and have not kept my covenant and my statutes as I commanded you, I will tear the kingdom from you** and give it to your servant. Nevertheless, for the sake of your father David I will not do this in your day; I will tear it out of your son's hand. Even so not the whole kingdom; I will leave him one tribe for the sake of my servant David and for the sake of Jerusalem, my chosen city.'" (1 Kings 11:1-13, *NEB*)

pr37» So because of the wrongs of Solomon, his kingdom was to depart from him, but because of a promise to David his father the kingdom would depart from only Solomon's son, not Solomon himself. Yet not *all* the kingdom would be taken from his son.

pr38» Now God said he would give the kingdom to one of his servants (1 Kings 11:11), and *Jeroboam* was that servant:

Jeroboam

pr39» "Jeroboam son of Nebat, one of Solomon's courtiers, an Ephrathite from Zereda, whose widowed mother was named Zeruah, rebelled against the king. And this is the story of his rebellion. Solomon had built the Millo and closed the breach in the wall of the city of his father David. Now this Jeroboam was a man of great energy; and Solomon, seeing how the young man worked, had put him in charge of all the labour-gangs in the tribal district of Joseph. On one occasion Jeroboam had left Jerusalem, and the prophet Ahijah from Shiloh met him on the road. The prophet was wrapped in a new cloak, and the two of them were alone in the open country. Then Ahijah took hold of the new cloak he was wearing, tore it into twelve pieces and said to Jeroboam, Take ten pieces, for this is the work of the L ORD and God of Israel: **I am going to tear the kingdom from the hand of Solomon and give you ten tribes**. But one tribe will remain his, for the sake of my servant David and for the sake of Jerusalem, the city I have chosen out of all the tribes of Israel. **I have done this because Solomon has forsaken me**; he has prostrated himself before Ashtoreth goddess of the Sidonians, Kemosh god of Moab, and Milcom god of the Ammonites, and has not conformed to my ways. He has not done what is right in my eyes or observed my statutes and judgments as David his father did. Nevertheless I will not take the whole kingdom from him, but will maintain his rule as long as he lives, for the sake of my chosen servant David, who did observe my commandments and statutes. But I will take the kingdom, that is the ten tribes, from his son and give it to you. One tribe I will give to his son, that my servant David may always have a flame burning before me in Jerusalem, the city which I chose to receive my name" (1 Kings 11:26-36, NEB).

pr40» "After this Solomon sought to kill Jeroboam, but he fled to King Shishak in Egypt and remained there till Solomon's death" (1 Kings 11:40, *NEB*).

Israel and Judah Split

pr41» Notice carefully that *ten* tribes were given to Jeroboam (1 Kings 11:31,35). Only one tribe was given to Solomon sons (V.32, 36, 13). Jeroboam was given the kingdom of Israel (1 Kings 11:37) — ten tribes of it.

pr42» So after Solomon died his son Rehoboam ruled. Then Jeroboam came back out of Egypt where he had fled from Solomon and joined in a revolt against Rehoboam — Solomon's son (1 Kings 12:1-18). "So Israel rebelled against the house of David unto this day" (V.19). Then Israel made Jeroboam "king over all Israel: there was none that followed the house of David, but the tribe of Judah only" (V.20). Only the tribe of Judah followed Solomon's son "with the tribe of Benjamin" who lived near Judah (V.21). It was the tribe of Judah (with Benjamin's tribe) that was not torn from Solomon's son and that did not revolt against the kingship of Solomon's son, Rehoboam.

pr43» Right after this revolt by the ten tribes of Israel, Solomon's son, Rehoboam, "assembled all the house of Judah, *with* the tribe of Benjamin ... to fight against the house of Israel..." (1 Kings 12:21). Notice the Bible calls the ten tribes under Jeroboam — the house of Israel.

pr44» Judah with the tribe of Benjamin under Rehoboam is called collectively, Judah: "Speak unto Rehoboam, the son of Solomon, KING OF JUDAH . . " (V.23). From this point on the tribes of Judah (Jews) and Benjamin were a separate nation from Israel.

pr45» The kingdom of Israel and Judah fought wars against each other from this point of separation and onward (cf. 2 Kings 16:1-6; 2 Chron. 16:1; etc.). In 2 Chronicles chapters 11 to 36, it shows the separate history of Judah as a distinctive nation apart from the nation of Israel. 1 Kings chapter 12 to 2 Kings chapter 25, shows each nation's history. These books of the Bible treat Judah and Israel as separate nations from the time of Solomon's death onward. (Note Ezek 37:19-22)

Israel Scattered

pr46» Now right after Jeroboam was made king of Israel, he began to change the laws of God to satisfy his own purpose. He made two calves of gold and said, "behold your gods, O Israel" (1 Kings 12:28). He changed the feast of tabernacles from the *seventh* month to the *eighth* month.

pr47» God then sent a prophet to Jeroboam (through his wife) telling him that because he did not keep His laws (for he changed a festival from the seventh month to the eighth month; etc.), and because he made molten images, and so on; that God would cut off Jeroboam's offspring (1 Kings

14:5-10) and "the LORD shall smite Israel, as a reed is shaken in the water, and he shall root up Israel out of his good land ... and shall scatter them beyond the river, because they have made their groves, provoking the LORD to anger. And he shall give Israel up because of the sins of Jeroboam, who did sin, and who made Israel to sin" (1 Kings 14:15-16).

pr48» Finally, after many years, "the king of Assyria took Samaria and carried Israel into Assyria" (2 Kings 17:5-6). Because of Israel's sins, Israel was taken captive into Assyria (2 Kings 17:7-8). In verses 9-17 it lists some of the wrong things that Israel did. "Therefore the LORD was very angry with Israel, and removed them out of his sight: *there was none left but the tribe of Judah only*" (V. 18). Only Judah (the Jews) was left with the tribe of Benjamin who dwelled with them in the land of Israel.

pr49» Because Israel followed in the ways of Jeroboam, they were removed to Assyria (V. 21-23). Then the king of Assyria brought in other peoples to fill up Samaria and they learned the ways of Jeroboam from one of the priests who was carried away but who returned to Samaria (2 Kings 17:24-34).

Judah Scattered

pr50» Next Judah was warned that it too would be going into captivity if it didn't turn away from its sin (see 2 Kings 21:1-14). Actually Judah sinned even more than Israel (Jer 3:6-11). "And the LORD said, I will remove Judah also out of my sight, as I have removed Israel, and will cast off this city Jerusalem which I have chosen, and the house of which I said, My name shall be there" (2 Kings 23:27).

pr51» And thus Judah went into captivity by the kingdom of Babylon (2 Kings 24 & 25). Now this fulfills Moses prophecy, "I call heaven and earth to witness against you this day, that you shall soon utterly perish from off the land whereunto you go over Jordan to possess it; you shall *not* prolong your days upon it, but shall utterly be destroyed. And the LORD shall scatter you among the nations, and you shall be left few in number among the heathen, whither the LORD shall lead you" (Deut 4:26-27). All twelve tribes thus went into captivity. The ten tribes of the kingdom of Israel were taken captive by Assyria, and the kingdom of Judah (with the tribe of Benjamin) went into captivity by Babylon.

Promises That Did and Did Not Come True

pr52» Now let's look at what promises of God came true up to the Babylonian captivity:

- Israel did possess the land of Canaan (the Middle East) for an agelasting time as promised in Genesis 13:15 and 17:8. For over 900 years they possessed this land before being driven out (note Joshua 21:43).

- Israel did have kings as the seed of Abraham was prophesied to have in Genesis 17:16 and 35:11.

- Israel did grow to a great population: "Your fathers went down into Egypt with threescore and ten persons; and now the LORD your *God has made you as the stars of heaven for multitude*" (Deut 10:22; 26:5; 1:10, see Neh chapter 9).

- Abraham's SEED was to possess the gates or cities of its enemies (Gen 22:17; 24:60) and that nations would bow down to it (Gen 27:29), and that it would spread out to the west, east, north, and south (Gen 28:14). This being typically fulfilled by David when he took the Philistines (west), and the Moabites (east), and Hadadezer -king of Zobah (north), and the land of Edom (2 Sam 8:1-3, 13-14). Also Solomon was paid tribute (1 Kings 10:25).

- That Israel did become a great nation (Gen 12:2; 18:18) with great glory could have been said to come true (relative to that time) in the reigns of David and Solomon, but only in a typical sense.

- Of Joseph's two sons (Ephraim and Manasseh), *Ephraim* did become a company of nations [peoples, tribes - Gen 48:3-5)] after Jeroboam (of the house of Ephraim - 1 kings 11:26) split from his father Solomon and formed the 10 northern tribes of Israel (1 Kings 11:26-36). This ten northern tribe nations was also called *Ephraim* in the books of Isaiah, Jeremiah, Hosea.

- That in Israel *all* families of the earth were blessed was only *very* typically true through the era of David and Solomon (note 1 Kings, chapter 10; Matt 6:29).

pr53» All these "fulfillments" were typical and only imperfectly represent the true fulfillment. We as Christians are to look to the higher meaning of scripture (see "Duality Paper" [BP4]).

Spiritual Promises of God

pr54» We have just seen in the first part of this paper the physical promises of God to Israel. These promises were typically fulfilled. These promises prefigured the real or intended promises.

pr55» But an antitypical fulfillment of prophecy will happen, "the kingdom of heaven is like unto a man that is a householder, which brings forth out of his treasure things new [Spiritual] and old [the physical]" (Matt 13:52). The kingdom of God will be set up on earth at Christ the God's physical return. This kingdom will bring in the old (the old physical blessings) and the new (the Spiritual blessings of God's Spirit).

Seed

pr56» In most of the promises given to Abraham, Isaac, and Jacob, the promises were pertaining to their "seed." This can and does mean their children. But the Bible uses the word "seed" in another and special way: "Now to Abraham and his seed were the promises made. He does *not* say, and to seeds, as of many; but as of one, and to your seed, which is Christ ... And if you be Christ's, then you are Abraham's seed, and heirs according to the promise" (Gal 3:16, 29). Hence Spiritually speaking Christ is *the* seed, and those of Christ are heirs according to the promise, they are counted as the seed of Abraham and they are the Spiritual Israel (cf Gal 6:16). And other scripture indicates one does not have to be a physical Israelite to become a Spiritual Israelite, for through being Spiritually baptized into Christ one becomes the real seed of Abraham (Gal 3:27-29, 16):

- "and if you are Christ's, then you are Abraham's seed, and heirs according to the promise."

Thus, all the promises made in the Bible to the physical seed of Abraham, Isaac, and Jacob (Israel) will come true to anyone Spiritually baptized into Christ's body. That is, will come true in a Spiritual sense.

pr57» Let me in outline form list many of the promises made to the "seed" of Abraham, Isaac, and Israel (Jacob). **We now know from the just mentioned scriptures that all these promises pertain to all people *in* Christ through Spiritual baptism.** These promises will be fulfilled in the truest sense beginning at Christ the God's physical return.

Promises To The *Seed*

pr58»

- The **land** of the Middle East is the Seed's. [Gen 12:7; 15:18; 17:8]
- The seed have the land for an **agelasting** time. [Gen 13:15; 17:8]

(But the new age will never end unlike the ages before it. See "Age Paper" [NM 7].)

- The seed is to be the heir of Abraham's **promises** (note Gal 3:29). [Gen 15:3-4]
- The seed is to be **numbered as the stars**. [Gen 15:5; 22:17; 26:4; Ex 32:13]

(Stars are symbolic of angels, Rev 1:20. The seed will equal the number of angels. See the *God Papers*, GP6, to understand this.)

- The seed is to be Spiritually **circumcised**. [Gen 17:9-14]

(That is Spiritually fulfilled in Spiritual baptism, Col 2:11-12; Phil 3:3.)

- In the seed all the nations will be **blessed** (cf Acts 3:25). You are in the seed when you are in Christ, for Christ is the seed. [Gen 22:18; 26:4; 28:14]
- The promises were given to Abraham because he **kept God's ways**; the same with the seed (Christians). One must follow Abraham's ways, which are God's ways to be the seed of Abraham (cf John 8:37-40). [Gen 26:5; 22:18]
- The **seed will spread around the world**, that is to the east, west, north, and south. [Gen 28:14; 13:14]

(The seed, the Christians, will be heirs of the kingdom of God that will spread around the world after Christ returns (cf Isa 2:2; Dan 2:44; 7:14, 27; Rev 11:15).

- The seed are to be **kings**. [Gen 17:6; 35:11]

(And the resurrected Christians, the seed, will be kings after Christ comes [cf Rev 1:6; 5:10; 20:4].)

- Israel, the seed, are to become a **holy nation** and a kingdom of **priests**. [Ex 19:5-6]

(Christians are now typically this (1 Per 2:9). Later they will antitypically be a holy kingdom of priests [Rev 5:10; 1:6].)

- The seed are and were **chosen**. [Deut 4:37; 10:15; Psa 105:6; 1 Chron 16:13; Isa 44:1]

(Christians are thus chosen [Eph 1:4].)

- The seed are to be **circumcised in heart** (mind, attitude). [Deut 30:6]

(Christians are Spiritually circumcised. They have the New Mind through Spiritual baptism [Phil 3:3; Col 2:11-12].)

- The seed will not pass through the **fire** to Molech. [Lev 18:21]

(This pictures that Christians will not pass through the lake of fire as Satan and his children will. Christians will not be dead during the 1000 year lake of fire [see "Thousand Years" paper (NM 15)].)

- The seed are shown **mercy**. [2 Sam 22:51]

(Hence Christians are the vessels of mercy. [Rom 9:23, see "Predestination Paper" (NM 8)])

- The seed is to **inherit the earth**.

(Thus the Christians (the meek), who are the seed, will inherit the earth [Matt 5:5].) [Psalm 25:13]

- The seed will have a **throne** for an agelasting period. [Psalm 89:4, 29, 36]

(The Christians have their throne for an agelasting time. The Christian throne is the Spiritual throne — the Spirit or New Mind. See *Mew Mind Papers*. But God's age does not end like other ages [See the "Reward" Paper (NM 11), and "Age Paper" (NM 7)].)

- The seed will "**rain**" on the earth at Christ's coming. [Isaiah 30:23]

(The coming of Christ the God with the resurrected saints is symbolically pictured as rain [cf Isa 45:8; Ho 10:12; Isa 32:15]. This is the "early rain" [James 5:7]. The "latter rain" is at the true end of creation.)

- The seed, the Christians, are God's **friends** (John 15:14). [Isaiah 41:8]

- The seed will be **gathered** at Christ's return. [Isaiah 43:5-6]

(Thus Christians will be gathered from the graves of the earth at Christ's return [cf Matt 24:31].)

- The seed will inherit the Gentiles, **all nations**. [Isaiah 54:3]

(This is pictured in Revelation 11:15; Dan 7:27; etc.)

- **Christ, the Seed, His Seed, and Seed's Seed**. God's word will not depart out of Christ, who is *the* seed, or Christ's seed (Christians), or the seed's seed. [Isaiah 59:21]

(The Christians are to be a Spiritual wife and mother [Isa 54:1-17, 13; Gal 4:27; Rev 19:7; 21:2, 9] while Christ will be a Spiritual husband and father [Isa 54:5; Isa 9:6; 22:21] in the kingdom of God. Together they will Spiritually have children [Isa 54:13; 44:3 and 65:23; 61:9; 59:21; Psa 102:28; etc.]. These children are those who are Spiritually begotten and/or born of God's Spirit [New Mind] in the new age [after the 1000 years].)

Other Promises

pr59» **We have just seen through the outlined scripture that the promises to Abraham's children (his seed), are Spiritually the same promises given to Christians**. Christians are of the seed of Abraham through Christ, Who is *the* seed of Abraham. But how are Christians the seed of Abraham through Christ? And what about the promises that David would "forever" have someone sitting on his throne (2 Sam 7:10-16), and what about the promise that the chief ruler would come from Judah (1 Chron 5:2), and what about the promise that the scepter (rulership) would not depart from Judah until Christ comes? (Gen 49:10) Let's examine these items in some detail.

Judah and the Scepter

pr60» As 1 Chronicles 5:2 said, the chief ruler would be of the tribe of Judah: He would be a Jew. And the chief ruler did come out of Judah, He was and is Christ. Christ will be King of kings when He returns to earth (Rev 19:16). And Christ was a Jew, for He was a seed of David who was a Jew of the tribe of Judah (Rom 1:3; Mat 1:1-17).

pr61» In Genesis 49:10 it says, "the scepter shall not depart from Judah ... until Shiloh [Christ] come." Notice the right of rulership for Israel would not depart from Judah. Christ has already come; thus for Genesis 49:10 to come true, the scepter need only be with Judah until the first coming of Christ. Today the scepter of physical Judah need not exist on earth for Genesis 49:10 to be fulfilled. So if we can trace this scepter to Christ's time, then we have established the fulfillment of another prophecy. **Thus we will trace the scepter up to Christ for this reason, but more importantly we will trace this to understand how one *in* Christ is a seed of Abraham**.

pr62» Also the *Spiritual* scepter of Christ will still exist and will exist up to Christ's physical return: "I am with you always, even unto the end of the age" (Matt 28:20). This speaks of Christ's Spirit being with the Spiritual Church until the end of the old age.

Promises to David

pr63» Now let us examine the scripture concerning the promise to David that his seed would "forever" rule on the throne of Israel. First we will list some of these promises, then we will try to trace the physical fulfillment. We will ascertain herein that these physical or typical fulfillments didn't come true perfectly. As with all typical or physical Biblical fulfillments of God's word, they never come *perfectly* true. God is a Spirit and speaks Spiritually to us. The Spiritual or antitypical or second fulfillment of prophecy always comes true perfectly. Thus the promises to David will come true perfectly antitypically, but only imperfectly true typically.

pr64» "I will set up *your seed* after you, which shall proceed out of your bowels, and I will establish *his* kingdom. He shall build a house for my [God's] name, and I will establish the throne of *his* kingdom for agelasting" (2 Sam 7:12-13).

> [Here we see where David's seed will establish the kingdom, and build God's house (the Church) and establish the throne for an agelasting period. Notice not "forever," but an agelasting throne. A throne is the symbol of ruling power. Solomon, David's son (his seed), established the kingdom for an age as a type of the antitypical agelasting kingdom

of God under Christ, who is the true seed of David. But of course the New Age will not end. See "Age Paper" [NM 7].]

pr65» "I [God] will be *his* [the seed's] father, and he will be my son. If he commit iniquity, I will correct him with the rod of men, and with the stripes of the children of men" (2 Sam 7:14).

[Here Solomon fulfills this, yet Christ the true seed of David was God's son in a truer sense than Solomon. Solomon is the typical Christ, yet Christ as the antitypical seed of David fulfills this position much better than Solomon. Although Christ didn't commit iniquity, God has "made him to be sin for us, who knew no sin ... and he was numbered with the transgressors" (2 Cor 5:21; Isa 53:12).]

pr66» "And your house and your kingdom shall be established for agelasting before you: your throne shall be established for agelasting" (2 Sam 7:16).

[Again we see this kingdom will last for an age. Solomon's kingdom did last for an *age*, but Christ the true seed's kingdom will last for an age of 1000 years under him as king of kings, and last beyond the 1000 years because his kingdom has no end, unlike previous ages (Luke 1:33, see "Age Paper" [NM 7]). Christ is the true SEED of David Who will rule over the seed of Abraham, Isaac, and Jacob (note Jer 33:15).]

Also notice these promises reiterated in Psalm 89:

- "Your seed will I establish agelasting" (V.4).

[Christ, the seed, will be established for the great age.]

pr67» When one reads about Solomon, one can see that Solomon is a physical type of Christ. He prefigures Christ. Solomon did many things typically and physically that Christ did/is/will-do Spiritually and antitypically. For example, Solomon built God's physical temple and established a rich, but small, kingdom for Israel. Christ the God is now building the Church, the true temple (1 Cor 3:16), and will establish the true kingdom of happiness and wealth beginning at his physical return.

Conditions

pr68» Solomon was the imperfect, typical seed. He didn't establish the *great* kingdom, because he didn't fulfill the conditions that were needed to be the leader of this great kingdom: "Hear the word of the LORD, O king of Judah, that sits upon the throne of David, you, and your servants, and your people that enter in by these gates: Thus says the LORD; Execute judgment and righteousness, and deliver the spoiled out of the hand of the oppressor: and do *no* wrong, do *no* violence to the stranger, the fatherless, nor the widow, neither shed innocent blood in this place. For *if* you do this thing indeed, then shall there enter in by the gates of this house kings sitting upon the throne of David, riding .... But if you will not hear these words, I swear by myself, says the LORD, that this house [Judah, verse 1] shall become a desolation" (Jer 22:2-5).

pr69» Notice these conditions, "do *no* wrong, do *no* violence." There has only been *one* person who ever lived that never did any violence, and that person was Christ: "he had done no violence" (Isa 53:9 with 2 Cor 5:21). It was Christ who only fulfilled these conditions for sitting on the throne of David, which is also God's throne (1 Chron 29:23; 2 Chron 9:8).

pr70» Notice other reiterations of this condition: 1 Kings 2:4; 6:12-13; 8:25; 9:4-7; 2 Kings 21:8; 1 Chron 22:13; 2 Chron 6:16. And as Jeremiah 22:5 said, the house of Judah would be desolate unless these conditions were fulfilled.

pr71» Notice because these conditions were never fulfilled by Solomon, his kingdom was taken away, for he didn't perfectly fulfill these conditions (1 Kings 11:6-12). "Howbeit I will not rip away all the kingdom; but will give one tribe to your son for David my servant's sake, and for Jerusalem's sake which I have chosen" (1 Kings 11:13). This last verse refers to the promise made to David that his seed (Christ) would establish the kingdom. In verse 36 it says what verse 13 did say, but in a different way: "And unto his son will I give one tribe, that David my servant may have a light all the days before me in Jerusalem ...."

pr72» Notice this verse didn't say that this "light" would all of the days *rule* in Jerusalem, but would be there in Jerusalem. Christ was physically born as a seed of David (Rom 1:3). This "light" (physical) in Jerusalem was the ancestors of Christ who lived in and around Jerusalem up to Christ's time, thus enabling Christ, the true seed, to be born of the physical seed of David. Even though most of Israel was scattered throughout the earth, a remnant lived in and around Jerusalem thus enabling Christ the true seed of Abraham, Isaac, Jacob, and David to be born as a seed of them (Mat 1:1-17).

Branch

pr73» Notice the prophecy concerning a person who would fulfill the conditions needed to establish the kingdom: "Behold, the days come, says the LORD, that I will raise unto David a righteous Branch, and a king shall reign and prosper, and shall execute judgment and justice in the earth .... And there shall come forth a rod out of the stem of Jesse, and a Branch shall grow out of his roots; and the spirit of the LORD shall rest upon him, the spirit of wisdom and understanding, the spirit of counsel and might, the spirit of knowledge and of the fear of the LORD; and he shall not judge after the sight of his eyes, neither reprove after the hearing of his ears" (Jer 23:5; Isa 11:1-3).

Christ: The Branch, The King, The Savior

pr74» Christ is this king; Christ is this Branch of Jesse; Christ is *the* seed of David. Therefore Christ fulfills or will fulfill the promises of God to David, Abraham, Isaac, and Jacob.

pr75» God promised David that Christ would sit on His throne (Acts 2:30). Typically, Solomon fulfilled this, but Christ is the true and intended king who was to sit on David's throne as Acts 2:30 and as Luke 1:31-33 prove: "and, behold, you shall conceive in your womb, and bring forth a son, and shall call his name Jesus [Savior]. He shall be great, and shall be called the Son of the Highest: and the Lord God shall give unto him the throne of his father David: and he shall reign over the house of Jacob into the ages; and of his kingdom there shall be no end."

pr76» Christ was born to be king (John 18:37). Speaking about Christ, "for unto us a child is born, unto us a son is given: and the government shall be upon his shoulder: and his name shall be called Wonderful, Counselor, the mighty God, the duration Father, the Prince of peace. Of the increase of his government and peace there shall be no end, *upon the throne of David, and upon his kingdom, to order it, and to establish it* with judgment and with justice from henceforth [from his birth, Isa 9:6; Luke 1:31-33] and for *olam* [the great age]" (Isa 9:6-7). It is Christ, not Solomon, who is the SEED to establish the kingdom; He was and is establishing it from His birth and onward. At His physical return He will take the kingdom of this world and make it His (Dan 7:9-14, 27).

Christ versus Satan; David versus Saul

pr77» Christ was even a king of Israel when he was only a human (John 1:49-50). But like David who was anointed king of Israel, Christ must wait until Satan's kingdom destroys itself much as David had to wait for Saul to destroy himself (1 Sam 16:1-3, 13 to 31:6). Christ was born to be king (John 18:33, 36-37).

pr78» After Christ's death and resurrection Paul tells us Christ is now "crowned with glory and honor" (Heb 2:9). Christ is now sitting on the throne of his father (Rev 3:21). This is dual: Christ is on his physical father's (David's) throne (Luke 1:32) which is also his Spiritual Father's throne or God's throne (note, 1 Chron 29:23; Rev 3:21). But as with David, who was appointed to be king of Israel, who had to wait for the anointed Saul to kill himself before he could take over the throne and rule, so too with Christ, He must wait until Satan, the anointed cherub (Ezek 28:14), destroys himself.

pr79» Satan who rules the world now is the antitypical of Saul. As Saul destroyed himself (1 Sam 31:1-6), so too will Satan and his kingdom destroy themselves in the Last War (see "Last War and God's Wrath" paper [PR5]). As David took over rulership of the kingdom after Saul destroyed himself, so too will Christ take over rulership when Satan destroys himself at the appointed time.

pr80» Although Christ is now the anointed king, He can't take over until Satan destroys himself. The typical example is Saul and David. Christ now has the throne, but is waiting for the end of Satan's kingdom. Christ received this right of rulership through being the seed of David's, and because he fulfilled the conditions of the right of rulership.

Spiritual Seed of Abraham

pr81» Today those in Christ are also the seed of Abraham because Christ is the seed of Abraham, and when we have Christ's Spirit (which is God's), then we are a part of Him. If Christ is a seed of Abraham, then so are we. As this paper clearly shows, Christ is the true SEED of Abraham, thus we are of that true SEED when we are in Jesus Christ.

Spiritual Jews

pr82» Today, those in Christ are also Jews because Jesus who came from the physical tribe of the Jews (through David) was a Jew. When we have Christ's Spirit, then we are part of him, we are in Him. We are Spiritual Jews. Thus, Paul writes: "For he is not a Jew that is one outwardly ... but he is a Jew that is one inwardly" (Rom 2:28, 29). Here Paul tells us that a physical Jew ("one outwardly") is not a real Jew, but the Spiritual Jew ("one inwardly") is a real Jew. A Spiritual Jew is a real Christian. Thus in the book of Revelation when it speaks of a "Jew," Spiritually it speaks of a real Christian (note Rev 2:9; 3:9; 7:5ff).

Spiritual Virgins

pr83» Jesus Christ was a sexual virgin: He never married, he kept all the laws of God, thus he never had sexual intercourse outside of marriage. He died a sexual virgin. Thus, following the logic above, those Spiritually in Christ are also considered Spiritual virgins. Therefore the "virgins" mentioned in the book of Revelation are real Christians (note Rev 14:4).

Christ The Mediator

pr84» Christ is the mediator between God and man. Christ is part man (son of man), and part God (son of God). He has both the physical and Spiritual essences in Himself (see the *God Papers*). If we have Christ's Spirit, since He is both Spirit and flesh, then we also have His flesh, we are *both* a son of Abraham, and a son of Christ the God when we have His Spirit.

Summarize: Jews and Israelites = Christians

By studying the above and scripture, after Christ's resurrection the only real Jews or Israelites were/are Christians. When you are in Christ, you are a Jew, you are an Israelite. Because the Jews did not bring forth the fruit required of them, their kingdom and their identity were in a sense taken from them and given to another people who will bring forth fruit required of them (Mat 3:10;7:17-19;12:33;13:8;21:19-21;21:34 [in context];John 15:4-8;Gal 5:22; etc.). But the Christians receive their fruit of good works through the Spirit of Christ: they are in Christ. Whatever Christ fulfilled, Christians will fulfill because they are in Christ. What this means is that the truest sense of the Old Testament prophecy will come true through Christians (the real Jews), not through physical Jews.

Notes for PR1

Three Orders/Divisions

pr85» The *three orders* or divisions of mankind can be seen typically in Joseph and his two sons, Manasseh and Ephraim. *Joseph*, the one set apart from his brethren (Deut 33:16), represents Jesus Christ, who was the first to be born of God (1 Cor 15:22-28). *Manasseh*, the one that was to become a great nation, represents the second group to be born of God, which are the Christians who lived in the old age. *Ephraim*, the one that was to become a multitude of nations, represents the third group to be born of God, which are the multitudes of peoples who will be born of God at the end of creation. They at that time will also become Christians — they will go into the Spiritual Body of Christ.

pr86» In these three groups will the great promises of God be Truly fulfilled. The promises to Israel are the promises that will be fulfilled to all of mankind through Jesus Christ our Lord, who has the NAME of God — the BeComingOne. (see in the *New Mind Papers* the "All Saved" paper [NM 13] and also "Three Orders of Creation" in "God's Appointed Times and Seasons" paper [NM 16])

Ur of the Chaldeans

pr87» Abraham (Abram) came from the "Ur of the Chaldeans" (Gen 11:31). The "Ur of the Chaldeans" mentioned in the Bible is not the city identified as "Ur" by many today. The contemporary "Ur" is hundreds of miles southeast of Haran and Ebla on *this* side of the Euphrates river. That is, on the side (this side) of the Euphrates river nearest Jerusalem. But the Biblical "Ur of the Chaldeans" was *across* the river Euphrates in northwestern Mesopotamia somewhere near Haran. Archeological finds and Biblical proof indicate this.

pr88» This "Ur of the Chaldeans" is most likely the same Ur that is mentioned to be "in the territory of Haran" in the Ebla Clay tablets discovered in 1975, not the Ur on *this side* of the river Euphrates southeast of the Mesopotamia region. The contemporary "Ur" is located in the southeastern territory of the Sumero-Akkadian Empire and had a different culture and language than Abraham's.

Ur of Abraham located near Haran in Mesopotamia

pr89» There is Biblical proof that the city of "Ur" that Abraham came from was near Haran:

- Abram, Lot, and Terah "went forth with them from *Ur of the Chaldees*, to go into the land of Canaan; and they came unto *Haran*, and dwelt there" (Gen 11:31).

- "Thus says the LORD God of Israel, your fathers dwelt *on the other side of the river* [Euphrates] in old time ... and I took your father Abraham from the other side of the river [Euphrates]" (Joshua 24:2, 3).

pr90» Thus, Abraham came from the *other* side of the river (from Jerusalem's viewpoint). That river being the Euphrates. But the contemporary so-called "Ur of Chaldeans" is on *this* side of the river (from Jerusalem's viewpoint).

- "The God of Glory appeared unto Abraham, when he was in Mesopotamia, *before* he dwelt in Haran" (Acts 7:2).

pr91» Abraham came from Mesopotamia. The word Mesopotamia means *"the country between the rivers"* (*Unger's Bible Dict.*, "Mesopotamia"). These rivers being the Euphrates and Tigris. But the contemporary "Ur" is not located *between* the rivers. Originally the word "mesopotamia" stood only for the northwestern region between the rivers Euphrates and Tigris (*Unger's Bible Dict.*, 3rd Ed., "Mesopotamia"). Albert Clay mistakenly wrote in 1907:

- "In former years Urfa, not far from Harran, was identified as the ancestral city of the patriarch [Abraham], but it is now [1907] fifty years since Rawlinson identified the mounds known as Mugayyar, in the southern part of the valley, as the home of Abraham. Ur is a very ancient city" (*Light on the Old Testament from Babel*, by Albert T. Clay, pub. 1907).

The former identification of Urfa as the area where the old Ur was located is much closer than the new and wrong identification of Ur.

Ur of the Chaldeans by the river Chebar

pr92» Abraham came "out of the land of the Chaldeans" (Acts 7:4). This is what Genesis 11:31 and other verses say:

- "And they went forth with them *from Ur of the Chaldees*" (Gen 11:31).

- "You the LORD God, who did choose Abram, and brought him forth *out of Ur of the Chaldees*, and gave him the name of Abraham" (Neh 9:7).

- "I am the LORD that brought you *out of Ur of the Chaldees*" (Gen 15:7).
- "The *land of the Chaldeans by the river Chebar . .* " (Ezek 1:3).

pr93» In Abraham's time the Biblical land of the Chaldeans where Ur was located was northwestern Mesopotamia. It was close to the Armenians (*Ramses II and His Time*, by I. Velikovsky, pp. 170, 168ff; note Gurney, *Hittites*, Chap VI; see endnote). The Biblical Chaldean language was the Aramean or Syriac language (Dan 2:4). The Biblical river Chebar was "in the land of the Chaldeans" (Ezek 1:3). This river C*hebar may* be the present day river K*habor* in northeast Syria near Haran and *Ur*fa and south of Armenia in Turkey. Later the Chaldeans moved southward to Babylon and were known in Ezekiel's time as the "Babylonians of Chaldea, the land of their nativity" (Ezek 23:15). But in contemporary literature the "Ur of Chaldeans" is located hundreds of miles in a southeastern direction from the Chaldeans' northwestern Mesopotamian homeland.

Land of Abraham's Nativity was the real Ur of the Chaldeans

pr94» The real Ur of the Chaldeans was the land of Abraham's nativity or birth:

- God told Abraham in Mesopotamia to "get you out of *your country, and from your kindred*" (Acts 7:3).
- Haran was a brother of Abram [Gen 11:27], and Haran died "in the land of his nativity [Hebrew, "his (place of) birth"], in *Ur of the Chaldees*" (Gen 11:28).
- When Abram went out of Ur he was told by God, "get out of your country, and from your kindred [Hebrew, "your (place of) birth"]" (Gen 12:1). And "get you out of your country, and from your kindred [Greek, "relations"]" (Acts 7:3).
- "The LORD ... took me from my father's house [family], and from the land of my kindred [Hebrew, '(place of) birth']" (Gen 24:7).

pr95» Abraham's birthplace, his nativity, was in *northwestern* Mesopotamia in the land of Syria or Aram or Padan-Aram (rivers of Aram):

- "And Abraham said unto his eldest servant of his house ... you shall go unto *my* country, and to *my* kindred, and take a wife unto my son Isaac ... and the servant took ten camels ... and went to *Mesopotamia* unto the city of Nahor [the name of Abraham's brother] ... and Isaac was forty years old when he took Rebekah to wife, the daughter of Bethuel the *Syrian of Padan-Aram*, the sister to Laban the Syrian [Hebrew — "Aramite"]" (Gen 24:2, 4, 10; 25:20).

pr96» Syrians are Aramites or Arameans who lived between the rivers (Euphrates & Tigris), in the land of Aram, northwestern Mesopotamia. This area was Abraham's birthplace. Abraham was called a Hebrew (Gen 14:13). Abraham the Hebrew came from across the Euphrates river. One of the fathers or patriarchs of Moses was Jacob (Israel) who was perishing from famine in Palestine before he went down to Egypt (Gen chap 42ff). Thus, Moses said, "My father was a perishing *Aramean*, and he went down to Egypt" (Deut 26:5, see Hebrew text).

pr97» **Review**. Abraham went forth out of Ur of the Chaldeans "to go unto the land of Canaan, and they came unto Haran and dwelt there" (Gen 11:31). This "Ur" was his homeland, his birthplace. He was born there with his brother Haran (Gen 11:27-28). When God spoke to Abraham in Ur of the Chaldeans, in Mesopotamia, he told Abraham to move away from his birthplace, his relatives, his kindred, and from his fathers house (family) (Gen 12:1; Acts 7:2-4, see above). Because Abraham spoke in a Semitic tongue, because his own country was the Ur of Chaldeans, because one of the Chaldeans' languages was a Semitic tongue (Dan 2:4 — "Syriac" or "Aramaic"), this is one reason why we can say that the real "Ur of Chaldeans" was located in northwestern Mesopotamia near Ebla and Haran (the name of Abraham's brother). It was not the southeastern "Ur" with its different language and culture. This southeastern "Ur" is actually spelled, "Urim" not *Ur* (*The Sumerians*, S. N. Kramer, pp. 28 & 298). But the "Ur of the Chaldeans" was probably the "Ur" mentioned in the Ebla tablets that was located "in the territory of Haran" (*Ebla Tablets*, p. 42; *Ebla*, by Bermant and Weitzman, 1979, p. 190; *Riv. Bibl.* [1977], p. 236).

Ebla Tablets' Proof

pr98» A Professor Paolo Matthiae of the Rome University has been excavating the Tell Mardikh (Ebla) since 1964. In 1968 he discovered a statue bearing the name Ibbit-Lim, a king of Ebla. The kingdom of Ebla was known to a few because Ebla is mentioned in Sumerian, Akkadian, and Egyptian texts (*Ebla Tablets*, pp. 11-12). Professor Giovanni Pettinato, University of Rome, is the epigrapher working on the tablets. He has written the book, *The Archives of Ebla* (1981) and wrote in such journals as *Biblical Archaeologist* (May, 1976).

pr99» The reports on the Ebla tablets reveal that the culture of Ebla had a Semitic language, "a forerunner of all the Canaanite dialects, which include Ugaritic, Phoenician, and Hebrew" (*National Geographic*, Dec, 1978, p. 749; *The Archives of Ebla*, by Giovanni Pettinato, 1981, pp. 56, 65). Many of the personal names in the Ebla tablets closely resemble Hebrew names: *Abramu* (Abraham), *Esaum* (Esau), and *Saulum* (Saul) (Nat. Geo. Dec, 1978, p. 736). The old city state of Ebla with its Semitic language was only about 100 miles from Haran, while the other and more southern "Ur" (Urim) with its different language was about 600 miles away — a large distance in those days. Along with the Biblical proof, we conclude that Abram, who spoke in a Semitic tongue, came from the "Ur of Chaldeans" which was much closer to Haran and Ebla than the southeastern "Ur." It was in this northwestern area where a Semitic culture existed. It was from this area that Abraham came from.

Ur was in the Territory of Haran

pr100» Clifford Wilson in his paperback book called *Ebla Tablets* writes of his disappointment on finding "a city of Ur is referred to in the trade tablets. It is described as being 'in the territory of Haran.'" (p. 42) Not only does the Ebla tablets mention Ur, but they say it is in the territory or locality of Haran. This is further proof that Abraham's city of Ur was near Haran in northwestern Mesopotamia, not the contemporary "Ur" hundreds of miles southeast of Haran and Ebla.

pr101» But Mr. Wilson was "somewhat disappointed." Why was he disappointed? "I am the producer of a number of audio-visuals on Bible backgrounds, and one of them is based on Sir Leonard Wooley's findings at the city of Ur" (Wilson, p. 42; and see C.L. Woolley, *Ur of the Chaldees*, 1929). It was the southeastern "Ur," first identified by Henry Rawlinson in the middle 1800's, that Wooley helped to popularize as being the "Ur of Chaldeans." Instead of Mr. Wilson seeing that he made a mistake, instead of reviewing the Biblical data as we have, Wilson comes up with a weak excuse to retain the contemporary "Ur" as the Ur of Abraham (p. 44).

Chaldeans Language Confusion

pr102» At one time the so-called "Syriac" language (dan 2:4) or the "Aramaic" language was called Chaldee. Notice "Chaldee" in such books as *The New Englishman's Hebrew and **Chaldee** Concordance*, or the *Hebrew and **Chaldee** Lexicon* by Gesenius. Before the mistaken identification of the southeastern "Ur" for the Biblical "Ur of Chaldeans," the Aramaic tongue was identified with the Chaldeans. "It [Aramaic] was formerly inaccurately called Chaldee (Chaldaic) because spoken by the Chaldeans of the book of Daniel (2:4-7:28). But since the Chaldeans are known to have generally spoken Akkadian, the term Chaldee has been abandoned" (*Unger's Bible Dict.*, "Aramaic").

pr103» Unger calls the former identification inaccurate because of the contemporary identification of the southern "Ur" as being the Biblical "Ur of Chaldeans." But this contemporary identification was mistaken as this paper makes clear. Outside of the Ebla evidence, the internal evidence of the Bible should have made it plain to Sir Leonard Woolley and the others that the "Ur of Chaldeans" was not some foreign culture to the Semitic Abraham, but Abraham's own culture and homeland.

pr104» It is of interest to note that the Chaldeans used at least two languages: the language used in Babylon was Akkadian-Babylonian, and the Syriac or Aramean language (*Ramses II*, p. 171 & Dan 2:4ff). The city state of Ebla also used two or more languages in their writings: the Semitic Paleo-Canaanite language, and the "Sumerian script, with Sumerian logograms adapted to represent Akkadian words and syllables" (*Ebla Tablets*, p. 24). "The schematic presentation of the verbal, nominal, and pronominal systems warrants classifying Eblaite in the West Semitic group .... For this reason I prefer to classify Eblaite as a Canaanite Language, thanks to its close relationship with Ugaritic, Phoenician, and Biblical Hebrew .... Eblaite becomes a chronological companion of Old Akkadian of the East Semitic group" (Pettinato, ...*Ebla*, p.65). But "the bilingualism of the tablets is only apparent. Though 80 percent of the words are Sumerian and only 20 percent are Eblaite, all of them were read as Eblaite. The Sumerian terms are in reality logograms which the scribes translated without difficulty into their own language when they read them" (... *Ebla*, by Pettinato, p. 57). It should be noted that there is no recorded evidence that the southeastern "Ur" had a Semitic culture or wrote with a Semitic script. Although one must be careful. The famous H.C. Rawlinson in about the 1850's mistakenly designated the Sumerian language as the "Akkadian" or "Scythian or Turanian" language (*The Sumerians*, p. 20). So you must be careful when studying old writings concerning the Sumerian language.

Babylonians and the Hittites

pr105» Velikovsky tries to connect the Babylonians with the Hittites (*Ramses II*, chapters IV ff). Gurney in his book, *The Hittites*, may in someway connect them:

- "Akkadian. This is the name now universally given to the well-known Semitic language of Babylonia and Assyria; to the Hittites, however, it was known as 'Babylonian'. It was widely used in the Near East for diplomatic correspondence and documents of an international character, and the Hittite kings followed this custom when dealing with their southern and eastern neighbours. Many Hittite treaties and letters are therefore wholly in Akkadian and were available in translation long before the great bulk of the archive of Boghazkoy had been deciphered. In addition, as mentioned above, Akkadian words are common in texts written in Hittite, but it is generally held that this is a form of allography .... Two languages only — Hittite and Akkadian — were used by the Hittite kings for their official documents" (Chap VI, pp. 125, 117).

pr106» ***Summarize***. The above Biblical evidence clearly indicates that the real "Ur of Chaldeans" was the Semitic speaking one, located in northwestern Mesopotamia. This "Ur" is mentioned in the Ebla tablets as being near Haran. The Ebla culture used a Semitic language and had similar names as the ones used by the Hebrews. The culture of Ebla was located near the city of Haran and near northwestern Mesopotamia at approximately the same time as Abraham lived. It was Abraham, a Semitic speaking Hebrew, who left his own homeland, where his relatives lived so as to go into the land of Canaan. Abraham's homeland was the "Ur of Chaldees" which is also close to or the same as Padan-Aram, located in northern

Mesopotamia. From his homeland, Abraham went to Canaan, by first going through and living in Haran for a while. But the contemporary "Ur" is located far from northwestern Mesopotamia; it had a different culture than Abraham's. Thus, this southern Ur (*Urim*) is not Abraham's own country.

PR2: Beast-System Paper

Ten Horns
Ten to Seven
1260 Days
Identity of First Three Beasts
Mean and Base Horn
Unity Power
Identity of the Fourth Beast
When is the Beast Set Up?
Daily Sacrifice
1290 Days
1335th Day
Beast Chart

System of the Beast

pr107» Who or what is the Beast? The "Beast" is described primarily in the 12th, 13th, and 17th chapters of Revelation, and in the book of Daniel. Notice carefully this Biblical description:

- And I stood upon the sand of the sea and saw a beast rise up out of the sea, having *seven heads* and *ten horns*, and upon his horns ten crowns, and upon his heads the names of blasphemy. And the beast which I saw was like unto a *leopard*, and his feet were as the feet of a *bear*, and his mouth as the mouth of a *lion*: and the *dragon* gave him his power, and his throne, and great authority (Rev 13:1-2).

pr108» This description of the "Beast" is symbolic. The very word "beast" is a symbol. We need to interpret the symbols in the Bible concerning the Beast, for they stand for something real. And when we know what all these symbols mean, we will know who or what the "Beast" is. The Bible interprets its own symbols and tells us what these symbols represent.

pr109» In the seventh chapter of Daniel, we find these same symbols described again. We see the beasts with the "seven heads," the "ten horns," and we see the "lion," the "bear," and the "leopard." And in the book of Daniel it tells us what these symbols represent.

pr110» God had given Daniel understanding in dreams and visions (Dan 1:17):

- Daniel said: In my vision at night I looked, and there before me were the four winds of heaven churning up the great sea (Dan 7:2, NIV).

As in Revelation, the "beasts" came up out of the sea:

- *Four great beasts*, each different from the others, came up out of the sea (Dan 7:3, NIV).

Four Beasts

pr111» And Daniel had a dream and vision in which he saw four great beasts:

- **(1)** The *first* was like a *lion*, and it had the wings of an eagle. I watched until its wings were torn off and it was lifted from the ground so that it stood on two feet like a man, and the heart of a man was given to it (Dan 7:4, NIV; note Dan 4:33-34, 'eagle feathers').

- **(2)** And there before me was a *second beast*, which looked like a *bear*. It was raised up on one of its sides, and it had three ribs in its mouth between its teeth. It was told, 'Get up and eat your fill of flesh!' (Dan 7:5, NIV)

- **(3)** After that, I looked, and there before me was *another beast*, one that looked like a *leopard*. And on its back it had four wings like those of a bird. This beast had *four heads*, and it was given authority to rule (Dan 7:6, NIV).

- **(4)** After that, in my vision at night I looked, and there before me was a *fourth beast* — terrifying and frightening and very powerful. It had large iron teeth; it crushed and devoured its victims and trampled underfoot whatever was left. *It was different from all the former beasts, and it had ten horns* (Dan 7:7, NIV).

pr112» So the first beast was like a "lion," the second was like a "bear," the third like a "leopard," and the fourth was so dreadful and terrible it could not be compared to any wild beast known to inhabit the earth, and it has ten horns.

Four Beasts = Four Kingdoms

pr113» Notice Daniel 7 where we see the *interpretation*:

- These great beasts, which are four, *are four kings* which shall arise out of the earth (Dan 7:17).

pr114» The word "king" is synonymous with *kingdom*, and is used in the sense that the king represents the kingdom over which he rules, for in verse 23 we read:

- The fourth Beast shall be the fourth *kingdom* upon the earth (Dan 7:23).

Notice also the word "kingdom" is used to explain the beasts in verses 18, 22, 24, and 27.

Seven Heads

pr115» There was only one head for the lion, one for the bear, but the third beast, the leopard, had *four heads*:

- After that, I looked, and there before me was *another beast*, one that looked like a *leopard*. And on its back it had four wings like those of a bird. This beast had *four heads*, and it was given authority to rule (Dan 7:6).

The fourth beast also had just one head (Dan 7:19-20, 'in his head'). Thus, there are seven heads on the Beast of Revelation.

Seventh Head With Ten Horns

pr116» Notice again that the fourth beast or kingdom is the seventh head. But out of this seventh head or kingdom comes the ten horns:

- "Then I wanted to know the true meaning of the *fourth beast* ... And concerning the ten horns in its head..." (Dan 7:19, 20).

- "The *fourth beast* is a fourth kingdom that will appear on earth ... And as to the ten horns, *out of this kingdom* shall arise ten kings" (Dan 7:23, 24).

pr117» This fourth beast with ten horns was different from the previous three kingdoms or beasts:

- "The fourth beast shall be the fourth kingdom upon earth, which *shall be diverse* from all kingdoms, and shall devour the whole earth, and shall tread it down, and break it in pieces" (Dan 7:23).

- "After this I kept looking in the night visions, and behold, a fourth beast, dreadful and terrifying and extremely strong; and it had large iron teeth. It devoured and crushed, and trampled down the remainder with its feet; and *it was different* from all the beasts that were before it, and it had ten horns" (Dan 7:7, NASB).

pr118» In the book of Revelation we note:

- "And I saw a beast coming up out of the sea, having ten horns and seven heads, and on his horns were ten diadems [crowns], and on his heads were blasphemous names. And the beast which I saw was like a *leopard*, and his feet were like those of a *bear*, and his mouth like the mouth of a *lion*" (Rev 13:1, 2, NASB).

pr119» The fourth beast of Daniel is the Beast of Revelation. The Beast pictures the previous three beasts incorporated within it (Rev 13:2). It has the *leopard*, which is the third kingdom (Dan 7:6, see above). It has the *bear*, which is the second kingdom (Dan 7:5, see above). It has the *lion*, which is the first kingdom (Dan 7:4, see above). It is different from the kingdom before it because it includes all of them in some sense, and because it has *ten horns*. The fourth kingdom will be as, if not more, rich, powerful, magnificent, than all the kingdoms before it. It will be so powerful that it will "devour the whole earth" (Dan 7:23). ["The whole earth" here means all the known earth at the time of the Biblical writer; in antitype it literally means all the earth.]

Ten Horns = Ten Kingdoms or Nations

pr120» Out of the great and dreadful fourth beast grew ten horns:

- It was different from all the former beasts, and it had ten horns (Dan 7:7).
- Then I wanted to know the true meaning of the fourth beast ... I also wanted to know about the ten horns on its head ... (Dan 7:19, 20).

pr121» What do the "horns" represent? Notice Dan 7:24: "and the ten horns out of this kingdom *are ten kings that shall arise*." Notice the ten horns, come *out of a fourth kingdom*. Since *king* in these prophecies stands for the *kingdom* he represents, and since the words are used interchangeably (Dan 7:17, 23), it follows that these ten horns are kingdoms or nations within the fourth kingdom or beast. These ten nations are represented by the ten "toes of the feet" of the image in Daniel 2:31-35, 42.

pr122» **Ten crowns**. Notice the ten horns of Revelation 13:2 had "ten crowns." These same horns with crowns on them are the same horns or kings indicated in Revelation 17:12: "and the ten horns which you saw are ten kings, which have received no kingdom yet [note, v. 10]; but receive power as kings one hour [Greek, "short period of time"] with the beast." When these kings receive power with the Beast for "one hour," or a short period of time, is when the Beast has ten crowns on its ten heads.

Ten to Seven

pr123» The Beast has ten horns in its seventh head, which is represented by the *ten* crowns of Revelation 13:1. But the Beast loses three. The following scriptures show that the Beast loses three horns or nations by them being "plucked up," "subdued," "broken," or "wounded to death."

pr124» Something strange happens to the fourth Beast: he loses three horns, or three kings, or three nations, or breaks three toes:

- "While I was thinking about the horns, there before me was *another horn*, an ignoble one {'little' #2192, 6810, & 6819: small in size or dignity; ignoble}, which came up among them; and *three of the first horns were uprooted* before it. This horn had eyes like the eyes of a man and a mouth that spoke boastfully. " (Dan 7:8)
- "And of the ten horns that were in his head, and of the other [horn] which came up, *and before whom three fell*" (Dan 7:20).

- "And the ten horns out of this kingdom are ten kings that shall arise: and another [kingdom] shall rise after them; and he shall be different from the first, and *he shall subdue three kings*" (Dan 7:24).
- "And the fourth kingdom shall be strong as iron ... and whereas you saw the feet and toes, part of potters' clay, and part of iron, *the kingdom shall be divided* ... the kingdom shall be partly strong, and partly broken*" (Dan 2:40-42).
- "Having seven heads and ten horns, and upon his horns *ten crowns* ... and I saw *one of his heads* [the seventh, with 10 horns] *as it were wounded to death*" (Rev 13:1, 3; see below, 'Eighth Head?').

pr125» Putting these scriptures together we see that the fourth kingdom or Beast, with its ten nations, will have three of its member nations: plucked up, subdued, broken, or wounded to death. Three nations will be subdued. They will be subdued by the "horn," that "shall subdue three kings" (Dan 7:24, 8, 20).

pr126» **Eighth Head?** "And here is the mind which has wisdom. The seven *heads* are seven mountains [or kingdoms], on which the woman sits. And there are seven kings [or mountains]; five are fallen and one is [remains of the third kingdom], and the other [7th mountain/kingdom] is not yet come; and when he comes [the 7th], he must continue a short space [time]" (Rev 17:9-10). Notice that the seventh kingdom ("mountain") when it comes will only continue a short time. But, "the Beast that *was, and is not*, even he is the *eighth* [kingdom or mountain], and is *out* of the seven [kingdoms or mountains] and goes into perdition [the lake of fire, Rev 19:19-20]" (Rev 17:11).

pr127» Now since the seven mountains or kingdoms are equated to the seven heads (Rev 17:9), then these are the heads that the woman sits on. But these verses say an eighth mountain will arise, and it is this mountain or kingdom that will go into the lake of fire. And it says this eighth is the Beast that was, and is not. And since it is the eighth mountain, then it must be the eighth head. But the Beast who was, and is not, has only seven heads (Rev 17:7).

pr128» **Deadly Wound**. Notice that in Revelation 13:3 that a head was as wounded to death, but its deadly wound was healed. This deadly wound will happen to the seventh mountain or kingdom of Revelation 17 with its ten horns or nations. And this "deadly wound" will subdue three of the ten horns (nations) of this seventh kingdom ("mountain") which is the ten-nation Beast (Dan 7:24). Thus, the eighth mountain or kingdom is the *healed* Beast of Revelation 13:3. It had ten horns, but three nations ("horns") will be subdued by the mean horn (Dan 7:20, 24).

pr129» In other words, "the Beast that *was* [the ten-nation Beast], and *is not* [the ten-nation Beast], even he is the eighth, and is out of the seven, and goes to perdition" (Rev 17:11). This Beast *was* [the ten-nation Beast], and *is not* [the beast with ten horns or nations], and *yet is* [the beast, but with only seven nations]. The "deadly wound" destroys the kingdom that *was* by subduing three nations ("kings"); the healing of this deadly wound creates a kingdom with seven nations as opposed to ten nations as before. The seven-nation Beast "is not" like the ten-nation Beast, "yet is" the same beast, but with three nations subdued.

First End-of-the-age Beast

pr130» At first, the seventh head of the Beast will have ten horns or nations. The seventh head, which is the fourth beast, is the head *after* the four heads of the third beast or kingdom. The seventh head is the fourth beast. This fourth beast is the *first* end-of-the-age Beast of Revelation with ten ruling or crowned horns (Rev 13:2; 17:12).

Second End-of-the-age Beast

pr131» But this first end-of-the-age Beast has a deadly wound whereby *three* horns, or kings, or toes, or nations are subdued. After this deadly wound the second Beast of Revelation comes alive with three of its former horns put down (Rev 13:3ff).

pr132» *Image of the Beast*. The seven-nation Beast is the "image" or likeness of the first Beast of Revelation (the ten-nation Beast). Therefore the "image of the Beast" is the seven-nation Beast (Rev 13:11-15). This is the true end-of-the-age Beast that rules superior in the last 1260 days of the kingdom of Satan.

1260 Days: the Last Days Before Christ Rules

pr133» The casting down of the three nations will be the "deadly wound" (see Rev 13:3). Notice that it is *after* the "deadly wound" when the Beast of Revelation, pictured in chapter 13, begins to speak "a mouth speaking great things and blasphemies" for 42 months or 3 and ½ years (Rev 13:5). This is what happens after three kings are subdued:

- "and he shall speak great words against the most high [blasphemy] ... until a time and times and dividing of time [3 and ½ years]" (Dan 7:25, 24).

pr134» The seven-nation end-of-the-age Beast rules the earth for 42 months; or a time, times, and dividing of time; or 1260 days (Rev 13:5; Dan 7:25; Rev 12:6, 14). It is during these 1260 days that the seven-nation Beast will speak blasphemies against God, and will seek to destroy God's Church (Rev 13:5-6; Dan 7:24-25; 12:7; Rev 12:6, 14).

pr135» The book of Revelation speaks *often* of a time period of 1260 days just before Christ returns:

- The 42 months of Revelation 13:5;
- and the 1260 days of Revelation 12:6;

- the time [1 year] times [2 years] and half a time [½ year] of Revelation 12:14;
- the 1260 days of Revelation 11:3;
- and the 42 months of Revelation 11:2

are the 1260 day periods mentioned in Revelation.

pr136» It is during these 1260 days or 42 months just before Christ physically returns that the Beast, in the truest sense, will reign great in the world (Rev 13:5; Dan 7:25; Dan 12:7).

pr137» After the 1260 days of the 'healed' Beast, then Christ returns and the 1000 years of the Kingdom of God begins. Note in context Daniel 7:8-9, 24-27; 2:42-45. We see in these scriptures the fourth beast of Daniel rules until he is destroyed and the Most High and his saints begin their rule. Christ begins his rule after the 1260 days as the above scriptures prove. Therefore the seven-nation Beast exists in the 1260 day period just before Christ returns.

Four Beasts or Kingdoms

pr138» These four kingdoms or beasts are also described in the second chapter of Daniel. King Nebuchadnezzar of the Chaldean Empire, who had taken the Jews captive, had a dream, the meaning of which God revealed to Daniel.

pr139» The dream is described in Daniel 2:31-35. The king saw a great image. Its head was of gold, its breast and arms of silver, its belly and thighs of brass, its legs of iron and its feet and toes were part iron and part clay. Finally, a stone, not with man's hands (but supernaturally) was cut out of the mountain, and this stone smote the image upon his feet and toes, thereby smashing the entire image together (v. 35a). Then the stone that smashed the image became a great mountain and filled the whole earth:

- "This is the dream; and we will tell the *interpretation* thereof to the king ... You art this head of gold. And after you shall arise another kingdom inferior to you, and another third kingdom of brass, which shall bear rule over all the earth. And the fourth kingdom shall be strong as iron: forasmuch as iron breaks in pieces and subdues all things; and as iron that breaks all these, shall it break in pieces and bruise .... And in the days of these kings shall the God of heaven set up a kingdom which shall not for olams be destroyed ... it shall break in pieces and consume all these kingdoms, and it shall stand for olams" (Dan 2:36-40, 44).

Nebuchadnezzar Until The Stone

pr140» There are four world-ruling kingdoms that begin with Nebuchadnezzar's kingdom. His kingdom was the Chaldean Empire which took away the Jews to Babylon. From Nebuchadnezzar's kingdom, which was the symbolical first beast of Daniel 7:4, or the symbolical tree of Daniel 4:20-23, or the golden head of the image of Daniel 2:32, 38, grew up or raised up the remaining kingdoms. And out of the fourth kingdom was to be ten kings or nations, which are symbolized by the ten toes on the image of chapter two of Daniel, or the ten horns of the fourth beast of chapter 7 of Daniel, or the ten horns of Revelation's Beast (Rev 13:1; 17:3, 12). The fourth kingdom will exist before Christ the Stone, and His kingdom will take over the world's governments, and fill the whole earth with the kingdom of God (cf Dan 2:32-45; Dan 7:2-14, 25-27).

pr141» *Christ Is The Stone*. The interpretation of the stone smashing the image on its toes is found in the 44th verse: "And in the days of these kings shall the God of heaven set up a kingdom, which shall not for olams ['never'] be destroyed: and the kingdom shall not be left to other people, but it shall break in pieces and consume all these kingdoms, and it shall stand for olams." The Stone is Christ and his kingdom. The interpretation of the Stone is given many places in the Bible, "Jesus of Nazareth ... *is the stone* which was set at naught of you builders, which is become head of the corner" (Acts 4:10-11).

pr142» The time when the Stone (Christ) takes over the kingdoms of the world "in the days of these kings," that is, the kings being the 'toes' of the image of Daniel, chapter two (Dan 2:43-44, 34). At Christ's physical return is when He shall destroy the Gentile kingdom (the Beast of Revelation, Rev 1:19-21; 11:15-19) in righteous warfare (Rev 19:11). The Stone will smite the image (the Gentile kingdoms) in righteousness, for "in righteousness he does judge and make war" (Rev 19:11). And righteous judgment or warfare is explained in Psalm 9:16, "the LORD [YHWH] is known by the judgment which he executes: the wicked is snared in the work of his *own* hands." In other words Christ the Stone will smite the image, by merely letting them or those of the Gentile kingdoms destroy themselves. This event is pictured in many places in the Bible. Here are two of them: "and was given to him that sat thereon to take peace from the earth," [How] "and that they should kill one another" (Rev 6:4). And, "for nation shall rise against nation, and kingdom against kingdom" (Matt 24:7). This is the Last War. See our paper on "Last War and God's Wrath" [PR5] for more on the Last War.

Fourth Beast

pr143» As we have seen the fourth beast is the seventh head of the seven-head and ten-horn Beast of Revelation 13:1-2. Out of this seventh head comes ten horns or nations who will rule as ten nations for "one hour," a short time period with the Beast (Rev 17:12). But the beast that causes the greatest trouble rules for 1260 or 42 months just before Christ's physical return. Just before these 1260 days three of the ten nations are subdued by the Beast (Dan 7:24-27, see above).

Identity of the First Three Beasts

pr144» Who were the first three beasts or kingdoms? Let's look at scripture and history to see.

pr145» *Image*. In the second chapter of Daniel, it identifies the head of the great image as king Nebuchadnezzar or the kingdom of Babylon (Dan 2:38). But in Daniel 2 it does not identify the second, third, and fourth kingdoms by name (Dan 2:39-40).

pr146» *Tree*. In the fourth chapter of Daniel, it identifies king Nebuchadnezzar with the tree, but it does not identify the bands of *iron* and *brass* left after the king is cut down. Remember, the third and fourth kingdom of the image in Daniel, chapter two, was made of brass and iron (Dan 2:39-40; see PR3 concerning this tree).

pr147» *Four Beasts*. In Daniel, chapter seven, it does not identify any of the beasts by name, except the clue of the eagle feathers (cf. Dan 7:4 w/ 4:33-34, 19-32).

pr148» *Seven-Head, Ten-Horn Beast*. In Revelation, chapters 12, 13, and 17 it does not identify the name of the kingdom involved except to tie this Beast of seven heads and ten horns with Daniel's beasts by its leopard, bear, and lion; Daniel's beasts were also like a lion, bear, and leopard (cf. Rev 13:2 w/ Dan 7:3-7) and they had/have seven heads and ten horns (see above).

pr149» *Ram, Goat*. But in Daniel, chapter 8, it identifies the second and third kingdom, or second and third beast, or the second through sixth head:

- "There stood before the river a RAM which had horns: and the **two** horns were high; but one was higher than the other, the higher came up last. I saw the RAM *pushing westward, and northward, and southward*, so that no beasts might stand before him..." (Dan 8:3-4).

- "The RAM which you saw having two horns are the kings of MEDIA and PERSIA" (Dan 8:20).

pr150» Thus the RAM with two horns (nations or kingdoms) is the Media-Persian empire with the two nations of Media and Persia. From its homeland it pushed westward (as far as Greece), northward (as far as the Caucasus Mts.), and southward (into Egypt), and while going westward took the land of Israel. It destroyed the Babylonian empire (Dan 5:24-31; see secular historical records). Through comparing various Biblical scripture, we can identify this RAM with the second beast of Daniel 7 and with the silver chest and arms of the great image of Daniel 2. *Media-Persia is thus identified, through comparison, as the second head of the seven headed beast.*

pr151» In Daniel, chapter 8, we read:

- "and as I was considering, behold, a he-GOAT came *from the west* ... and the-GOAT had a notable horn between his eyes ... and he came to the RAM that had two horns ... and I saw him come close unto the RAM ... and smote the RAM, and broke his two horns ... Therefore the he-GOAT grew very great: and when he was strong, the great horn [see v. 5] was broken; and *in its place came up four notable ones toward the four winds of heaven*" (Dan 8:5-8).

- "And the rough GOAT is the king of GRECIA: and the great horn that is between his eyes is the first king. Now that being broken, whereas four stood up in its place, *four kingdoms shall stand up out of the nation*, but not in his power" (Dan 8:21-22).

- One of the last kings of Persia "shall stir up all against the realm of GRECIA. And a mighty king [Alexander the Great] shall stand up, that shall rule with great dominion, and do according to his will. And when he shall stand up, his kingdom shall be broken, *and shall be divided toward the four winds of heaven*; and not of his posterity, nor according to his dominion which he ruled; for his kingdom shall be plucked up, even for others beside these" (Dan 11:2-4).

pr152» Thus, the he-GOAT was the kingdom of Macedonia. History identifies this empire as the one under Alexander the Great who came from the west and destroyed the Media-Persian empire and took its territory. After Alexander "grew very great," after "he was strong," he "was broken" and four kingdoms came up in the place of Alexander's kingdom.

pr153» Alexander the Great died shortly after he conquered a great territory from the Indus river near India to Greece and south into Egypt. The four kingdoms that came from Alexander's kingdom came from four of his generals not from his posterity (his physical heirs). After more than 20 years of struggle among successors of the empire, by the year 301 BC (according to conventional chronology and history) four generals and their territories were:

- **(1)** CASSANDER reigning over Macedon and Greece;
- **(2)** LYSIMACHUS reigning over Thrace and Bithynia (Asia Minor);
- **(3)** PTOLEMY reigning over Egypt and Palestine;
- **(4)** and SELEUCUS reigning over Syria, Babylonia, and territory to the east as far as the Indus river (Seleucus took over Syria and Babylon from

general Antigonus, but Antigonus was never called "king" in the territory he controlled militarily. Antigonus was a power behind some who through struggle were attempting to be successors to Alexander's rule; see *Babylonian Chronology* by Parker and Dubberstein, 1971, pp 19 & 20).

pr154» **Greek Culture**. These four kingdoms did not have the unified power of Alexander's empire: "but not in his power" (Dan 8:22). But because of Alexander's conquest, the culture of Greece was spread to the four winds or four directions of the compass. A unified currency was established, the Attican coin measure, and thus a world economy or vast economic area was created. Greek became the universal language (*Koine*) over a wide area, cities were established, and libraries built. The *Septuagint* or a Greek text of the Bible, was also a result of the third beast — the Grecian Empire. *It is these four kingdoms of the four generals that are counted as the four heads of the third beast* (Dan 7:6), *which are the third, fourth, fifth, and sixth head of the seven headed beast.*

Babylon — The First Beast

pr155» The four beasts of chapter 7 of Daniel are the same four ruling Gentile powers that are identified by the interpretation of the "image" of Nebuchadnezzar's dream (see above). The *first was Nebuchadnezzar's kingdom*, the Chaldean Empire, called "Babylon" after the name of its capitol city (Dan 2:32, 38; and see above). This kingdom symbolically had one head.

Media-Persia — The Second Beast

pr156» The *second kingdom* which followed we know from history. It was the Persian Empire, often called Media-Persia, composed of Medes and Persians. Notice the Biblical description of the Medes taking over the kingdom of Babylon. This kingdom symbolically had one head. See Daniel 5:28-31; 5:1-31; 8:3-4, 20, and see above.

Greece With Four heads — Third Beast

pr157» The *third world kingdom* was Greece, or Macedonia under Alexander the Great, who conquered the great Persian Empire. But Alexander died after his swift conquest, and his four Generals divided his vast Empire into four regions: Macedonia and Greece; Thrace and Western Asia; Syria and territory east to the Indus River; and Egypt. These Generals were the "four heads" of the third beast of Daniel 7:6. Notice the scripture on this in Daniel 7:6; 8:5-8, 21-22, and see above.

Six Heads = Babylon, Media-Persia, And Greece

pr158» The first three beasts or kingdoms have six heads. Thus the fourth beast or kingdom must have the seventh head.

Who Or What Is The Seventh Head?

pr159» *Roman Empire?* There are presently many theories on the identity of the seventh head or the fourth world kingdom of Daniel. Some say it is the revival of the Roman Empire, but this is not so. Some argue that Rome was too important to be left out of Daniel's vision of world-empires, but Daniel never mentions Rome. It is argued that the terrible character of the fourth kingdom is best fulfilled by Rome, but I say it is best fulfilled by a nuclear armed nation(s). Some argue that the Roman theory is favored by the statement in Dan 2:44, "in the days of these kings [fourth kingdom with ten "toes" or ten "horns"] shall the God of heaven set up a kingdom," for the Roman Empire was ruling Palestine when Christ first appeared. But remember, even after Christ's resurrection the kingdom of God had not yet been set up for at that time his apostles asked him, "will you at this time restore again the kingdom" (Acts 1:6). Christ's apostles were asking about restoring Israel's kingdom, which was the kingdom of God in a typical sense (see PR1). His apostles at that time were thinking physically about physical Israel, but Christ when he spoke of the Kingdom of God was referring to Spiritual Israel (PR1). Christ had not yet at that time set up the Kingdom of God on earth. Prophesy tells us the kingdom will only be set up when the time of the Gentile kingdoms is ended and Christ returns (Dan 7:23-27; 2:44; Luke 21:24; Rev 11:2; PR2 & PR3; see *Biblical Hermeneutics*, by Milton S. Terry, chapter 22). Let's look to scripture for the answer.

Mean and Base Horn

pr160» From Daniel 7:8, 20 we see that the "mean horn" {'little'= # 2192, 6810, 6819, mean, ignoble, base, diminished in size or behavior} with the mouth that spoke great things and ruled the 1260 days before Christ's return is the same horn spoken about in Daniel 8:9 and is "the king of fierce countenance" (Dan 8:23). This horn subdues three kings (Dan 7:8, 20, 24). This is the horn, which grows exceeding great, *toward the south, and toward the east and toward the pleasant land*" (Dan 8:9). The pleasant land is the land of Israel. It was Alexander the Great that came from the west to conquer Media-Persia (Dan 8:5). It is the debased horn that comes, and in some way grows great in reference toward the South, East, and pleasant land (Dan 8:9).

pr161» **It is the horn that comes "out of *the* one from them"** (Dan 8:9, Hebrew text). **The "them" being the four notable ones or four kingdoms that spread out toward the four winds of heaven** (Dan 8:8, 22). It is in the "latter time of *their* kingdom" that the evil king will appear (Dan 8:23). "Their kingdom" was the Grecian empire. But this kingdom was spread out to the four winds of heaven (Dan 8:8; 11:4). Yet out of the one of the dissipated kingdoms will come the base horn.

pr162» In an imperfect sense, Antiochus IV Epiphanes was 'the one of them' ("them" being the four kingdoms that came from Alexander's kingdom). And it was this kingdom that was great towards the south (Egypt), east (to the Indus R.), and the pleasant land or the land of Israel (see *Encyclopedia of Biblical Prophecy*, by Payne, pp 389-390; *The Interpretation of Prophecy*, by Tan, pp. 323ff; Clarke's commentary, Vol 4; etc.). Antiochus IV Epiphanes made great havoc in the land of Israel (Josephus, *Antiquities of the Jews*, Book 12, Chap 5 ff). But this is not the true meaning of these scripture, for one thing it never had ten horns (kingdoms) united to it.

Unity Power

pr163» The phrase, 'the one,' from 'out of *the one* from them' in Daniel 8:9 has two senses in Hebrew. Antiochus IV and his Seleucidan Empire was in a sense from the former four kingdoms of Greece under Alexandra the Great: he was one from them. But the Hebrew text also indicates a *unity* of the remains of the Alexandrian Empire:

- "out of *the* one from them," or "out of the unity from them" (see Hebrew text). In the Hebrew text 'the one' (#259, *ha 'echad*) means 'the **unity** from them.' (Hebrew text: compare Gen 32:8 (9); 34:16; 41:25; Exo 12:49; 24:3;Jud 20:1, 8; 1 Sam 11:7; 2 Sam 2:25; etc.)

pr164» The real sense of this scripture is that there will be a unification of the dispersed four kingdoms of the four generals of Alexander. Out of the *unity* of the old and dispersed Grecian empire comes the Beast. The unification character of the Beast is indicated by the previous empires being included in some way in the Beast of Revelation. Thus we see that the Beast in Revelation 13:1-2 included Babylonian (lion), Media-Persian (bear), and the Grecian empire (leopard). The second kingdom, the Persian one, took over the territory of the first kingdom, Babylon. The third kingdom (Grecian empire) took over the second kingdom's territory. The fourth kingdom, with its ten nations, will in turn in some way control the territory of the former kingdoms. But when we look at the maps of these kingdoms we see that the second kingdom took somewhat different territories than the first, and the third took somewhat different territories than the second. Thus, the fourth kingdom's territory will not have *exactly* the same territories as the beasts before it. **The fourth beast with ten horns will control or have great influence in the land through a treaty or as a league of nations united for some common purpose.**

pr165» The seventh head is then a **unity** head or unifying head. The seventh head has ten nations or horns. Its existence is just before the time of Christ's kingdom. The Bible does *not* give us the names of these ten kingdoms, but it does give the **number** of the nations who will join into an end-of-the-age united league. It is out of the unity of these kings that the

Beast will come. It is out of the unity of the ten nations that the Beast will show itself, and this Beast will subdue three of the ten nations exactly 1260 days before Christ's return. This Beast becomes great in reference to the east, the south, and the pleasant land. But in a higher sense the whole world is the future land of Spiritual Israel. In the truest sense it is the spiritual Beast that becomes great in *all* the earth (see PR3 & "Seed Paper" [PR1]).

Kings of the North and South

pr166» In a sense the kings of the north and south are represented by the two legs on the great image of Daniel, chapter two. The king of the north being the Seleucidan kingdom. The king of the south being the Ptolemaic kingdom. Both these kings struggled over the land of Israel. In Daniel, chapter 11, is a description of the struggle between these two kingdoms (see *Encyclopedia of Biblical Prophecy*, by Payne, pp 389-390; *The Interpretation of Prophecy*, by Tan, pp. 323ff; Clarke's commentary, Vol 4; etc.).

pr167» But *antitypically* the king of the north and king of the south indicate the divided kingdom of the Beast. *All* the kingdoms of the world in the old age belong to the influence of the spiritual Beast. Thus all the kingdoms are divided against each other (see "Last War and God's Wrath" paper [PR5]). Typically, chapter 11 of Daniel occurred over decades, but antitypically the battles will be in the true time of the end before Christ's return, especially at the very end — the Last War. The Beast will be great in the "glorious land" (Dan 11:16, 24, 41, 45; 8:9) and the "place" of the sanctuary (Dan 8:9, 11). But in an antitypical or higher sense, the "place" of the sanctuary are the real Christians — those with God's Spirit inside them. The Beast will go into the physical place of the physical sanctuary, but in the higher sense of the scripture the Beast goes against the Spiritual sanctuary. Chapter 11 can be interpreted in a dual sense (see PR3 and "Last War" paper [PR5]).

Identity of the Fourth Beast

pr168» We have seen that the first end-of-the-age Beast is an accumulation of world powers into a ten-nation league of nations, a united league of ten nations united by treaty, written or oral. The Babylonian (lion), Media-Persian (bear), and Grecian (leopard) kingdom were old-world powers who came to control the land of Israel. The third beast (Grecian empire) was spread out to the four winds. But near the end-of-the-age it will be unified. That is, a unification of *world powers* will occur, since the first three beasts represent known world powers. This unification will be of ten nations.

Identified by the Number of Nations Unified

pr169» As of now, the identity of each of the ten nations cannot be ascertained. They *may* include the people or territory of Greece, or Babylon, or Persia, but not necessarily so. The scripture says the "Beast" becomes great in reference to the south, to the east, and to the glorious land (Dan 8:9). Thus, it becomes great to the land of Israel, and to the east and south of it. Until the ten nations join together no one will be able to identify the ten nations exactly. But before they join you can be sure of the NUMBER of the Beast or the number of the nations of this united force or empire. At first there will be ten; later, after 30 days there will be seven (see 1290 Days, below). **Thus the identity is ascertained, not by the *name* of the nations, but by the *number* of nations that are unified.**

pr170» The unification of *ten* nations is but the first of an end-of-the-age Beast. There is a second end-of-the-age Beast and it has *seven* nations. The seven-nation league comes into existence 1260 days before Christ's return.

When Is The Beast Set Up?

pr171» Now we know what is the Beast of Revelation. The Beast in the truest sense will be fulfilled during the 1260 day period just before Christ physically returns. But *when* is the ten-nation league going to be set up? We know by our study that during the 1260 day period only *seven* nations will be with the individual Beast, who will be the shadow of Satan himself (see above & PR3). Sometime *before* the 1260 days a ten-nation league must be set up that will give its power to the system of the Beast (Rev 17:12-13). At the 1260th day before Christ appears physically, the seven-member Beast will take over; but when is the ten-nation league to be set up?

pr172» Now the Bible is dual, type and antitype. The prophecy of the Bible is dual: typical and real fulfillments. It is the time of the end when the prophetic fulfillments will happen in the truest sense.

Daily Sacrifice

pr173» Now in Daniel it speaks about the mean horn and the DAILY SACRIFICE, and the "abomination that makes desolate" (Dan 8:9, 13, 23-25; 11:31; 12:11). The "abomination that makes desolate" is also spoken of by Christ when he was telling His disciples about His return (Matt 24:15). What is the "daily sacrifice," and the "abomination that makes desolate?"

pr174» Now typically we know what the daily sacrifice was. It was the Israelite's twice daily religious sacrifice of animals (Num 28:1-8). Antiochus IV Epiphanes in a sense stopped these sacrifices (Josephus, *Antiquities of the Jews*, Book 12, Chap 5 ff). Now what did these sacrifices represent?

pr175» As Hebrews 10:1 and 8:4-5 projects, these sacrifices were "the example and shadow of heavenly things," or spiritual things since the Bible uses the words "heaven" and "spiritual" interchangeably (1 Cor 15:44-49; see "Duality Paper" [BP4]). What is the heavenly, or Spiritual, or antitypical meaning of the daily sacrifices?

pr176» Now the Bible speaks about Christians being "*living* sacrifices," or "*spiritual* sacrifices" (Rom 12:1; 1 Pet 2:5). Further the Bible calls Christians "sheep for the slaughter" (Rom 8:36) in that they suffer for doing what is right, as Christ suffered, or was sacrificed for what was right (1 Pet 3:14, 17; 4:1; 3:17; Heb 10:14; 9:23, 26; Isa 53:10; 2 Cor 5:21).

pr177» Christians and Christ were/are "*living* sacrifices," or "*Spiritual* sacrifices." They were/are living sacrifices because they have the **living** Spirit inside them. The sacrifices or sufferings of Christians are somewhat like the others (Job 15:20; 31:3) except Christians have the living Spirit, and they suffer for their good (1 Pet 3:14, 17).

pr178» Yet there are also *dead* sacrifices offered by those labeled the "dead" by the Bible. The old sacrifices were for the remembrances of sin (Heb 10:3). These sacrifices were for remembrances of sin, for many of mankind's problems, sacrifices, and sufferings are because of his sins. It is wrong behavior that causes mankind's ills. And sin is merely wrong behavior, or behavior that man does to others that he does not really want done to himself. The "dead" sacrifices are the sacrifices of those with only the dead spirit, the other-mind.

pr179» Therefore the antitypical "daily sacrifice" is the daily suffering of all mankind. And when Daniel speaks of the daily sacrifice being taken away (Dan 8:11; 11:31; 12:11), he means, Spiritually or antitypically, the daily sacrifice of mankind by the hand of sin (or Satan) will be taken away. We are to understand God by taking the higher, or Spiritual, or antitypical meanings of Biblical scripture since God is Spirit and speaks to us Spiritually (John 4:24; 6:63; Phil 3:19; Col 3:1-2). And the time when the "daily sacrifice" is taken away is at Christ's physical return, for it is at that time and after that time that man's daily sacrifice will be taken away.

Now we know the truest meaning of what Daniel was speaking of when he spoke about the daily sacrifice being taken away. And we know when it will be taken away — at Christ's physical return.

pr180» *Abomination of Desolation*. In Daniel 12:11 it speaks about the "abomination that makes desolate" being "set up" ["to give" or "to bestow" in Hebrew]. The Hebrew word translated "abomination" means "a detestable thing." Now this "abomination" is an "abomination that makes desolate." It is a detestable thing that destroys.

pr181» In Daniel 8:9-13, 23-25, it speaks of the "mean horn" as destroying the daily sacrifice through transgression, and speaks of the "*transgression of desolation*." And Daniel 9:26-27 speaks about an end-of-the-age war that makes desolation. And in Daniel 11, which antitypically speaks of the "latter days" (note Dan 10:14 & Dan 11:40), it speaks about the "abomination that makes desolate" and about the abomination taking away the daily sacrifice. Therefore by putting these verses together, Daniel is saying that the *abomination is* the despicable horn, or as we show in PR2 and 3 (*Beast Papers*) he is also the end-of-the-age Beast described in Revelation. He is a detestable thing, for he speaks lies, kills, and plays like he is God, yet he is merely the shadow of Satan. And the Abomination makes desolate by the means of the end-of-the-age war in which he is a principal participate (Dan 9:26-27; see God's Wrath). But because after this Last War, Christ with his peace comes, and thereby sin and evil is put away, then, in a sense, the Abomination of Desolation through the Last War also takes away man's daily sacrifice.

pr182» Or, it is through the LAST great sacrifice of mankind in this Last War (Isa 34:6; Zeph 1:8; Ezek 39:17; Rev 19:17-21) that man's sacrifice will be stopped by Christ the God, the Messiah (Matt 24:22; John 3:17) with His righteous wrath (see "God's Wrath" paper [PR4]).

1290 Days

pr183» The "abomination" is the *individual* Beast or the *system* of the Beast. And according to Daniel 12:11 it is set up 1290 days from (away from) when the daily sacrifice is taken away. The real daily sacrifice is taken away at Christ's return. Since the abomination can't be "set up" *after* Christ returns, then it is set up *before* Christ returns. It is set up *before* Christ's physical return. It is set up (or given or bestowed on the world) 1290 days *from* when the daily sacrifice is taken away, or from before the time of Christ's return. (It is the abomination or detestable thing that destroys that is set up on the 1290th day before Christ's return.)

pr184» But we have seen that for 1260 days the Beast of Revelation will rule before Christ returns, and that this Beast will be of seven nations. Therefore it is the ten nations, or a first end-of-the-age Beast that will be set up 1290 days before Christ physically returns. And it will exist for 30 days as ten nations with one mind (Rev 17:13). This is the "one hour" (a short period of time) that the ten nations will be together. But these nations' power goes to "the horn that looked more imposing than the others and that had eyes and a mouth that spoke boastfully" and the seven-member league (Dan 7:20, NIV). This leader takes control through his deceit and craftiness (Dan 7:23-25) 1260 days before Christ returns, as explained in PR2 & 3 (Beast Papers). Thus, the ten-nation league will rule for 30 days, *from* the 1290th day before Christ physically returns *to* the 1260th day before Christ returns. This **"backward count"** of the 1290 days is not an unusual method of counting. For example, the Greeks and Romans counted days in their month backward at times:

- "In this [Grecian] system, the count in the last decade [of the month] was backwards, i.e., counting from high to low towards the end of the month ... " (*Greek and Roman Chronology*, P. 60).

- "The designation of the days within the month was made by a peculiarly Roman system. The first day of the month was called *Kalendae*, the 5th (or 7th in a 31 day month), was called the *Nonae*, and the 13th (or 15th in a 31 day month) was called the *Idus*. These are the named days, and other days in the month were designated by counting back from these named days, counting inclusively" (*Greek and Roman Chronology*, p. 154).

2300 Evenings and Mornings Sacrifices or 1150 Days

pr185» In Daniel, chapter 8, it speaks of "evening morning two thousand and three hundred" (Dan 8:14, 26; v. 14 "day" = "evening-morning" in Aramaic [Hebrew]). In context with verses 11, 12, and 13, verse 14 is speaking about the daily sacrificeS: one in the evening and one in the morning. "This is the offering made by fire which you shall offer to the LORD; TWO lambs ... The one lamb shall you offer in the morning, and the other lamb shall you offer at even" (Num 28:3-4; see Exo 29:38ff). There were *two* sacrifices each day. Verse 14 spoke of 2300 evening and morning sacrifices: One in the evening and one in the morning equals two per day. 2300 evening-morning sacrifices equals 1150 days.

pr186» The 2300 evening-mornings in verse 14 is the answer to the question between the two holy men in verse 13: "How long shall be the vision concerning the daily sacrifice, and the transgression of desolation, to give both the sanctuary and the host to be trodden under foot?" (Dan 8:13) But in verse 9 and 11 it speaks of the evil horn going towards the pleasant land and casting down the *place* of the sanctuary. Since we know that the daily sacrifices, in its highest meaning, is taken away at Christ's coming, then the scriptures concerning the 2300 evening-morning sacrifices speak of the 1150 days *before* Christ's return when the place of the sanctuary is "cast down" or "trodden under foot."

1335th Day

pr187» There is also something important to happen on the 1335th day before Christ returns when he who reaches this date is blessed (Dan 12:12).

[**NOTE**: The 1335th day mentioned in Daniel 12:12 is the 1335th day before the antitypical daily sacrifice is to be taken away. This sacrifice is taken away at Christ's return. See the Beast Papers [PR2, PR3] and the "End of the Age" paper [PR7] to understand this: to understand the 1335th day one must understand our rendering of the 1290th and 1260th day.]

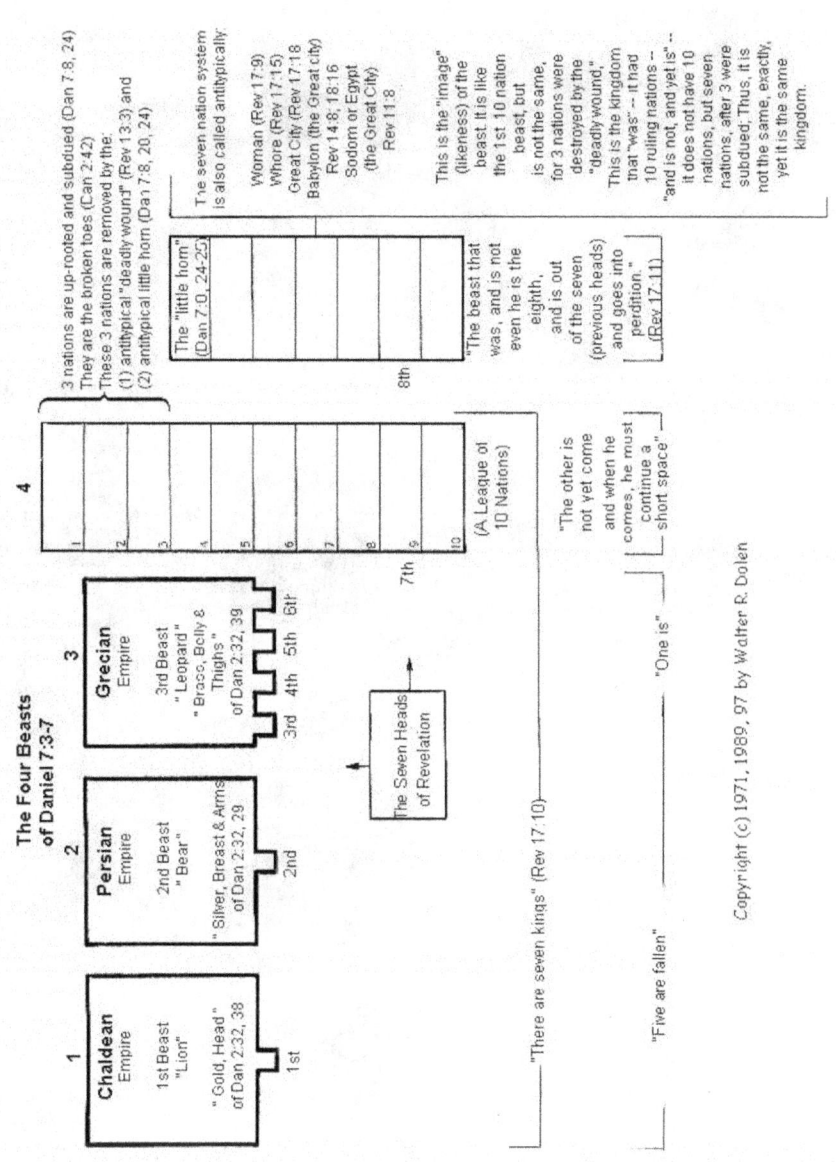

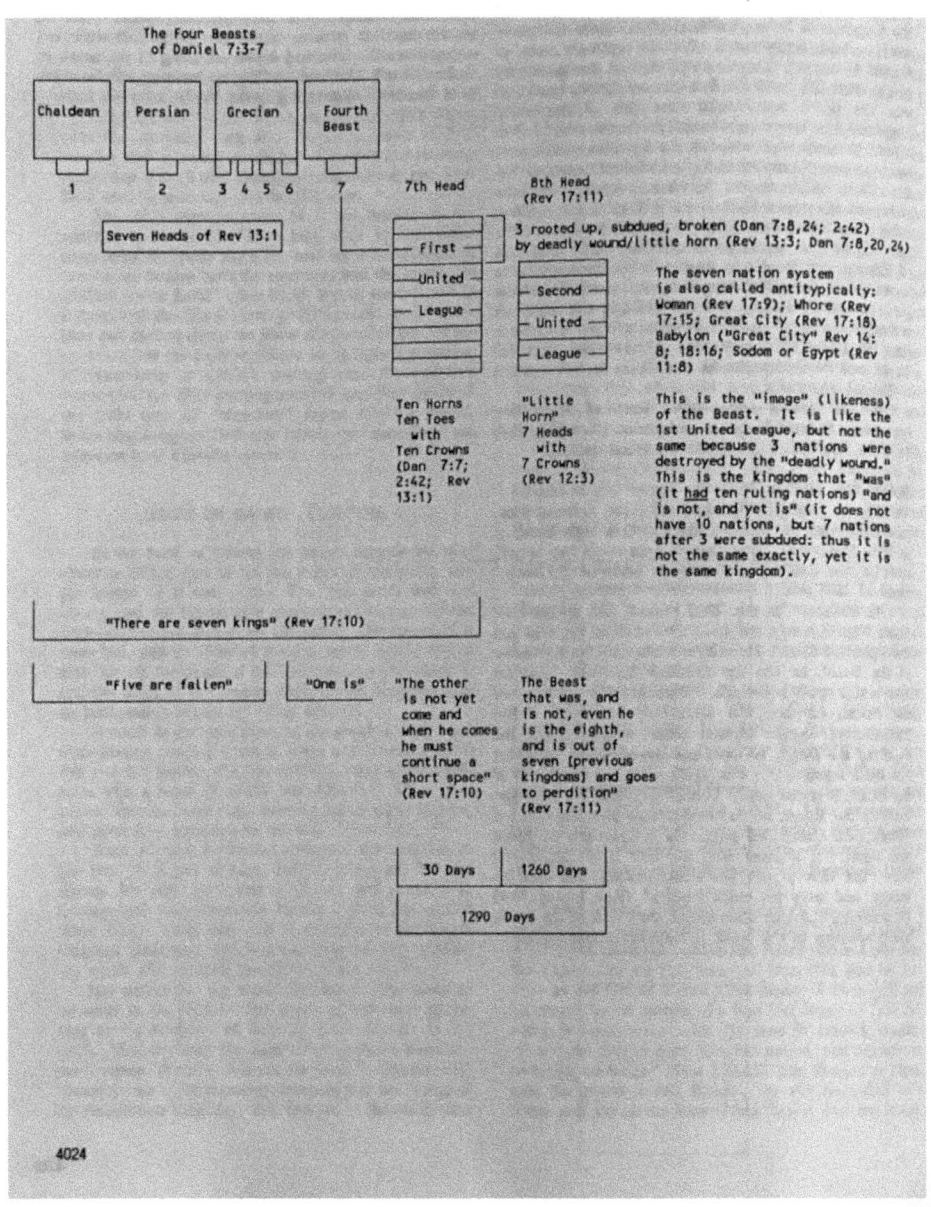

PR3: Beast-Man Paper
False-Prophet
Antichrist
Mark of the Beast
Beast and Church in the 1260 Days
Tree of Daniel

Individual Beast

System of the Beast versus Beast-man

pr188» From PR2, we see that the first Beast of Revelation will have ten nations with ten leaders or "kings." These ten leaders of the ten-nation league will be in a council of ten, they "receive power as kings one hour [a short period of time] *with* the Beast" (Rev 17:12). This "Beast" represents:

- (1), the whole *system* of the Beast (the league of nations);
- and (2), the man who is called the 'little' (diminished in size or behavior) horn by the Bible.

These ten leaders will share their power with each other (with the system of the Beast), and with the Beast-man. Thus the ten leaders are, in some way, in power with the Beast-man. But they "shall give their power and strength unto the Beast" (Rev 17:13; 17:17). At first the power of these nations will be given to the *system* of the Beast. Yet, because of this, later, at some point the Beast-man will gain all power. At some point the individual Beast will have the authority of the system of the Beast.

Last False-Christ

Abomination of Desolation

pr189» Although there are many who have/do/will claim to be Christ (Mat 24:5,24), there will be only one last false-Christ,

- "And I beheld another beast coming up out of the earth; and he had two horns like a lamb [false Lamb of God], and he will speak as a dragon [Satan Rev 12:9]" (Rev 13:11).

This same person will eventually claim to be God (2 Thes 2:4, 1-12; Dan 11:37; 8:11); he is the false-Christ of Revelation 13:11 who will make fire come down out of heaven (Rev 13:13 – the fire of the Last War and other wars before it). He is also called the abomination of desolation by Daniel and Christ (Dan 11:31; Mat 24:15; Mark 13:14) and by comparing Daniel 11:31 with Daniel 8:9-11 we see this same person is also the "little horn." He will come up among a diminished group, with seven kings or leaders instead of ten (Dan 11:23), and he will give life to the image of the Beast (Rev 13:15). The image of the Beast is the eighth kingdom, the league of seven nations — that is of the likeness or "image" of the seventh kingdom (see PR2 of the *Beast Paper*; Rev 17:10-11).

pr190» Now this false-Christ, or this individual Beast-man, after he receives all the power of the system of the Beast will rule as the speaker of the system of the Beast for 1260 days (Rev 13:5, 15; Dan 7:25). Thus, 1260 days before Christ the God physically returns, the false-prophet, who will eventually claim to be God, will exercise the power of the first Beast. The first Beast is the ten-nation league that exists immediately before this individual and his dictatorial-like rulership (Rev 13:12, 5). Those who do not honor this Beast-man will be destroyed (Rev 13:15). Thus, this is one reason the Church will be destroyed at the very end by the Beast (see PR6).

Little Horn

pr191» This Beast-man is the mean "horn" that is greater, and he is the one that will do the speaking for the whole kingdom (the system of the Beast). He is the horn with the eyes and mouth (Dan 7:20; Rev 13:5). He speaks for the system of the Beast. He will do all the speaking because at some point the other leaders of the ten member council or league, passively or overtly, will give him the power of the system of the Beast. The "diminished horn" or 'little[1] horn' in another sense is also the system of the Beast — the seven-nation Beast, because it was made smaller or diminished by three nations from its former ten nation status.

Man with the Number Six Hundred Sixty Six – 666

pr192» The individual Beast-man will have a name that calculates to six hundred and sixty six (Rev 13:18; see http://becomingone.org/666). Not 6 - 6 - 6, not three 6's in a row, but as in the Greek text, six hundred sixty six. In the Greek language and in the Hebrew language, each letter had a numerical value, with the exception that Hebrew vowels were not written and thus they had no numerical value. You can find the value of these letters by looking them up in a reliable dictionary, or reliable Greek and Hebrew grammars, or in various manuals of style such as the University of Chicago's *A Manual of Style* (1969):

- "Numbers, when not written out, are represented in ordinary Greek text by the letters of the alphabet, supplemented by three special characters …. The entire series of Greek numerals is shown in table 9.3." (pp. 232-233)

Or you can find the values of the letters by going to PR11.

---

[1] See Hebrew text

Beast-man = Last Antichrist = Last False-Prophet = Little Horn = Man of Sin = Abomination of Desolation = Man with the Number 666

Metonymical Names for the Same Person

pr193» The Bible uses many different names to depict the same evil person. When you use many different names to picture the same person, you are using metonymy. Metonymy is a figure of speech "by which one name is used instead of another, to which it stands in a certain relation" (*Figures of Speech Used in the Bible*, by E.W. Bullinger, p. 538). The last false-Christ (Rev 13:11; 19:20), is also the last false-prophet, is also the Beast-man, and is the man with the number six hundred and sixty six (Rev 13:18). By comparing scripture we see he is also the "little horn" who will do major destruction to people, nations, and eventually to the whole world (Dan 7:1-25; 8:24; 9:27; 11:31,38-44; Rev 13:4,13). It is because of the great destruction caused by his misuse of power that the world will say, "Who is like unto the Beast? Who is able to make war with him?" (Rev 13:4) It is his *lying* wonders or "miracles" of his great fire-destruction against some nations that will put fear into much of the world and cause it to follow him (2 Thes 2:9; Rev 13:13-17, 7). The evil behavior of the Beast-man reveals the power behind him. The verses about the Beast-man are dual: in the typical sense, they indicate the physical man of sin, but in the antitypical or spiritual sense, they reveal the power behind the man, and that power is Satan. The physical false-Christ or prophet is merely the shadow of Satan (2 Thes 2:9; Dan 8:23-24; 11:36-39), he is the "lamb" who speaks as Satan or for Satan (Rev 13:11; 12:9). In so many words, he will say he is the Christ (note the "lamb" of Rev 13:11), this "man of sin" will say he is God (remember Christ is God) while standing in the holy place or temple (2Thes 2:4; Dan 11:36-38; Mat 24:15; Isa 14:12-14; Ezek 28:17).

pr194» This Beast-man will eventually say he is God after he is given the power of the Beast system for the forty two months or 1260 days (Rev 13:5; Dan 7:25; see "1260 Days..." in PR2). At the very end he will say he is God through his words and actions (2 Thes 2:4). During his 1260 day rulership he will hope to change the times and the law (Dan 7:25). Those are some of the blasphemies he will say and do during his 1260 day rulership (Rev 13:5-6; Dan 7:25; 11:36). Yet even though this Beast-man is alive today, even up close to the time he is to do these things, he will not realize he will do these exact things (Isa 10:5, 7, antitypical meaning). But he, through his great desire for power and through his deceit, will contrive to put himself into a position of great power with the help of the evil power. It is the power of Satan that will enable and empower the individual Beast-man and the system of the Beast (Rev 13:4; Hab 1:11, 5-10; 2 Thes 2:9). But the Beast-man willfully goes along with this evil power within him, and thus he is sent to the fire to be destroyed at the very end of Satan's kingdom (Rev 19:20; 20:10).

Antichrist

pr195» There are many antichrists:

- "Children, it is the last hour; and just as you heard that the antichrist is coming, even now many antichrists have appeared; from this we know that it is the last hour" (1John 2:18)

We know it is the last hour or times after "many antichrists have appeared." But there is a specific Antichrist that will come: "you heard that [the] antichrist is coming." Since "anti" is translated from a Greek word that means either against or before, then this specific Antichrist will be against Christ and will exist just before Christ comes.

pr196» We see the Antichrist, with his many different names, warring, in words and deeds, against the Church and against Christ:

- I kept looking, and that horn was waging war with the saints and overpowering them.... He will speak out against the Most High and wear down the saints of the Highest One, and he will intend to make alterations in times and in law; and they will be given into his hand for a time, times, and half a time. (Dan 7:21,25)

- And through his shrewdness He will cause deceit to succeed by his influence; And he will magnify *himself* in his heart, And he will destroy many while *they are* at ease. He will even oppose the Prince of princes, But he will be broken without human agency. (Dan 8:25)

- And he opened his mouth in blasphemies against God, to blaspheme His name and His tabernacle [Church], *that is*, those who dwell in heaven. 7 It was also given to him to make war with the saints [Church] and to overcome them, and authority over every tribe and people and tongue and nation was given to him....And I saw the beast and the kings of the earth and their armies assembled to make war against Him [Christ] who sat on the horse and against His army. (Rev 13:6-7; 19:19)

pr197» This last Antichrist, is also called by other metonymical names such as:

- the "little horn" that speaks (Dan 7:8,11,20-25; 8:9-12, 23-25)
- the "abomination of desolation" (Dan 11:31-45; 9:27; 12:11; Mat 24:15; Mark 13:14)
- the "man of sin" (2Thes 2:4)
- the "son of perdition" (2Thes 2:4)
- the "false-prophet" (Rev 19:20 w/ 13:11-18)
- the "Beast" (Rev 13:3-7,11-14; 19:20)
- man with the number, six hundred sixty six (Rev 13:18)

70 Weeks
69 Weeks

pr198» In Daniel 9:24-27 it speaks about the 70 weeks. As we indicate in the "Last War and God's Wrath" paper [PR5], these 70 weeks can indicate either 70 weeks of days or 70 weeks of years. In the "Last War and God's Wrath" paper we show you the interpretation of the **70 weeks of years** [Dan 9:2, 24-27; Mat 18:22] In this paper we will show you the interpretation of the **70 weeks of days**. Let's look at the scripture:

- <24> Seventy weeks are determined {divided} concerning your people and upon your holy city, to finish the transgression, and to seal up sins, and to make atonement for iniquity, and to bring in righteousness of olams, and to seal up the vision and prophecy, and to anoint (the) holy of holies [most Holy]. <25> Know therefore and understand, that from the going forth of the commandment {word} to restore and to build Jerusalem unto (the) anointed prince {leader, ruler, 'one in front'} shall be seven weeks, and threescore and two weeks: the street shall be built again, and the moat {trench}, even in troublous times. <26> And after the weeks, threescore and two, shall (the) anointed one be cut off, but not {nothing} for himself {'and not for him'}: and the people of the prince {leader, ruler}, who is to come [see Isa 55:4], shall destroy the city and the sanctuary; and his end thereof shall be with a flood, and unto the end of the battle, desolations are decreed. <27> And he shall confirm a covenant with many for one week: and in the midst of the week he shall cause the sacrifice and the offering to cease, and upon the wing [extremity] of abominations (comes) the desolator that makes desolate [11:31], but at the full end that (which is) decreed shall be poured out upon the desolator (Dan 9:24-27, BCB).

pr199» This can be interpreted two ways and should be interpreted both ways. The anointed one is interpreted by many as Jesus Christ, but the 'he' in verse 27 is interpreted by some as the Antichrist. They believe that the Antichrist will make an agreement (covenant) for one week of years, that is for seven years, but in the middle of the seven years he will break this agreement (p. 223, Biederwolf). In such books as *The Millennium Bible*, by William E. Biederwolf (pp. 217ff) various interpretations are listed, both the Messianic and anti-Messianic interpretations. (See PR11 In *Prophecy Papers: Biblical Prophecy*, Expanded Edition, 2018, where we reproduce these pages.) In fact, this obscure and difficult scripture has to do with both the Messiah and the anti-Messiah. The real Messiah, Jesus Christ, was born approximately 2,000 years ago (see *New Chronology Papers*). He died after three and one-half years of teaching, on a Wednesday, a Passover on the 14 of Nisan of the Jewish Calendar. At His death, in one sense sacrifice and the offering ceased (Dan 9:27) because His was the perfect and fulfilling sacrifice (study Hebrews chapter 9 & 10; note Heb 10:18 & Zech 11:10). Christ was cut off after three and one-half years of confirming a new covenant (Heb 8:6ff; see *New Chronology Papers*; *Handbook of Biblical Chronology*, Finegan, pp. 280-285; see Dan 9:26; Isa 22:25; Zech 11:10). His two witnesses will fulfill the rest of the seven years in their 1260 days (Rev 11:3-4; Zech 4:11-14; see "Two Witness" paper [PR8] & "Last War" [PR5, pr284 ff]). Christ began his three and one-half years of confirming the new covenant starting at his 'Baptism' which was **69 weeks of years (483 years)** [Dan 9:2, 24-27; Mat 18:22] after a word had gone out to rebuild Jerusalem (see New Mind Papers & "Last War" paper [PR5]). Jesus Christ fits the scripture in Daniel 9:24-27. But also the Antichrist will fit these scriptures. The Antichrist may be a participant of an agreement or covenant. He will be the false-Christ who will manifest himself in the last 1260 days of the Old Age (Rev 13:11-18, 'like a lamb'; 1 John 2:18; 2 John 2:7; 2 Thes 3-4; Matt 24:15; Dan 11:36-39, 31-32; 8:9ff). There will be an order to restore and build Jerusalem **69 weeks of days (483 days)** before the false Messiah comes (Dan 9:25-26). This Antichrist will sit down in the 'temple' of the God pretending that he is the God (2 Thes 2:4; Dan 11:36; 8:23ff; Ezek 28:2; etc.). He is the false messiah projected in one meaning of Daniel 9:25-26. He will kill the two witnesses **3 ½ days** after he declares his false Messiahship and **3 ½ days** before the Real Messiah comes and saves the world from total destruction. As noted before, the real Messiah is also projected in Daniel 9:25-26. The vagueness of this scripture has something to do with the cherubs, the right and left side of the True God (see *God Papers*).

Mark of the Beast

pr200» "And he caused all, both small and great, rich and poor, free and bond, to receive a mark in their right hand, or in their foreheads: And that no man might buy or sell, save he that had the mark, or the name of the beast" (Rev 13:16-17). As indicated in our *God Papers*, and in our *New Mind Papers*, when one is in the NAME of God, he has the Spirit of God. Therefore, when one has the *name* of the Beast, he has the spirit of the Beast. As just shown this spirit is Satan's. When one has the *name of the Beast*, he has the spirit of the Beast. But furthermore, in the highest sense, when many have the *mark of the Beast*, they have the spirit of the Beast "in their forehead." The spirit of evil is the mark of the beast; it is the power behind the Beast. Those who worship the Beast, do so because they have the mind of Satan (see "Old Mind" paper [NM 21] for information on Spirit and mind). It is those with God's Spirit who have "the victory over the Beast [Satan], and over his image, and over his mark [spirit]" (Rev 15:2-3; 20:4). By knowing the true meaning of the mark of the Beast, many sections in the book of Revelation make sense.

Monetary System

pr201» The system of the Beast may initiate a monetary system whereby people have to have some kind of physical mark (such as an invisible mark(s) only seen by some electronic device) on their foreheads or right hand in order to buy or sell (Rev 13:16-17). But it is no sin to submit to such a monetary system as long as you are not forced to sin to get the physical "mark." The true and higher meaning of the mark of the Beast is *the spirit of the Beast*.

Beast and Church in the 1260 Days

pr202» It is during the 1260 days that the seven-nation end-of-the-age Beast will speak "great things," or "great words against the Most High," or "great things and blasphemies," or "in blasphemy against God, to blaspheme his NAME, and his tabernacle, and them that dwell in heaven" (Dan 7:8, 20, 25; Rev 13:5-6). Sometime during this period the Beast:

- will "*persecute* the woman"; will *blaspheme* God's tabernacle; "will make war with the Lamb ... and they that are with him"; will "wear out the saints of the most High"; will "make war with the saints"; will "destroy the mighty and the holy people"; will cause "the sanctuary and the host to be trodden under foot"; and so forth (Rev 12:13; 13:6; 17:14; Dan 7:25, 21; 8:24, 13).

pr203» As our "Last War God's Wrath" paper [PR5] indicates, the true woman, tabernacle, those with the Lamb, the saints, the holy people, and the sanctuary are the true Church of God. As the "God's Wrath, An Outline" paper [PR6] indicates the Beast makes final war against the Church at the end of the 1260 days, for during the 1260 days the Church is in the wilderness (Rev 12:6, 14), that is the wilderness of the people (Ezek 20:35-36), that is in the wilderness of spiritual Egypt (Ezek 20:36; Rev 11:8; see "God's Wrath, An Outline" paper [PR6]). And during these days the two witnesses will teach (Rev 11:3, see Two Witnesses [PR8]). Only near the end of the 1260 days, or 3 ½ days before Christ returns, are the two witnesses killed, and thereafter at Christ's return is the resurrection (Rev 11:11-12) at "the same hour" as the destruction of the city or Church (Rev 11:13) and the beginning of God's kingdom (Rev 11:15). But during this time period (and before it) some in the Church:

- "And those who have insight among the people will give understanding to the many; yet they will fall by sword and by flame, by captivity and by plunder, for days. Now when they fall they will be granted a little help, and many will join with them in hypocrisy. And some of those who have insight will fall, in order to refine, purge, and make them pure, until the end time; because it is still to come at the appointed time" (Dan 11:33-35, NASB).

Tree of Daniel

Kingdom of the Enemy

pr204» In the fourth chapter of the book of Daniel we read about a TREE that is "in the midst of the earth, and the height of it was great. The tree grew, and was strong, and the height of it reached to heaven, and the sight of it to the end of all the earth: The leaves of it were fair, and the fruit of it were much, and in it was food for all: the beast of the field had shadow under it, and the fowls of the heaven dwelt in the branches, and all flesh was fed from it" (Dan 4:10-12).

pr205» It reads in the next three verses about a "holy one" from heaven coming down to earth and breaking down this tree but leaving the "*stump of his roots in the earth*, even with a band of *IRON* and *BRASS*." This is to prove "that the most High rules in the kingdom of men, and gives it to whomsoever he will" (Dan 4:17). Then in verse 22, Daniel interprets the meaning of this tree: "It is you, O King, that has grown and become strong: for your greatness is grown, and reached to heaven, and your dominion to the end of the earth" (Dan 4:22). Thus, this tree is symbolic of the king's kingdom (Babylon), and it is cut down by God to show the world who controls the affairs of the world.

pr206» But notice that the most High leaves "*the stump of his roots in the earth*." The stump of the roots of the king or his kingdom of Babylon would remain in the earth. Now we know that after the Babylonian kingdom, the Persian Empire "raised up itself" (Daniel 7:5). Therefore we can reasonably conclude that the stump of the Babylonian kingdom, that was left in the earth after the tree or kingdom of Babylon was destroyed, did grow into another tree or kingdom which is the second Beast or world kingdom. Why can we reasonably conclude this?

Band of Iron and Brass

pr207» When the "holy one" cut down Nebuchadnezzar's tree or kingdom, he left "the stump of the roots, even *with a band of IRON and BRASS*" (Dan 4:15, 23). What is this band of IRON and BRASS?

pr208» In the book of Daniel the second chapter, Daniel explains the image that Nebuchadnezzar saw in a dream: "You are this head of gold. And after you shall arise another kingdom inferior to you, and another *third kingdom* of *BRASS*, which shall bear rule over all the earth. And the *fourth kingdom* shall be strong as *IRON*" (Dan 2:38-40). The "image" of Daniel chapter 2, was made up of a head of *gold*, its breast and arms of *silver*, its belly and thighs of *BRASS*, and its legs of *IRON* (Dan 2:31-33). This image is representative of all the world-ruling kingdoms as are the four Beasts of Daniel chapter seven. But notice that the third kingdom was of *brass*, and the fourth kingdom was of *iron*. Remember that when the tree of Daniel 4 was cut down, in its stump or roots was a band of *IRON* and *BRASS*.

pr209» In other words, in the stump or roots of the TREE was the life for: (1), the third world ruling kingdom, the BRASS of the "image" is the BRASS band of the roots of the tree; and (2), the fourth kingdom, the IRON of the "image" is the IRON band of the roots of the tree.

Who or What Is the Stump?

pr210» Remember that the last kingdom in the chain of Gentile kingdoms will be the Beast described in the book of Revelation with its seven heads and ten horns. And in Revelation 16:13 we read of a spirit coming out of the Beast. Who is this spirit?

pr211» "And there appeared another wonder in heaven; and behold a great red [fiery] DRAGON, having SEVEN HEADS AND TEN HORNS, and seven crowns upon his heads ... And the great DRAGON was cast out, *that old serpent, called the Devil, and Satan*, which misled the whole world" (Rev 12:3, 9). So we see that Satan has misled the whole world? Also we see that Satan is described as having seven heads and ten horns – the same as the Beast of Revelation, chapter 13, which is nothing but an accumulation of the Beasts in Daniel 7:4-7.

pr212» "And I stood upon the sand of the sea, and saw a Beast rise up out of the sea, having SEVEN HEADS AND TEN HORNS ... And the Beast which I saw was like unto a *leopard* [3rd Beast of Dan 7:6], and his feet were as the feet of a *bear* [2nd Beast of Dan 7:5], and his mouth as the mouth of a *lion* [1st Beast of Dan 7:4, which is synonymous with the tree in Daniel, chapter 4]: and *the dragon gave him his power, and his throne, and great authority*" (Rev 13:1-2). The dragon or Satan gave his power to the Beast. We see here that both Satan and the Beast have seven heads and ten horns, and that part of the Beast of Revelation 13 is the first Beast of Daniel 7, which is synonymous with the tree of Daniel 4, and that Satan gives the Beast its power.

Kingdom of Satan

pr213» By putting together all the information above, how could anyone otherwise conclude than that the Beast is the kingdom of Satan and that it has misled the whole world. And furthermore, that the symbolic tree of Daniel 4 is part of Satan's kingdom, and that the stump of the roots left from the first tree had grown again and was cut down again each time one of the world kingdoms had come up after its predecessor had fallen. Since the roots of a tree are the foundation of a tree, then we see from Revelation 13:2 that Satan is the foundation of the Beast. So we can conclude that the stump of the roots of the tree in Daniel 4 is nothing other than Satan and his spiritual power. Satan is the root of the tree or kingdom of Satan. The kingdoms of this age are Satan's as we see in Matthew 4:8 where Satan shows Jesus his "kingdoms of the world, and the glory of them." But we see in Revelation that the Beast is finally destroyed and the kingdom of God rules from then on (Rev 19:20; note Dan 7:9, 14). See the "Thousand Years and Beyond" paper [NM 15] for details on the seven times of Daniel, chapter 4.

pr214» **Seven Crowns**. Notice that the great red dragon, Satan (Rev 12:9), had seven heads and ten horns and that his heads had *seven* crowns on them (Rev 12:3). The seven crowns indicate Satan's power over all seven heads of all the four beasts of Daniel.

pr215» **In the truest sense the Beast of Revelation represents Satan's kingdom and power throughout all the ages of his kingdom** (Rev 13:2; 12:3, 9; 17:15, 18; 18:2-3, 24; see "Last War and God's Wrath" paper [PR5]).

See PR 11 for more information on the Beast-man.

[Page Name: Beast's Character]

Characteristics of the Individual Beast [1]

Individual Beast: Coming with the power of Satan
A Deceiver – A Liar – with Cunningness
1. Whose coming is according to the working of Satan in all [Satan's] power, signs, and wonders of **falsehood** and in all **deceit** of unrighteousness (2 Thessalonians 2:9, 10; Rev 13:2; Dan 8:24a)
2. He [Devil] was a murderer from the beginning, not holding to the truth, for there is no truth in him. **When he lies, he speaks his native language**, for he is a liar and the father of lies." (John 8:44)
3. And in the end of their kingdom, when the rebellion are come to the full, a king of strong presence, and skilled in **double-dealing** shall stand up.... And through his **cunningness** also he shall cause deceit to prosper in his hand (Daniel 8:23, 25)
4. And it **cast the truth to the ground**; and it practiced, and prospered (Dan 8:12)
5. And after the league made with him he shall work **deceitfully** (Dan 11:23)
6. He shall corrupt by **flatteries** (Dan 11:32) But he shall come in peaceably and obtain the kingdom by **flatteries** (Dan 11:21)
7. And the Beast... he **deceived** them (Rev 19:20) Who **deceived** them (Rev 20:10; 12:9)
8. And there was given to it a mouth, speaking great things and blasphemies [**lies about God**] (Rev 13:5)
9. It **deceives** them that dwell on the earth (Rev 13:14)

PR4: God's Wrath, What is it?

Righteous Judgment

Definition of God's Wrath

pr216» What is God's wrath? The Bible speaks about "the great day of his wrath," "the wrath of the Lamb," and "the wrath of God," and so forth (Rev 6:16-17; 15:1). People picture in their minds after reading the book of Revelation a God pouring out fire and damnation on the people of the earth. They read about the seven seals, the seven trumpets, and the seven plagues of Revelation and see a wrathful God getting even for man's wrongs. What is God's wrath? By only reading the book of Revelation can you know what the Bible means when it speaks of God's wrath?

- "For as the heavens are higher than the earth, so are my ways higher than your ways, and my thoughts than your thoughts. For my thoughts are not your thoughts, neither are your ways my ways, says the LORD" (Isa 55:9, 8).

pr217» God's ways and thoughts are *not* man's ways and thoughts. Man's heart is "deceitful above all things" (Jer 17:9). What man thinks about God is many times quite different from what the truth is. What man does is to project his own ideas onto God. When God says through the Bible that there is a "wrath of God," man thinks of *man's wrath* and projects this onto God's behavior. But "the wrath of man works *not* the righteousness of God" (James 1:20). God's ways are not like man's ways (Isa 55:8-9). God's wrath isn't what the deceitful heart of man (Jer 17:9) thinks it is.

pr218» Man teaches as the true doctrines the commandments of men (Mark 7:7), not the commandments of God. Man teaches as true the precepts of men (Isa 29:13) as opposed to the precepts of God. Man teaches what comes "out of their own hearts" as "the word of the LORD" (Ezek 13:2).

pr219» For example, God says "their *fear* toward me is taught by the precept of men" (Isa 29:13). Remember God's thoughts and ways are *not* like man's (Isa 55:8-9). Then what is the fear of God? The Bible interprets itself:

- "The fear of the LORD is to hate evil: pride and arrogance, and the evil way" (Prov 8:13).

pr220» The fear of God is to hate the wrong ways. Not to hate those who do evil, for nothing of itself is evil (Rom 14:14), but to hate the wrong ways of man. This is the fear of God. We hate evil behavior, for it is what harms us, not the God. Isn't this almost opposite to what many teach as the fear of the LORD? Man thinks it means fearing God as one fears to be killed.

pr221» What we are saying here is that God's ways and thoughts are not like man's. What some verses of the Bible at first glance seem to say is on more research quite different. The Bible uses many metaphorical expressions to describe God. More than some of the Old Testament is poetry. To find out the Spiritual essence you must have the New Mind or New Spirit.

Does this mean that God has purposely made the Bible difficult?

pr222» No, for in the places where God through his word has come right out and said something, man has changed the meaning of the words used in order to suit man's own motives. For example, there are words in over 400 verses in the Bible that mean "agelasting" which has evolved through misusage to be wrongly translated as "eternal." This twisting of the scriptures has caused much misunderstanding of the Bible. Thus, when God comes right out and says something, man changes the meaning of the words. *So God has used symbolism, not necessarily to hide, but more correctly to preserve the truth for the latter days.*

pr223» Most people have read God's word without the New Mind. When people speak of God's wrath, they think of it as if it were man's wrath. They make God out to be a hypocrite, for God has told us to give good for evil (Rom 12:21, and to love our enemies (Matt 5:44). What does it mean to love our enemies? Does this mean pouring fire over their heads as some picture God doing at his return to the physical dimension? If we can know what love is, we know how to love our enemies. What is love?

pr224» **Love Is**. "Love is patient; love is kind and envies no one. Love is never boastful, nor conceited, nor rude; never selfish, not quick to take offense. Love keeps no score of wrongs; does not gloat over other men's sins, but delights in the truth. There is nothing love cannot face; there is no limit to its faith, its hope, and its endurance. Love never comes to an end" (1 Cor 13:4-8, NEB).

pr225» Now if God is love as the Bible pictures him (1 John 4:8), then will God lose his *patience* with his enemies and kill them with fire at the end of the age? Remember, God is the almighty, the All Powerful. God created the whole heaven and earth by his words. All God has to do to correct his enemies is to *change* them. All He has to do is give them the New Mind, and instead of being bad, they will be good. Will God lose his patience? Will God be angry with his enemies? In other words is God's wrath like man's wrath? If it is, then God is like us, a hypocrite. He tells us to love our enemies, he tells us to give good for evil, then at the end he does what we shouldn't do, at least this is what many say God will do.

Will God come to destroy his enemies, or will he come to do good, to love his enemies? Let's let God, through his word, answer.

Christ Comes to *Save* Mankind

pr226» One of Jesus Christ's names means savior or Jehovah's savior (Jesus): "the Father sent the Son to be the savior of the world" (1 John 4:14). And, "you shall call his name Jesus [savior]: for he shall save his people from their sins" (Matt 1:21). And, "except those days ['the last days'] should be shortened, there would be no flesh saved: but for the elect's sake those days shall be shortened" (Matt 24:22). "And except that the Lord had shortened those days, no flesh would be saved: but for the elect's sake, whom he has chosen, He [God] has shortened the days" (Mark 13:20). Does this sound like God is coming to destroy?

pr227» When some didn't receive Christ the disciples asked, "do you wish that we command fire to come down from heaven and consume them even as Elijah did? But he [Christ] turned, and rebuked them, and said, You know not what manner of spirit you are of [at that time the disciples hadn't yet received the Spirit of God]. For the son of man is not come to destroy men's lives, but to save them" (Luke 9:54-56).

pr228» God through Jesus Christ will come to save mankind from destroying himself as these scriptures show. Then what is God's wrath? What does the Bible mean by God's wrath?

Righteous Judgment

pr229» The day of wrath is also called a day of trouble, of distress, of desolation, of darkness (Zeph 1:15), and further called a day or hour of judgment (Joel 3:12; Rev 14:7; 18:8, 10). God's wrath is the judgment on the society that the other-mind (Satan's influence) has created on earth. It is the appointed day of righteous judgment (Act 17:31). Paul calls the day of wrath, "the day of wrath and revelation of the righteous judgment of God" (Rom 2:5). And, "the LORD: for he comes, for he comes to judge the earth: he shall judge the world with righteousness" (Psa 96:13; 98:9; 1 Chron 16:33). "And in righteousness he does judge and make war" (Rev 19:11).

pr230» Notice God comes to judge the world righteously. God's wrath, God's judgment is righteous, not unrighteous like man's wrath (see James 1:20). What is righteous wrath or judgment? "For all your commandments are righteousness" (Psa 119:172). Righteous wrath, righteous judgment does not include direct mass killing of inherently weak human beings by the all-powerful God as some accuse God of planning for the end of this age. Evil will be punished. But not in the manner projected by many. What is God's wrath, or God's judgment at his return to the physical dimension?

- "The LORD is known by the judgment which he executes: the wicked is snared in the work of his own hands" (Psa 9:16).

pr231» That is a Biblical definition. In other words the wicked judge their own self, they are snared in the works of their *own* hands.

- Again, "the heathen are sunk in the pit that *they* made: in the net which *they* hid is their own taken" (Psa 9:15).
- "The wicked in his pride does persecute the poor: let them be taken in the devices that *they* have imagined" (Psa 10:2).
- The "transgressors shall be taken in their *own* naughtiness" (Prov 11:6).
- "The wicked is snared by the transgression of *his* lips" (Prov 12:13).
- "Woe unto the wicked it shall be ill with them: for the reward of *his* hands shall be given him" (Isa 3:11).
- "According to *their* deeds, accordingly he will repay" (Isa 59:18).

How Will God Repay Their Deeds?

pr232» "Will you render me a recompense [reward]? and if you recompense me, swiftly and speedily will I *return* your recompense upon your own head ... For the day of the LORD is near upon all the heathen: as you have done, it shall be done unto you: your reward shall return upon your own head" (Joel 3:4; Obad 1:15; check context).

pr233» When one comes to understand that at Christ's coming all the peoples of the world will try to destroy Christ and his people (Rev 17:14, "and they that are with him;" Rev 19:14, 8, "his army" clothed in white; see Matt 25:40), then one understands God's "wrath." As we will prove in the notes and in PR4 and PR5, the world will go mad through the other-mind's (Satan's) influence, which man agrees with, and through circumstances (Rev 16:13-16; 12:4, 13; Jer 51:7; 25:15, 16) the world will be burning up because an instant super-war will have begun. At that time God will *save* mankind from their madness, or thus from their sins (Matt 1:21). Man will be in the process of destroying the world, and their own deeds (use of war weapons) are blowing them off the earth when Christ comes to save (cf Isa 29:6; Matt 24:22; John 3:17). Their *own* deeds (war, nuclear bombs, etc.) are returning on their *own* heads, for all nations will go mad at that time, as the Bible emphatically manifests, and will be committing cosmocide.

pr234» Thus, "the LORD is known by the judgment which he executes: the wicked is snared in the work of his *own* hands" (Psa 9:16). God comes to save, for He is love. The transgression of the built-in law of the universe (cause and effect) will destroy the transgressors of that law, or will destroy them, if God doesn't come to save. How is God's "wrath" poured out on the earth? It is poured out by man himself against himself.

pr235» We will now show you many verses in the Bible where it describes nations and peoples destroying each other during the Last War. When read in the higher sense (see "Duality Paper" [BP4]) the following verses are in context at the day of the LORD:

- "Violence in the land, ruler against ruler" (Jer 51:46).
- "Evil shall go forth from nation to nation" (Jer 25:32).

- "The Egyptians against the Egyptians: and they shall fight every one against his brother, and every one against his neighbor; city against city, and kingdom against kingdom" (Isa 19:2).
- "For nation shall rise against nation, and kingdom against kingdom" (Matt 24:7).
- "Every man's sword shall be against his brother" (Ezek 38:21).
- "By the swords of the mighty will I cause your multitude to fall" (Ezek 32:12).
- "And the horses and their riders shall come down, every one by the sword of his brother" (Hag 2:22).
- "They shall lay hold every one on the hand of his neighbor, and his hand shall rise up against the hand of his neighbor" (Zech 14:13).
- "And the ten horns which you saw upon the beast, these shall hate the whore, and shall make her desolate and naked, and shall eat her flesh, and burn her with fire" (Rev 17:16).

pr236» The horns of the beast destroy the whore (the woman of Rev 17:1, 4). And who is the woman? The woman is the great city (Rev 17:18). And what is the great city? The great city is Babylon (Rev 14:8). Since the "Beast" represents spiritual Babylon, then in other words, the Beast of Revelation destroys itself.

pr237» Now why will mankind begin to destroy themselves? "And in the latter time of their kingdom [man's kingdom], when the transgressors are come to the full..." (Dan 8:23). At the End transgression will be full. The ultimate end of transgression of the built-in laws of the universe is death. Mankind has chosen death and will die, or more correctly will die if the Spiritual Jesus (the SAVIOR) does not come to save the world (Matt 24:22).

pr238» **What is God's Wrath?** It is man's own transgression of God's built-in laws. If some of mankind kill, some of mankind will be killed. If some lie, then some will be lied to. And so on and so forth. See the "Freedom & Law Paper" [NM 17].

pr239» God himself does not have the "freedom" to be wrathful towards man, as man thinks of wrath. God's "wrath" is not like man's wrath (James 1:20). **God's wrath is to let the built-in laws of the universe deal with man's misbehavior** (Psa 9:16). When man goes against God's built-in laws, they are in fact following the ways of destruction. And it is the ways of destruction that destroy man. The laws of God, in and of themselves, do not destroy. But when one goes against them, they are in fact following the way of death and destruction. There is actually a law of sin or a way of destruction (Rom 7:23, 25). And it is the following of this law of sin that destroys man.

pr240» Man does not sin against God when they sin, but against themselves (Prov 8:36). Each sin is a transgression of the built-in laws of the universe. And each transgression of these laws is "rewarded" by an effect. And the effects of these transgressions are all around us today. The misery of life was/is/will-be caused by the transgression of the universe's built-in laws. And as we have noted the transgression of these laws, is in reality, the positive doing of the law/way of destruction, the law of sin.

Spiritual Influence

pr241» As we noted so far that mankind will begin to destroy itself in the Last War. What is the reason man will perform this madness? As we've shown in the "Old Mind Paper" [NM 21], mankind is now being misled by enemy spirits in their minds. Not only is the present age the age of man, but it is also the age of Satan who is the enemy of mankind. The present age is the age of man/Satan. It is the wrath or madness of satanic spirits at the time of the Last War that will mislead man into beginning to destroy themselves. Notice the following Biblical verses for the proof that it is the satanic spiritual power (the other-mind) that is behind man's madness:

- Now, *why* will Egypt fight against itself, and its neighbors; city against city, and kingdom against kingdom? (Isa 19:2; Matt 24:7) [The antitypical Egypt is Satan's kingdom, see PR5]

- *Because* the SPIRIT of Egypt (Satan) is a perverse spirit and has "caused Egypt to err in every work thereof" (Isa 19:14, 13).

- Notice that the wrath against typical Egypt, when God led typical Israel out of Egypt, was caused by "evil angels" (Psa 78:49, 43-51). Thus, from the antitypical Egypt (Satan's kingdom) the antitypical Israel (the Church, Gal 6:16) will be saved from the wrath of the satanic spirits, or the wrath of the devil (Rev 12:12).

pr242» **Wine**. Notice further proof that the Last War's madness is caused by the satanic spiritual influence in man's mind that man now agrees with:

- "Babylon [Satan's kingdom, see the Beast Papers] is fallen, is fallen, that great city, *because* she made all nations drink of the wine of the wrath of her fornication [spiritual fornication]" (Rev 14:8).

- "Babylon has been a golden cup in the LORD's hand, that made all the earth drunken [of Babylon's cup]: the nations have drunken of her wine; therefore the nations are mad" (Jer 51:7).

pr243» What is this *wine* that the nations are drunk on that makes them mad and causes them to fall? (Rev 14:8-10; Jer 51:7-8)

- "Stay yourselves, and wonder; cry you out, and cry: they are drunken, but not with wine; they stagger, but not with strong drink. For the LORD has poured out upon you the *spirit* of deep sleep, and has closed your eyes" (Isa 29:9-10).

pr244» This spirit of deep sleep is the satanic spirit that God gave to man (see "Old Mind Paper" [NM 21]). It is the mad Satanic spirit that man is drunk on. This is the opposite wine (spirit) from which God's children drink, the new wine (Zech 9:17; Luke 5:37). Notice once again: It is "the *spirit* of the kings of the Medes" that is raised up against Babylon for the "vengeance of his [God's] temple" (Jer 51:11).

pr245» On the day of the wrath besides great madness there will be great fear (Rev 6:15-16; Ezek 32:10, 7-9) because of the cruel angels that are sent through Egypt (Satan's kingdom) (see Ezek 30:2-3, 9; Prov 17:11, "angel" is translated "messenger" in the KJV). Also note and compare with the previously mentioned examples, Revelation 16:12-16.

pr246» Now we have shown you one more dimension of the cause of the wrath of Satan (God's "Wrath"): The satanic influence of Satan's spirits that are misleading mankind (Rev 12:9). Now let's show another facet concerning the question as to why man destroys himself. That is, man will destroy himself, if there is not a Jesus (Savior) to save mankind from his own madness.

Pride

pr247» At the End of the old age will come "the son of perdition," (2 Thes 2:3) or the "false prophet" (Rev 19:20; 13:11-18), or the "little horn" (Dan 7:8, 20, 24-25; 8:9-12, 23-25). If you will read the verses quoted you will see that this antichrist has one obnoxious quality — pride. This false prophet is not only one person, but he epitomizes mankind as a whole at the end of the age — filled with pride of *self*. Notice how God describes mankind at the end of the old age: "in the last days perilous times shall come. For men shall be lovers of their *own* selves ... proud ... heady, high-minded" (2 Tim 3:1, 2, 4). And what is pride a shadow of?

pr248» "How art you fallen from heaven, O Lucifer ['O wail'], son of the morning! ['son of darkness'] how are you cut down to the ground, which did weaken the nations! For you have said in your heart, I will ascend into heaven, I will exalt my throne above the stars of God: I will sit also upon the mount of the congregation, in the sides of the north: I will ascend above the heights of the clouds; I will be like the most High" (Isa 14:12-14). Lucifer is another name for Satan. Notice how he wants to become "the most High," and notice how much *pride* he manifests in these verses.

Why is false pride destroying mankind?

- when pride, then shame (Prov 11:2)
- the way of a fool is right in his own eyes (Prov 12:15)
- contention comes through pride (Prov 13:10)
- pride before destruction, a haughty spirit before a fall (Prov 16:18)
- before destruction a haughty man (Prov 18:11-12)
- high looks, and a proud heart is transgression (Prov 21:4)

pr249» Why are pride and high looks wrong?

- "For who makes you to differ from another? and what have you that you did not receive? now if you did receive it, why do you boast, as if you had not received it?" (1 Cor 4:7)

pr250» In other words, all of us have received what we have mentally, physically, and spiritually from the outside — from our parents (genes, training), from our teachers, or from our spiritual fathers (God, Rom 8:14, 16; or Satan, John 8:44).

pr251» Why is pride wrong? It is wrong because man receives *all* from outside of him. Even man's life has nothing to do with him, it comes from outside of him. The trouble with mankind's pride is that man is lying to himself, if he has pride in himself, because everything that mankind is comes from outside of man. Mankind is lying to himself when he has pride in himself. And the problem with lying to oneself is that one loses reality. Reality is what is real, or true. Because mankind has false pride, he has lost contact with reality — the true or real. In other words, man has lost contact with God (the truth) because of his false pride in himself. Man has lost contact with the ways of happiness (God's law of love), thus, he is in confusion. Mankind is confused when it comes to finding happiness because he has lost the truth (God). And because mankind is in confusion, he is destroying himself. Another name for God's law is harmony. Another name for confusion is disharmony. Because man has false pride, he has lied to himself concerning the truth (God). Because mankind has lied concerning the truth, he has not found the truth (God). Because he has not found the truth, he is in disharmony. Because man is in disharmony, he is destroying himself.

Destruction Comes From God Himself?

pr252» Now some verses in the Bible seem to say that fire comes from God, instead of from man/Satan's kingdom fighting against itself. Let's examine some of these verses in question:

- "Our God shall come, and shall not keep silence, a fire shall devour *before* [immediately preceding; he comes to *save* mankind from that fire] him" (Psa 50:3).

Now notice one mistranslation:

- "And fire came down *from God* and devoured them" (Rev 20:9).

Some translators thought they were clarifying this verse by saying the fire came from God, for they knew not about the super weapons of the latter days. But that phrase ('from God') is not in most old Greek texts of the New Testament. But even if the phrase 'from God' does belong here it means that because God has predestinated all things that are now happening, in a sense the fire does come from God (see "Predestination Paper" [NM 8]).

Anger of the Lord

pr253» Now in this part we showed you how God is a person of love. And a person of love is a person who loves even his enemies. But the Bible speaks of the ANGER of God.:

- "The LORD will not spare him, but then the *anger* of the LORD and his jealousy shall smoke against that man, and all the curses that are written in this book shall lie upon him" (Deut 29:20).

pr254» What is the *anger* of God that destroys? Is the True God a destroyer? Notice 2 Samuel 24:1:

- "and again the *anger* of the LORD was kindled against Israel, and *he* moved David against them to say, Go, number Israel and Judah." But this verse is qualified by 1 Chronicle 21:1 which points out that the "he" of 2 Samuel 24:1 is Satan. Thus, by comparing we see that the "*anger* of the LORD" is Satan — not the True God. The anger of God is Satan as we proved by comparing the just mentioned verses. Hence, each time one sees the "anger of the LORD" in the Bible he knows the Bible speaks of Satan. (See the *God Papers* for a deeper understanding of the anger of the God.)

pr255» Notice how Sodom and Gomorrah were destroyed (read Gen 19:24-29). Now did God destroy these cities? Is God a destroyer? (In a sense the God is somehow or someway a destroyer and a creator of evil. [Deut 32:39; Isa 45:7] But in this age it is true to say that Satan is the destroyer and the true God the healer.) It was God's "anger" and "wrath" that overthrew Sodom and Gomorrah: "like the overthrow of Sodom, and Gomorrah, Admah, and Zeboim, which the LORD overthrew in his *anger*, and in his *wrath*" (Deut 29:23). As we have just shown you the "anger" of the LORD is Satan. And in *God's Wrath* we showed you that God's "wrath" is in reality Satan's wrath.

pr256» Since in some sense God's power is everywhere, everything that exists is *of* God. This is one reason the Bible speaks of the anger *of* God, the wrath *of* God, and so forth. But the Bible qualifies this, and tells us that the true God only uses his power for good. It is Satan who is the destroyer. Since Satan is a spirit being who came into being *from* God, then Satan is also *of* God (see the *God Papers*).

pr257» The writers of the Bible wrote as if they knew that everything was *of* God. Thus, the writers of the Bible told their readers that God destroyed Sodom, and so forth without qualifying that it was Satan that did the destroying. This cannot be understood in the fullest sense unless you have read and understood the *God Papers*.

PR5: Last War and God's Wrath

Simultaneous Events
Day of the Lord
Great City
Seventy Years
Two Witnesses
Pattern of Last War
Greater Detail
Seals
Trumpets
Vials

Faulty Translations

pr258» In PR5 we examine the book of Revelation. This book of the Bible is highly symbolic. It is a very difficult book to understand because of its symbolism. But the Bible does interpret its own symbols. In order to ascertain the meaning of the symbols of Revelation one must be knowledgeable of the rest of the Bible, for the symbolism can be found scattered throughout the Bible. For example, information on the Beast of Revelation can be found in the book of Daniel (see Beast Papers [PR2, PR3]). In order to understand the book of Revelation, one must understand the rest of the Bible. One must know something about type and antitype. One must know about looking for the higher *meaning* in scripture. The truest meaning in the book of Revelation is its antitypical or Spiritual meaning. The same can be said of the rest of the Bible, but it is especially important in understanding the book of Revelation.

Aorist Verbs & Other Timeless Verbs

pr259» One must also know that the book of Revelation is full of the *aorist* verbs. The aorist verb is a verb of action, not time. An aorist verb by itself tells us nothing about the *time* of the action. It speaks of action without denoting the duration of the action or time of the action:

- "The aorist stem presents action in its simplest form (*a-oristos* 'undefined'). This action is simply presented as a point by the tense. This action is timeless ... The aorist is a sort of flashlight picture, the imperfect a time exposure" (pp. 824, 1380 in, *A Grammar Of The Greek New Testament*, by A.T. Robertson; see also such books as, *Do It Yourself Hebrew and Greek*, by E.W. Goodrick, pp. 4.4-4.5).

pr260» In fact, in Greek, the aorist, present, and perfect is timeless:

- "These ideas (punctiliar, durative, perfected state) lie behind the three tenses (aorist, present, perfect) that run through all the moods ... The present is also timeless in itself as in the perfect ... These three tenses (aorist, present, perfect) were first developed irrespective of time. Dionysius Thrax erred in explaining the Greek tenses from the notion of time, and he has been followed by a host of imitators. The study of Homer ought to have prevented this error" (p. 824, A.T. Robertson).

- "The terms aorist, imperfect, and perfect (past, present, future) are properly named from the point of view of the state of the action, but present and future are named from the standpoint of the time element. There is no time element in the present subjunctive, for instance. But the names cannot now be changed, though very unsatisfactory" (pp. 825-826, A.T. Robertson).

Because of errors some Greek verbs were misnamed; many today read the idea of *time* into Greek verbs, when they should read the state of the *action*.

Simultaneous Events

pr261» We will in this paper make it plain that many events in the Book of Revelation (the seals, trumpets, and vials, etc.) do not depict *sequential* events. In a way the Book of Revelation was written in the same manner as the movie *Mystery Train* (1989, Directed by Jim Jarmusch).

pr262» The movie *Mystery Train* portrays three separate stories of people in a hotel in Memphis Tennessee during one night through three sequential movie scenes, but it does not tell its viewers that these three separate adventures happened on the same night. At first the viewers think they are separate adventures on separate nights.

pr263» The first story was about a Japanese couple's trip to Memphis to visit Graceland, the home of Elvis. The movie shows the Japanese couple coming to Memphis on a train and their escapades before renting a hotel room (27) and after leaving the hotel room. The second story was actually of two separate women, one from Rome, who was stranded in Memphis, and the other a woman who had just broken up with her boy friend. Both women by chance end up in room 25 in the same hotel as the Japanese couple, but the movie does not indicate that they were spending the same night in the hotel as the Japanese couple. The third story was about three men, one of whom happens to be the boy friend of one of the two women in room 25. They eventually hid that same night in room 22 after one of them shot a man at a local liquor store. It isn't until the movie gets into the third story that you begin to see that all three groups are in the same hotel on the *same* night.

pr264» You begin to see that each group was in the hotel on the same night by subtle hints in the movie:

- the repetition of the same song by Elvis (*Blue Moon*);

- the reiteration of events and conversation between the manager and the bellhop
- the same train passing by in each story
- the Japanese couple being overheard by the two women
- and then the gun shot from room 22 that all the separate groups re-act to in different ways, all without any interaction between the three groups of people renting different rooms in the same hotel the same night.

pr265» The three stories were told sequentially, but they occurred in parallel time periods. This is what is happening in the Book of Revelation. Again and again with subtle hints Biblical evidence projects to us that the seals, trumpets, and vials happen all at once. This was one reason John used the aorist verb in describing events in the book of Revelation. The use of the aorist verb and other timeless verbs (verbs of action not time) helped John to describe many *simultaneous* events. Under the subtitle 'But Simultaneous Action is Common also,' A.T. Robertson in his Grammar states: "Indeed this simultaneous action is in exact harmony with the punctiliar meaning of the aorist tense." And he states, 'in many examples only exegesis [interpretation] can determine whether antecedent or coincident action is intended ....' Many events in the book of Revelation were *written* sequentially, but they actually transpired in parallel time periods. The Greek text of the Book of Revelation superficially appears sequential only as the movie *Mystery Train* superficially appears sequential. An understanding of the Greek aorist verbs (and other timeless verbs) and the discernment of the reiteration of simultaneous events in the Book of Revelations makes it plain that the Book of Revelation describes many simultaneous events not just sequential events. In the rest of this paper we will make this plain.

Day of the Lord

pr266» Furthermore, the whole vision of John was concerning the "day of the Lord." The "day of the Lord" has two senses: the regular seventh day — the weekly Sabbath; or the antitypical seventh day — the 1000 years. John was in Spirit "*in* the Lord's day," and was told to "write the things which you [John] saw and the things which are and the things which shall be after these things" (Rev 1:10, 19). In John's vision he saw things that occurred in the 1000 years — the antitypical Sabbath (Rev 20:2-3). He also saw things that happened before the 1000 years (Rev chap. 2 & 3). And he saw things that happened after the 1000 years (Rev 20:7; 21:1, 4, 6; 5:13 & note Psalm 148 150 & "All Saved" paper [NM 13]; etc).

pr267» In order to understand the book of Revelation we need to synthesize most of the Bible. Why? "Son of man, what is that proverb that you have in the land of Israel, saying, The days are prolonged, and every vision fails? Tell them therefore, Thus, says the Lord GOD; I will make this proverb to cease, and they shall no more use it as a proverb in Israel; but say unto them, *The days are at hand*, **and the effect of *every* vision**" (Ezek 12:22-23). *All* the visions of the Bible will be fulfilled in the last years of the old system of man. Visions in the past that appeared to fail will come true soon.

pr268» The vision of the Beast in Revelation and Daniel are for the end time (Dan 12:4, 9). But we know the time is truly *near* when we truly hear and understand all the book of Revelation (Rev 22:10; 1:3).

Here Some, There Some

pr269» Another principle a person needs to understand is related in Isaiah 28:9-10: "Whom shall he teach knowledge? and whom shall he make to understand doctrine? them that are weaned from the milk, and drawn from the breasts. **For precept must be upon precept, precept upon precept; line upon line, line upon line; here a little, and there a little**." The truth of Revelation is scattered throughout the Bible. We must put all these scriptures together. This is much like the truth of Jesus Christ's first coming. Scripture on this event is scattered throughout the Bible. When all the prophetic scriptures on Jesus Christ are put together we see just how much of the Bible pointed to Jesus Christ (see, *Messianic Prophecies of the Bible*, by Lockyer; etc.). Yet the Jews in Jesus Christ's time could not see these prophecies as pointing to Jesus Christ. We must not be like those Jews. We must be the Jews with the New Mind that see all the scriptures that point to the Last War and the return of Christ.

Higher Meaning

pr270» Furthermore one must understand that the Bible is dual — there is a shadow/physical/type of the real/Spiritual/antitype. This is manifested by comparing the following verses (Rom 1:20; Heb 8:5, 9, 23-24; 10:1; and all of Hebrews 8:1 to 10:21). And this is proven by the repeated consistency of duality throughout the Bible (see "Duality Paper" [BP4]). God through the Bible asks us to look for and seek after the higher or spiritual or real or antitypical meaning in the Bible. Compare the usage of "heaven," "earth," and "spiritual" in Isaiah 55:9 with 1 Cor 15:44-49; Phil 3:18-19 with Col 3:1-2. Thus, "heaven" = spiritual, and we should look to the above/heavenly or spiritual meaning of scripture (see "Duality Paper" [BP4]).

pr271» What is an example of taking the higher meaning? Notice in the book of Hebrews 12:22-23 where it calls the Spiritual Church: "mount Zion," or the "city of the living God," or the "heavenly Jerusalem." In other words, these terms are metonymical for the Church. Most of the time when we read Zion, Jerusalem, or city of God we know it means literally a city, as well as Spiritually, the Spiritual city or Church. This is duality: type (the physical city) and antitype (the Spiritual city or Church). Also the Church is called the holy temple (Eph 2:21), thus, anytime the Bible uses the word "temple" (meaning holy temple) we know it can mean the physical and/or Spiritual temple. The Spiritual temple is the Spiritual Church of God. But God wants us to look to the heavenly, or Spiritual, or antitypical meaning (Col 3:1-2; John 4:24; 6:63). When Revelation 11:1 says to measure the temple of God, we then know it means antitypically to go measure the Church or count its members.

pr272» Now God's wrath and the day of the Lord are mentioned throughout the Bible. We need to tie-in the events of the Old Testament with the things in the book of Revelation because of the principle in Ezekiel 12:22-23, and because we would be taking Revelation out of context from the whole Bible if we did not use the rest of the books to amplify the book of Revelation.

Great City

pr273» In Revelation 11:8, speaking of a few days before Christ's return, it says the two witnesses "shall lie in the street of the *great city*, which spiritually [or antitypically] is called *Sodom* and *Egypt*, where also our Lord was crucified." Now we know the Lord was not crucified in the physical Sodom or Egypt; it was near physical Jerusalem. Yet Christ was killed in the *antitypical* Egypt, or Sodom, or great city which is Satan's spiritual kingdom. Therefore the physical Jerusalem was in the spiritual kingdom of Satan, for all the kingdoms and lands of the world are now, in this old age, Satan's kingdoms (Matt 4:8-9).

pr274» Notice that the spiritual or antitypical Sodom and Egypt are both called "the great city" (Rev 11:8). The spiritual Sodom, Egypt, and the great city are each just different names for each other. They are metonymical terms. Each term speaks of the same thing. What is the great city?

pr275» "And the *woman* which you saw is that *great city*, which reigns over the kings of the earth" (Rev 17:18). The antitypical woman who sits on the Beast *is* the great city (Rev 17:1, 9, 18). Who is the Beast? The Beast is Satan's kingdom (see the "Beast-Man Paper" [PR3]). Thus, the woman is metonymical to the spiritual great city, which is the antitypical Sodom and Egypt. Yet we know women are symbolical to churches (Eph 5:22-25). Thus, the woman on the Beast symbolizes the church essence of the church/kingdom of Satan, and she is metonymical to the spiritual great city, Sodom, and Egypt.

pr276» Notice also in Revelation 14:8, "Babylon is fallen, is fallen, that *great city*, because *she* made all the nations ..." Babylon is also the "great city."

pr277» Therefore according to the book of Revelation, the spiritual great city, Babylon, Sodom, Egypt, and the antitypical woman on the Beast are metonymical for each other.

pr278» Notice after it says the woman is the great city, that it describes the great city as Babylon (Rev 17:18; 18:1-24). In describing Babylon in chapter 18 it says, "and saying, Alas, alas, that *great city*, that was clothed in fine linen, and purple, and scarlet, and decked with gold, and precious stones, and pearls!" (Rev 18:16) Compare this with the description of the *woman* in Revelation 17:4, "and the woman was arrayed in purple and scarlet color, and decked with gold and precious stones and pearls." The city and the woman are clothed alike. This is another proof that the antitypical woman and Babylon are one and the same — each term merely adds more detail to the other term.

pr279» Just as the Bible uses many terms to describe Satan (the devil, dragon, serpent, etc.), it has used many terms to describe the same system of Satan. These terms are metonymical names for Satan's "Beast" system.

Metonymical Names For The Antitypical Beast, Or The Kingdom of Satan

pr280»

- Great City [Rev 17:18; 11:8]
- Woman or Whore (the great city) [Rev chap 17; 17:18]
- Babylon (the great city) [Rev 14:8; 18:16]
- Sodom (the great city) [Rev 11:8]
- Egypt (the great city) [Rev 11:8]
- All Kingdoms Are Satan's — The Beast

pr281» If you have read the papers on the "Beast" you know that the Babylonian kingdom was the first Beast of Daniel, chapter 7, which is pictured as part of the "Beast" of Revelation, chapter 13. Further, we know that the Beast of Revelation will encompass at once all the characteristics of all the "Beasts" of Daniel because the book of Revelation's Beast encompasses the same characteristics as Daniel's four Beasts (Rev 13:2; Dan 7:4-6, "lion," "bear," and "leopard"). Thus, since Babylon was the first Beast of Daniel, then we know the antitypical Babylon will belong to the antitypical Beast of Revelation, for the Beast of Revelation will encompass all the Beasts of Daniel at once. **The Beast of Revelation in its truest meaning encompasses all of Satan's kingdoms**. Therefore the Beast is the spiritual or antitypical great city, Sodom, Egypt, Babylon, and the Woman. All these terms describe the same church/kingdom of Satan. Each term adds another detail to the overall description of the final Beast kingdom. The woman in Revelation 17 merely tells us that the system of Satan also includes a church. Revelation calls this church, the synagogue of Satan (Rev 2:9, 3:9).

pr282» *Church of Satan*. A church is an assembly of people who worship the same god: the church of Satan worship their god Satan even though they *think* they are worshiping the true God. To be in the church of Satan you need not ever go *to* church; an atheist with the spirit of Satan is in the church of Satan and worships Satan.

pr283» *A Principle of Interpretation*. Now since the Bible is dual, then what the Bible says concerning the day of the Lord or God's wrath towards the physical or typical Egypt, Sodom, and Babylon, can be used to synthesize the story about the Last War. We know now that when the Bible describes the "wrath" on the physical Egypt and Babylon, in the antitypical meaning, it is speaking about the "wrath" on the Beast of Revelation, for the antitypical Egypt and Babylon belong to the Beast of Revelation.

Seventy Years And Seventy Weeks

pr284» Let us further synthesize the Old Testament with the New Testament through the "seventy weeks" and "seventy years." In Jeremiah 25:9-14 it speaks about the land of Israel and the nations around it serving Babylon during a seventy year period, but "when **seventy years** are accomplished, I will punish the king of Babylon, and that nation." All that Jeremiah has prophesied against Babylon will happen after the seventy years.

Wine Cup

pr285» But the next verse speaks about the wine cup that all nations are to drink. And in Jeremiah 51:7-8 it speaks about this same wine cup, calling it a golden cup. Also in Revelation 18:3; 14:8-10 it speaks of the same cup poured out on Babylon. By reading Jeremiah 25:27-33 and comparing this with Revelation, one knows that this great slaughter of nations didn't happen to the *full* extent shown in Jeremiah 25:15-33. Only a typical event happened. The true slaughter of nations in this chapter of Jeremiah will happen in the Last War. There is an antitypical seventy years, and after those seventy antitypical years then the cup of wrath will be poured out to the *full* extent mentioned in Jeremiah, chapters 25 and 51.

Cyrus

pr286» "To fulfill the word of the LORD by the mouth of Jeremiah, until the land had enjoyed her sabbaths: for as long as she lay desolate she kept the sabbath, to fulfill **threescore and ten years**. Now in the first year of Cyrus king of Persia, that the word of the LORD spoken by the mouth of Jeremiah might be accomplished, the LORD stirred up the spirit of Cyrus king of Persia, that he made a proclamation throughout all his kingdom, and put it also in writing, saying, Thus says Cyrus king of Persia, All the kingdoms of the earth has the LORD God of heaven given me; and he has charged me to build him a house in Jerusalem, which is in Judah. Who is there among you of all his people? The LORD his God be with him, and let him go up" (2 Chron 36:21-23; see Ezra 1:1-3).

pr287» Thus, after the seventy typical years Cyrus came to build a house for the LORD God of Israel in Jerusalem (Ezra 1:3). Now the Bible is dual and God tells us to look to the higher meanings. Is there an antitypical meaning to this verse? Notice that the Hebrew word translated "Cyrus" means *sun* and that this is the symbol of the returning Christ (Mal 4:2; see *God Papers* on sun and moon symbolism). Further the antitypical house of God which Cyrus was to build is the Church (Eph 2:19). And who is building this house? — Christ (Heb 3:3-6). Is Cyrus a typical Christ? Does this mean that after the antitypical seventy years that the antitypical Cyrus (Christ) will return and claim "all the kingdoms of the earth" for himself? (2 Chron 36:23) Then will the antitypical Cyrus (Christ) be King of kings? (Rev 19:16) Is this a dual story? We answer yes, for all the Bible is dual. And there is an antitypical Cyrus and he will destroy the antitypical Babylon as did the typical Cyrus destroy the typical Babylon. But Christ, the antitypical

Cyrus, will destroy the antitypical Babylon righteously as explained in the *God's Wrath*, PR4.

pr288» Notice: "that says of Cyrus, He is my shepherd, and shall perform all my pleasure: even saying to Jerusalem, You shall be built; and to the temple, Your foundation shall be laid" (Isa 44:28).

pr289» What is the antitypical Jerusalem and the antitypical temple? They are the Church (Heb 12:22; Eph 2:21; see "New Jerusalem" in [NM 18]). What are the foundations that are to be laid?

pr290»

- The righteous are an agelasting foundation (Prov 10:25)
- Zion (the Church, Heb 12:22) a foundation, a tried stone (Isa 28:16)

The wife (the Church, Rev 19:7) of Christ will be laid with stones of fair colors, and her foundations with sapphires (Isa 54:11).

pr291» Cyrus is a shepherd. Who is the chief shepherd? Christ is the chief shepherd (1 Pet 5:4). What does the Hebrew word translated Cyrus mean? It means the *sun*. Who is the antitypical sun? Or what is the sun symbolic of? It is symbolic of Christ (Mal 4:2). Then in the higher or antitypical meaning of Isaiah 44:28 it says Christ will come to do what Cyrus did typically after the seventy years of Israel's captivity? Isn't Cyrus a typical Christ?

pr292» "Thus says the LORD to his *anointed*, to Cyrus" (Isa 45:1). Who is the LORD's true anointed? It is Christ, the Messiah, who is the anointed. Compare Psalm 2:2-7 with Hebrews 1:5, 9 to prove Christ is the Anointed of the LORD. Thus, Cyrus is a typical Christ. And after the seventy antitypical years, Christ will return with God's "wrath" as explained previously in PR4.

pr293» What we are doing remember is tying-in the Old Testament's Babylon, Egypt, and Cyrus with what is about to come on this old age. We are tying-in the Old Testament with the book of Revelation in order to have a detailed description of the Last War as well as to explain the book of Revelation. Now we need to know what the antitypical seventy years are.

Antitypical Seventy Years

pr294» "In the first year of his reign [Darius], I Daniel considered by books the number of the years, whereof the word of the LORD came to Jeremiah the prophet, that he would accomplish *seventy years* in the desolation of Jerusalem" (Dan 9:2).

pr295» Daniel is speaking about the same seventy years we have been writing about. Then Daniel begins to pray for his people asking forgiveness (v. 3-19). And while he was praying Gabriel came to him (v. 20-21). And Gabriel said he came to give Daniel skill in understanding.

pr296» Now Daniel was seeking through prayer two things: (1) for mercy on Israel (v. 18, 13); and (2) for understanding of the truth (v. 13). He had considered the seventy years mentioned in Jeremiah. Now what was there to consider if these seventy years were a literal seventy years of desolation? It is true that *some* came back to Jerusalem after this seventy years (Ezra). But did the following happen to the full extent: "that after seventy years be accomplished at Babylon I will visit you, and perform my good word toward you, in causing you to return to this place" (Jer 29:10, 11-14). Sure it is true in one sense. But many Jews didn't return and God hasn't visited his people in the truest sense of Jeremiah 29:10-14. When will the LORD visit his people? He will visit at the day of the LORD when the enemies have destroyed themselves and He begins to gather all the peoples of Israel back to their land (Obad 1:15; Isa 13:6-14:3; Joel 2:31-32).

pr297» Daniel was considering and perceiving the seventy years of Jeremiah. Then Daniel began to seek through prayer (v. 3) the true understanding of these seventy years (v. 13). While he was praying Gabriel came to give him understanding (v. 21-22).

pr298» Gabriel: "at the beginning of your supplication [v. 3] the commandment came forth, and I am come to show you [the truth of the seventy years as explained just previously]; for you art greatly beloved: therefore understand the matter, and consider the vision. *Seventy sevens* [KJV, "weeks"] *are determined upon your people and upon your holy city* [Jerusalem], *to finish the transgression...*" (v. 23-24). Let's stop here.

pr299» In many translations it uses the word "weeks" for a Hebrew word [#7620 — *shabuwa*] that means, *sevens*. It is like the word, *heptad*, which means a group of seven. In Hebrew, the seventy *sevens* could mean seventy sevens of days (70 weeks) or seventy sevens of years.

pr300» Why was Jerusalem desolate: "Yea all Israel have transgressed your law, even departing, that they might not obey your voice; therefore the curse is poured upon us" (Dan 9:11). The seventy *years* of desolation was caused by transgression and Daniel was praying for mercy (v. 18, 13), and understanding as to the truth. Gabriel came to give understanding, and said seventy *sevens* are determined for the people of Israel to *finish* their transgression. Thus, if the seventy years of desolation was caused by transgression, then the desolation in the truest sense will not end until the seventy sevens are completed.

pr301» *483 Years or 69 weeks*. Now Gabriel goes on to say an anointed one would come after sixty-nine sevens (KJV, "weeks") from the "commandment to restore and to build Jerusalem" (v. 25). This is dual. The scripture in Daniel 9:24-27 is ambiguous. It can be understood in two ways: (1) anti-Messianic; and (2) Messianic. That is, the anointed prince can be either the Messiah Prince or the coming false anointed prince. By reading, *Second Coming Bible*, by William E. Biederwolf, (pages 219-225, Baker, 1972; also known as *The Millennium Bible*) you can see some of the two different interpretations given these scriptures down through history. The Messianic interpretation has the Messiah coming after 69 weeks of years: 483 years "from the going forth of the commandment." By various interpretations this commandment was: (1) Cyrus' (Isa 44:28; Ezra 6:14); (2) Darius' degree in the second year of his reign (Ezra 6:12) (3) The degree of Artaxerxes in his seventh year (Ezra 7:1, 7, 11 ff); (4) or the degree of Artaxerxes in his twentieth year (Neh 2:1,7). According to the Messianic interpretation, since after sixty-nine sevens of days Christ did not come, then Daniel 9:25 means sixty-nine sevens of years. The sixty-nine sevens of years equals 69 times 7 years, or 483 years. After 483 years the Messiah appeared as the prophecy in Daniel indicated. This is when Christ was baptized. See our *Chronology Papers*.

pr302» ***7 Years Cut in Half***. And the Messiah was to "confirm the covenant with many for one seven: and in the midst of the seven [seven days or seven years] he shall cause the sacrifice and the oblation [offering] to cease" (v. 27). Furthermore in the middle of the seven (7 years) of "confirming the covenant" he was cut off (Dan 9:26, 27; Isa 22:25; Zech 11:10).

> (The "he" in verses 26 and 27 refers to the Messiah; the "covenant" being the new covenant. Matt 26:28; Mal 3:1; Jer 31:31-33; Heb 9:26; Heb 10:7-9; see *Chronology Papers*. In the second sense 'he' refers to the Antichrist. See "69 Weeks" in the "Beast-Man Paper" [PR3])

pr303» Christ's first ministry of confirming the covenant lasted 3 ½ years. Thus, 69 ½ sevens of years of the 70 have been fulfilled. A week of years is seven years. Therefore one-half of seven years is 3 ½ years. At Christ's death this prophecy was cut off since 3 ½ years after Christ died the transgression of Israel didn't cease as Daniel 9:24 indicated. There are still 3 ½ years left in Daniel's prophecy.

pr304» Notice that "the end [of the prophecy] thereof shall be with a flood, and unto the end of the war [the Last War] desolation are determined" (v. 26). Further, note that Christ the Messiah would confirm the covenant for one seven, or one seven year period (Dan 9:27). But so far he has taught only for 3 ½ years. **Where are the other 3 ½ years?** If we find it, we will know when the transgression of Israel will cease and when the Last War will take place. We will also know when the end of the antitypical seventy years of Jeremiah will end since in explaining the seventy years Gabriel used seventy sevens. (The 70 antitypical years are the 70 sevens, or 70 sevens of years.) Also if we can locate these 3 ½ years we will know *how* Christ will confirm the covenant during these 3 ½ years.

Two Witnesses In Their 1260 Days

pr305» Now who will confirm the covenant of Christ these last 3 ½ years? We know it isn't Christ himself, for he won't return to earth until *after* the 3 ½ years (see Beast Papers [PR4, PR5, PR6]). There will be an agent or agents for Christ these 3 ½ years. Who?

pr306» "And I will give power unto my two witnesses, and they shall prophesy a thousand two hundred and threescore days [3 ½ years], clothed in sackcloth. These are the two olive trees, and the two candlesticks standing before the God of the earth" (Rev 11:3-4).

pr307» It will be the two witnesses who will preach 1260 days (3 ½ years) "before the God of the earth." Or as Zechariah 4:14 says, "these are the two anointed ones, that stand by the Lord of the whole earth." These two persons who come in the spirit of Moses and Elijah will teach as agents for Christ (see the "Two Witnesses" paper [PR8]).

pr308» It is during these 3 ½ years of teaching by the two witnesses that the Church will be in the wilderness (Rev 12:6, 14), will be in trial (Dan 11:33-35; 12:10; Rev 3:14-19) for the 3 ½ years (Dan 12:7). Hence, the Church will be in the spiritual wilderness for 3 ½ years during the Beast's misrule (Rev 13:5; Dan 7:25; 12:7; Rev 12:6, 14). And during this 3 ½ years of misrule by the Beast the Church will be tried: some during the 3 ½ years will be physically tried, but all will be physically tried at the end of the 3 ½ years, and all will be spiritually tried throughout the 3 ½ years (as well as throughout their life) by the spirit of Satan, that other mind (see "Old Mind" paper [NM 21]).

pr309» What is the antitypical Jerusalem? It is the Church (Heb 12:22). What is the antitypical Babylon which makes Jerusalem desolate? The antitypical Babylon is the Beast. Thus, the antitypical Jerusalem or the holy city (the Church) will be as good as desolate during these 3 ½ years under the antitypical Beast (Rev 11:2). They will physically be under the Beast (Satan's kingdom) and spiritually tried by it (see "Old Mind Paper" [NM 21]). And at the end of the 3 ½ years they will be physically desolated (see below, see PR6).

pr310» **Hence**, by putting this together, the last part of the seventy sevens of years will be the 3 ½ years when the Beast of Revelation, the antitypical Babylon, will rule the earth. (The spirit of the Beast rules all the earth; the seven nation Beast rules great in the earth and great in the Middle East.) And it is after these 3 ½ years, that Cyrus (Christ) will return and become King of kings.

To Review

pr311» So far then, we have tied-in the seventy years of Jeremiah and the seventy weeks of Daniel to the story of Revelation. Also we have shown that Cyrus was a typical Christ. We've shown you that the two witnesses are agents of Christ to confirm the covenant in Christ's place the last 3 ½ years. We have shown you that physical Egypt and Babylon were types of the Beast of Revelation, which is the kingdom of Satan. We have shown you that the antitypical woman of Revelation 17 is a dimension of the Beast, both church and kingdom at once. We are thus showing you the Spiritual meaning of the Bible.

Old Wars as Pattern of the Last War

pr312» All the battles of the Old Testament happened as examples, but during the last 3 ½ years they will happen again in the antitype, or truest sense. Much of the Bible is for the next few years, that is, the years just before and during the 3 ½ years or 1260 days (1 Cor 10:11; Heb 10:1; Ezek 12:22-23).

pr313» Thus, after this 3 ½ year period, which fulfills the antitypical seventy years of Jeremiah or the seventy sevens or weeks of Daniel, then Christ (Cyrus) will come to build the temple (Church/ kingdom) of God (2 Chron 36:23; Isa 44:28), and to subdue the nations (Isa 45:1; Rev 17:14). He will come at the Last War (Dan 9:26) to *save* mankind from destroying themselves (Matt 24:22; John 3:17). He will *not* come to destroy nations, but to save them from their own transgression as shown previously in PR4. Transgression will be at its full as Daniel explained (Dan 8:23). The ultimate end of transgression is death (Deut 30:15). Thus, when the world has reached its height of transgression God will come to *save*.

pr314» But Christ comes only when the world is in the process of destroying itself. One-third of the world's population at that point will have died in the war (Rev 9:18), *and* one-fourth of the earth will have been destroyed by the Last War (Rev 6:8).

All Nations Destroyed

pr315» Now Jeremiah 25:12-13 said *all* the nations written about in his book would receive all that God pronounced against them in Jeremiah's book by the completion of the seventy years. As explained, the end of the antitypical 70 years is after the 3 ½ years just before Christ's rule. The nations included in the destruction includes the antitypical Babylon, Egypt, the Medes, all the kings or rulers of the North, and so forth (Jer 25:12-26). All these nations will drink of the wine cup of fury (Jer 25:15-17); there will be a great slaughter throughout the land (Jer 25:26, 32-33).

pr316» In Ezekiel it speaks about a group of nations from the north who will come down and gather for God's wrath (see Ezek 38:15, 18-20). These are the peoples of Gog, Meshech, and Tubal. Along with these will come Persia, Cush, Phut, Gomer, and Togarmah (Ezek 38:2-6; see Dan 11:44 & Rev 16:12). They all will be destroyed at Christ's coming according to the higher meaning of Jeremiah 25:12-38 and according to Ezekiel 38:18-22; 39:2, 11. These nations are also the same nations as shown in Revelation 16:12-16; 9:11-18; 19:19; 20:8-10, and which Daniel 11:44 speaks about.

Pattern of the Last War Throughout Bible

pr317» Yet not only are all the nations spoken about in Jeremiah to be destroyed, but all nations mentioned in all the prophecies. The nations' destruction is mentioned in most of the Bible, and these prophecies speak about all nations being destroyed because of God's "wrath." Thus, we can use most of the Bible to describe the details of the Last War (see Ezek 12:22-23).

Day of Trouble

pr318» For example, much of the book of Psalms speaks about the day of the LORD. In the book of Psalms time and time again it speaks of a "day of trouble" with the LORD coming and saving God's people. All these scriptures can add to the details of the Last War.

Wicked and Evil Ones

pr319» Then in the book of Job it speaks about the wicked ones and their fate. All these scriptures can also be used to describe the Last War. In fact anywhere in the Bible where it speaks about evil or the wicked's fate can be used, for many of the Biblical prophecies are all at once completed on the day of the LORD (Ezek 12:22-23). The day of the LORD is the climax of evil, the fullness of transgression, and also its *end*. It is also the beginning of God's rulership

All Evil and War Destroyed

pr320» The following verses in their higher meaning or antitypical meaning prove there will be no more evil from the time God takes over:

- they shall not learn war any more [Isa 2:4; Mic 4:3]
- violence no more [Isa 60:18]
- no evil seen any more [Zeph 3:15]
- affliction *not* to rise a second time [Nah 1:9]

pr321» Thus after this climatic Last War there will be no more confusion, no more war, no more evil. As Psalms 37:38 and Jeremiah 51:48-49 show the transgressors will be destroyed *together*.

How Long Will The War Last?

pr322» But how long will this Last War last. Some have said that God's "wrath" will be poured out over a period of time. As we've shown you in PR4, God's wrath is the wrath of Satan, his age, and his people. Some say the Last War may take a year or more.

pr323» But this can't be, for when antitypical Babylon (the Beast) is destroyed so too will the other nations be destroyed (Jer 25:12-26; Jer 51:48-49). The Beast will be destroyed after 3 ½ years of misrule (Rev 13:5; 19:20). It is during these 3 ½ years that the Church will be in the wilderness (Rev 12:6, 14). The Church of this old age is not the utopia or the New Age: the Church consists of those belonging to the New Age because they have the Spirit of the New Age. Since no one (except Christ) is allowed to enter the temple (kingdom of God, or the New Age, see notes) until the last plague is poured out (Rev 15:8), the last plagues will be poured out at the *end* of the 3 ½ year period.

Wrath: All At Once

pr324» How long is the Last War? How long is God's wrath? There are at least 12 verses in the Bible that say in their higher meaning that the end of this age and its way will come in *one day*, *one hour*, in an *instant*, *at once*, *swiftly* and *speedily* as a overwhelming flood (Nah 1:8; Zeph 1:18; Mal 3:5; Isa 29:5; Isa 42:14; Luke 18:8; Rev 18:8, 10, 19; Dan 9:26; Isa 47:11; Joel 3:4; Isa 10:17). The destruction will come just before or near the beginning of the day of the LORD. But it will happen in an instant, at once. Hence *the seals, trumpets, and plagues of Revelation will happen all at once.*

Greater Detail

pr325» Now let's go into some greater detail. After this we will construct what will happen in the 3 ½ year period and thus explain the book of Revelation. Let's now continue to simplify and synthesize the book of Revelation.

Angel and Angels of Revelation

pr326» Notice that the shout of the voice of Christ sounds like a *trumpet* (cf 1 Thes 4:16; Rev 4:1; 1:10). God's voice also is described as *thunder* (Job 37:4-5). And his voice is as the sound of *many waters* (Ezek 43:2). And the "seven thunders" of Revelation 10:3 is nothing other than the seven trumpets, for God's voice is like a trumpet, thunder, and many waters. These terms are merely metonymical of each other.

pr327» The angel of Revelation 10:1-4 that uttered "with a voice, as when a lion roars: and when he had cried [with *a* voice], seven thunders uttered their voices," is Christ's *own* angel.

pr328» Notice this angel had a rainbow on his head, and his face was as it were the sun, and his feet as pillars of fire (Rev 10:1). This rainbow is of God's throne (Rev 4:3; Ezek 1:28), not just any angel's throne. This angel's face looked like the sun which is the way Christ's face is described (Rev 1:16). He swore by him who created the heaven and earth (Rev 10:6).

pr329» Another proof yet that this angel is Christ's own is to compare the following verses:

- "A lamb [Christ] as it had been slain, having seven horns and seven eyes, which are the seven Spirits of God sent forth into all the earth" (Rev 5:6).

pr330» All these seven eyes (Spirits) are on the Lamb, and the Lamb is Christ (John 1:29). These seven Spirits are of Christ. Note also:

- "Seven lamps of fire burning before the throne, which are the seven Spirits of God" (Rev 4:5).

pr331» Now spirits are angels (Heb 1:7). Thus, these seven Spirits are seven angels. Also, the seven lamps (flames) must burn on a lamp stand. And sure enough there are seven golden candlesticks (lamp stands), and these hold the seven lamps or spirits or angels (Rev 1:20). And as Revelation 1:20 shows these seven candlesticks indicate the seven churches of Revelation, chapters 2 and 3. These seven lamps (flames) are the seven spirits or angels of the seven churches. Notice Hebrews 1:7 where flames of fire are equated to spirits or angels. These seven spirits or angels are shown throughout the book of Revelation blowing trumpets, talking to John, and so forth. Now we know these seven angels are the seven eyes of the Lamb (Christ); they are of Christ (cf. Rev 4:5). **That is, they are of Christ's Spiritual Body that will eventually fill all in all** (1 Cor 12:12, 27).

pr332» Notice Zechariah describes these seven same eyes upon *one stone* (Zech 3:9). In Zechariah 4:7 it calls this same stone the *headstone*: "and he shall bring forth the headstone thereof with shouting." The head or chief stone is Christ (Eph 2:20). Thus, this is another proof that these seven eyes or angels are of one, Christ. Revelation uses seven angels to describe Christ or the Spiritual Body of Christ. Hence, the angel of Revelation 10:1-4 is Christ and his voice sounds like seven thunders, and his voice is metonymical for the sound of a trumpet or many waters. Remember there is Christ the individual and the Body of Christ with many individuals.

Things We Should Understand

pr333» Revelation is a poetical, symbolical rendition of the end-of-the-age events. It seems mystical only if the reader doesn't understand Biblical symbolism. The Bible uses many metonymical terms to describe the same things or events. Revelation is understandable only *if* one knows that the seals, trumpets, and plagues happen all at once. And the only way one knows this is to use the whole Bible to unveil the book of Revelation. But the only way to properly do this is to study the whole Bible.

pr334» Next one must know all the terms used to describe the Church, for example the first-fruits, the bride, the woman of Revelation 12:1-2; the temple, new Jerusalem, etc. Also, one must know that the seven angels are merely the manifestations of Christ, and that his "voice" is metonymical for many waters, trumpets, thunders, and shouts. What he speaks with his voice is the Word of God, and the physical Word of God is in the Bible. Further one must know that the lake of fire is the beginning and aftermath of an instant atomic (and other super weapons) war that is beginning to burn up the earth at the return of Christ to the physical dimension, and it is this fire that will burn for an agelasting time (Matt 25:41), and this age is for one-thousand years (Rev 20:1-3).

pr335» One must know that many prophecies will be fulfilled to the fullest extent at the end of the age (Ezek 12:22-23). And we must know the Beast of Revelation is the kingdom of Satan/man which will at once encompass all the qualities of the four Beasts of Daniel 7. And we must know that the Revelations's woman, great city, Babylon, Egypt, and Sodom are all a descriptive part of the end-of-the-age's Beast. Thus, what the Bible says about the typical Babylon, Egypt, and so forth can be used to describe the end-of-the-age events since many prophecies are to be fulfilled near or at the end of the age.

God's Throne

pr336» Now let's identify one spiritual meaning of God's throne. Revelation 3:21 pictures Christ sitting on a throne of his Father. In Isaiah 66:1 God describes his throne as being heaven: "the heaven is my throne." But what is heaven representative of? It represents the Spiritual dimension. Compare the use of "heaven" and "earth" with "spirit" and "flesh" in, Isaiah 55:9; Phil 3:18-20; Col 3:1-2; 1 Cor 15:44-49; and Hebrews 9:23-24.

pr337» Now Christ says we can sit on his throne, which is his Father's (Rev 3:21), which is heaven, which is the Spiritual dimension. Thus, Christians can put on the Spiritual dimension as Christ did (see the *God Papers*). Also notice that Christ's throne is like a fiery flame (Dan 7:9), and fiery flames are equated to spiritual beings (Heb 1:7). What is God's throne? It is Spiritual life. This is one higher meaning of God's throne. In other words, God's throne is *not* like man's throne, just as the fear of God is different from what man thinks. Those ruling in the 1000 year age won't be sitting around on thrones, but they will act and behave as Christ did on earth. They will be the *servants* of the new world.

Seals, Trumpets Plagues, and 1260 Days

pr338» Now let's synthesize the seals, trumpets, and plagues (vials) of Revelation.

- The Church of God (Rev 3:7-13) will be in the spiritual wilderness of the Beast for 1260 days (Rev 12:6, 14).
- The Beast is to rule these 1260 days (Dan 7:25; Rev 13:5).
- The Beast is destroyed after these 1260 days (Rev 14:8-10; Rev 16:19; 19-20).
- These 1260 days (3 ½ years) are the last ½ week of Daniel's prophetic seventy weeks (Dan 9:24-27).
- It is also the last half of Christ's "week" of confirming the covenant with many, through his two witnesses (Dan 9:26-27, & see above).
- It is the 3 ½ years that the Church (Rev 3:14-22) is tried (Rev 3:18-19; Dan 11:33-35; 12:7, 10; Mal 3:2-3, see previous qualifications).
- The end of the seventy weeks of years of Daniel will come on as a flood, with war (Dan 9:26).
- "Then, in the end [of the 70 weeks; at the end of the 3 ½ years], what has been decreed concerning the desolation will be poured out" (Dan 9:27, *NEB*).

What is poured out?

- the vials of Revelation 16
- the "wine of wrath" or "cup of wine" (Rev 14:10; 16:19; 18:6, 8; Jer 51:7-8; 25:15-17)
- the angel's censer (Rev 8:5)

pr339» Thus, God's "wrath" is poured out at the end of the age. This word is translated "consummation" in Daniel 9:27 in the KJV and "end" in the NEB, but in Hebrew it means, *full* end. Therefore, at the *full* end of the 3 ½ years the wine of wrath is poured out. Then the Beast will be destroyed while the Church will be saved (Dan 12:1), and the rulership of God will commence (Rev 11:15).

pr340» This is also confirmed by Jeremiah's seventy years, and the seventy weeks of Daniel 9. At the end of these antitypical seventy years, Cyrus (Christ) will physically return and be King of all nations.

pr341» Thus, Christ can't return physically until after the 3 ½ years. The Church is not "born" of God until after the 3 ½ years. The Beast isn't destroyed until after the 3 ½ years. The cup of wrath (vials) is not poured out until after the 3 ½ years.

pr342» Yet Revelation 11:15 says after the seventh trumpet (which is, in the word flow of Revelation, before the vials of Revelation 16), Christ will come and take over the nations, and the Church will be "born" of God. But as we've shown above these vials are poured out after the 3 ½ years, and at that time the Church is to become the kingdom of God, and at that time Christ is to return physically. Is this another Biblical contradiction? No!

Wrath All at Once

pr343» Notice that in the higher or antitypical meaning of the following scriptures that the wrath is to happen all at once:

- as an overrunning flood [Nah 1:8; Dan 9:26]
- speedy riddance [Zeph 1:18]
- in one day [Isa 10:17; 47:9; Rev 18:8]
- at an instant, suddenly [Isa 29:5; 1 Thes 5:3; Isa 47:11; Eccl 9:12; Jer 51:8; Psa 73:19]
- destroy and devour at once [Isa 42:14]
- as in a moment [Psa 73:19]
- avenge them speedily [Luke 18:8]
- as a whirlwind [Psa 58:9-10]
- in one hour [Rev 18:10, 19]
- swiftly, and speedily [Joel 3:4]

Then all nations will be destroyed *together*:

- the transgressors are destroyed together [Psa 37:38]

pr344» Because of Babylon's sin against the Church (Israel), then in or "at Babylon [the antitypical Babylon] shall fall the slain of all the earth," thus, of all the nations (Jer 51:49, 48).

No War Or Evil Will Be Around After The Kingdom of God Takes Over:

pr345»

- they shall not make war anymore [Isa 2:4; Mic 4:3]
- violence no more [Isa 60:18]
- affliction not to rise a second time after the end of the wrath [Nah 1:9]
- No one shall see evil anymore [Zeph 3:15]
- hail (from the super weapons — Rev 16:21) to sweep away the lies [Isa 28:17]

Summarize

pr346» Thus, by putting these verses above together, the seals, trumpets, and vials must:

- happen all at once, in an instant;
- no war or evil will be thereafter;
- all destroyed together, that is, evil and the nations' power will all be destroyed together;
- all this will happen *after* the 3 ½ years;
- Christ will physically return after the 3 ½ years to *save* mankind from his own wrath against himself (Matt 24:22; Luke 9:56);
- the Church will be born after the 3 ½ years;
- and the kingdom of God takes over after the 3 ½ years.

pr347» The seals, trumpets, and vials picture events that happen all at once, in a very short period of time. They are not sequential events. They merely amplify with different words and events this greatest of great points in time. This is the reason the book of Revelation is filled with the *aorist* verb (and other timeless verbs). This verb is one of action, not of time. The aorist verb and other timeless verbs cannot be translated correctly into English, thus the confusion.

Similarities of the Seals, Trumpets, and Vials

pr348» Now let's show the similarities between the seals, trumpets, and vials as well as show you the meaning of the symbolism of these events. After this, in PR6, we will list many groups of verses so you can help further to confirm for yourself what we have been putting forward in this paper.

Seals

First Seal

pr349» The first seal was opened and John heard, "as it were the noise of thunder" (Rev 6:1). As we've shown before God's "voice" sounds like, or is metonymical for, thunder, many waters, and trumpets. Thus, another meaning of the noise of thunder is the sound of a trumpet. What John heard was the first trumpet when the seal was opened. Remember John was "in Spirit on the Lord's day." John was transfigured to the day of the Lord. This is spiritual Lord's day which exists for 1000 years (see "Thousand Years And Beyond" paper [NM 15]).

pr350» Then in verse two John sees a white horse with one on it with a bow, "and a crown was given unto him: and he went forth conquering, and to conquer."

Four Horses

pr351» These four horses mentioned in the sixth chapter of Revelation are the same horses as in Zechariah 1:8 and 6:1-8. Notice these four horses are commissioned to go "to and fro through the world" (Zech 1:10-11; 6:5, 7). And these four horses are called four spirits or winds of heaven, which go forth from standing before the Lord of all the earth (Zech 6:5).

pr352» Now in the book of Job it speaks about Satan coming at certain times and standing before the LORD (Job 1:6; 2:1). Notice that Satan is like the four horses or spirits, he goes to and fro through the earth (Job 1:7). Satan's job, one might say, is to go to and fro through the world trying mankind. Now what is the meaning of these four horses of Revelation and Zechariah?

pr353» Notice the four horses are associated with the "Beasts" in Revelation chapter 6. These four "Beasts" should be translated "living creatures." These are the same four living creatures as the ones described in Ezekiel 1:5-28; 10:1-22. These living creatures describe a part of the throne of God. This throne of God describes the total characteristics and powers of God as the Beast of Revelation describes the total powers (rulership) of Satan (see the *God Papers*, GP9). But if this is so, what part of God's power do the living creatures signify?

pr354» They signify the four Beasts of Daniel 7, for again in Daniel "Beast" should be translated "living creature." These living creatures of God's throne are the living creatures ("Beasts" — KJV) of the seventh chapter of Daniel. These living creatures are the world-ruling kingdoms of the earth. And these kingdoms are a part of God's power (throne) because all kingdoms were given their predestinated power by God (John 19:10-11; Dan 4:32-37; 2:20-21; etc.).

pr355» ***God's Power Over the World's Kingdoms***. It is God who has the overall power over the world's kingdoms. Notice that God cut Nebuchadnezzar off as a leader of Babylon, "to the intent that the living may know that the most High rules in the kingdom of men, and gives it to whomsoever he will, and sets up over it the basest of men" (Dan 4:17). And again, "by me [God] kings reign, and princes decree justice. By me princes rule, and nobles, even all the judges of the earth" (Prov 8:15-16).

pr356» God is the overall head ruler of the world's nations in that all power comes from God (Dan 4:25; Jer 27:5). But the true God (the Becoming-One) himself does not do any wrong, for the true God *is* love (1 John 4:8).

[*Remember* here that all the works were done from the beginning (Heb 4:3). The creation is like a wound up clock ready to ring at the appointed time. God through knowing ahead of time the outcome has planned it in such a way so as to best form within man the true knowledge of right and wrong. So in a sense, since God planned it this way he has the authority over the parts therein. Yet he himself has not done any harm, but Satan — the opposite force of the True God — has been doing the destruction. What God did was create a situation whereby, through cause and effect, he was able to determine the outcome. Since he created man's mind with its limits, and created the degree of effect for each cause, and created the parts of the creation (man, spirit, earth, etc.); he knows the outcome as does one who builds a clock and then sets it to ring at a certain time (see the *God Papers*).]

pr357» Now we showed you how the four horses go "to and fro through the earth," (Zech 6:7) just as Satan goes "to and fro" through the earth (Job 1:6-7). And we pointed out that the four horses are associated with the four living creatures ("Beasts" — KJV) in Revelation 6, which are the same living creatures as the ones described in Ezekiel, chapters 1 and 10. Yet we know that the four living creatures ("Beast") of Daniel 7 are the successive rulership of Satan's kingdom since Satan is at this time the ruler of the world (under God who has allowed Satan's rulership for a higher purpose). Therefore Satan goes "to and fro" through the earth trying it by the medium of the world's kingdoms which are the four living creatures ("Beasts") of Daniel 7. And since the four horses are associated with the four living creatures, and also go throughout the world, then the four horses are just another metonymical name for the four living creatures.

pr358» The four horses are like the four living creatures ("Beasts") of Daniel 7 which are the four living creatures of Ezekiel 1 and 10 and the four living creatures of Revelation. These four horses, which indicate the four Beasts of Daniel 7, will at the end of the age be the final Beast pictured in Revelation 13:1-2.

pr359» *Four Winds; Four Horses*. These same four horses, which are called the four spirits (winds) of heaven (Zech 6:2-5), are also indicated by the four horns of Zechariah 1:18-21 which are the "horns of the Gentiles" (v. 21).

pr360» *Four Horns of Brazen Altar*. Now "horns" in the Bible are symbolic of kingdoms (see Dan 7:24). These are the four world ruling kingdoms of Daniel 7. These four kingdoms are also indicated by the four horns on the Brazen altar of Moses' tabernacle. The fire and sacrifices of this altar indicate two things:

- the trial and sacrifices the whole world has been going through because of these four horns (kingdoms of Satan);
- the lake of fire, by which these four Beasts will be destroyed, thus fulfilling God's righteous judgment (Psa 9:15-16).

pr361» Notice the angel takes a censer full of fire off the altar and casts it to the earth (Rev 8:5). This pictures the lake of fire being poured on the earth through the atomic Last War. But let's get back to the first seal.

First Seal

pr362» Who is riding on this first horse, the horse being symbolic of Satan's kingdom? Notice he has *A* crown, and he went to conquer. It is Christ with his golden crown (Rev 14:14) on his white horse, and his making war in RIGHTEOUSNESS (Rev 19:11).

pr363» Christ is making war in righteousness, as explained before in PR4, by letting the wicked destroy themselves. Christ is pictured on top of this horse because all power and authority is his (Matt 28:18); he has the power over this horse (kingdom); he allows man to begin to destroy himself, yet he will save man from man's own madness. The first seal, thus, pictures Christ allowing the horse to begin to make war.

Second Seal

pr364» Now the second seal shows us how the war is fought "they should kill one another." As shown previously mankind will make war on themselves. They will go mad at the end and begin to commit cosmocide.

Third Seal

pr365» The third seal pictures judgment — the scales or balances. Also the third vial pictures judgment (Rev 16:4-7). This is judgment of nations (Joel 3:12). This is the righteous judgment of God on Babylon (see, Rev 14:7; 18:10). This seal also pictures the famine of Babylon which comes upon it in one day, in one hour, or one moment of time (Rev 18:8, 10).

Fourth Seal

pr366» The fourth seal pictures Death (satan) and the destruction of one-fourth of the earth. This indicates the scope of the destruction by the Last War. It is over one-fourth of the earth's surface. All the destruction was caused by the sword (war), hunger, and death.

Fifth Seal

pr367» The fifth seal is reflective and qualitative. it pictures all those saints killed under the power of the horses (Satan's kingdoms). Daniel 7:21, 24; 11:33-35; and Daniel 12:7, 10 picture the same thing. They are told to rest a while until the full number of the saints are killed.

> [*Remember* this is the fifth seal. The whole instantaneous wrath is amplified into seven parts of three sets of descriptions — the seals, trumpets, and vials; yet the Bible also describes events leading up to this time, and events happening after it (Rev 1:19). The end of the wrath isn't until the action of the last (7th) seal, or trumpet, or vial is completed.]

Sixth Seal

pr368» Now the sixth seal shows the sun becoming black. This is described elsewhere in the Bible, but it speaks of it as the sun and moon being darkened (Isa 13:10), and Ezekiel 32:7 says why it will be darkened: "and when I put you [Pharaoh — a type of Satan] out, I will cover the heaven, and make the stars thereof dark; [*how*?] I will cover the sun with a cloud." The same clouds are pictured in the fifth trumpet as the smoke that came out of the bottomless pit (caused by the bombs) that made the air and sun dark (Rev 9:2).

pr369» Also in the sixth seal it speaks about the stars falling on the earth. Now if any of the stars ever fell on the earth, the Earth would blow up. This is symbolic. God tells us to look to the higher meaning (Col 3:1-2). Stars are representative of angels (Rev 1:20). This merely speaks about the one-third of the total angels who belong to Satan being cast into the bottomless pit at the Messiah's return (Rev 12:4; 20:1-3; Isa 34:4; 14:12, 15; Ezek 28:7-8, 17; 31:16).

pr370» Verse 14 speaks of *every* mountain and island being moved out of their places. Now this can't be because only one-fourth of the earth will be affected by the Last War (Rev 6:8). There is a higher meaning here. Now mountains are symbolic of nations or kingdoms (Rev 17:9-10). Although the earth will be greatly shaken by this Last War (Isa 24:19-21), the higher sense of this verse tells us every kingdom of this world will be put down; then the rulership of God will take over (Rev 11:15).

pr371» Verses 15 and 16 show people hiding themselves in caves and so forth. This pictures the great fear surrounding this day of wrath (Isa 2:10, 19, 21; Ezek 32:10). One reason for this fear is that about three days before this the two witnesses were killed. For 3 ½ years these two have been teaching what the world was about to do to itself — commit cosmocide. They have been telling them that the New Age or the kingdom of God is coming. Revelation 11 pictures the world as if it were relieved that these prophets died. The world will probably hope what they were saying was wrong, yet subconsciously (the other-mind) they will know that these prophets are right. The spirit in man (the other-mind) knows it will at some time be tormented (Matt 8:29; Mark 5:7). But also they think they will be *destroyed* in the lake of fire (Mark 1:24; Job 15:22).

pr372» Man, and the enemy spirit in man, as the hours tick off after the prophets are killed will remember their last words that the Messiah will come within 3 ½ days after they are killed (Rev 11:9-12). The spirit in man knows it will be tormented once the Messiah returns. This is the reason for the great fear as the hours tick away toward Christ's physical return. This is why people go into caves to hide from the Lord. Even though the two witnesses will tell the world that Christ will come to save or free mankind, they will not believe it, for they have the spirit of fear in them (2 Tim 1:7; Rom 8:15). Not only was Christ's first stay on this earth marred, but his return will be even more so, "his visage was so marred more than any man" (Isa 52:14). People now think God will come with fire and damnation, and this idea won't change much over the next few years.

Seventh Seal

pr373» Now when the seventh seal is opened, "there was silence in heaven about the space of half an hour" (Rev 8:1). This "half an hour" is translated from a Greek word. It merely indicates a very short period of time. This is also pictured in Revelation 7:1-3. As the Last War begins, in the middle of it God will stop it for a short moment and seal his elect, by writing his NAME on their foreheads (Rev 14:1). They at that moment are born of God in the middle of the lake of fire caused by the super weapons. Now let's explain the trumpets and vials.

Trumpets

pr374» Before the first trumpet is blown we see an angel with a golden censer filled with fire out of the altar. This altar has four horns indicating the four Beasts of Daniel 7 or the four horses of Revelation and Zechariah. On this altar a continuous fire was always going (Lev 6:13). This pictures the continuous fire or trial of mankind caused by Satan's spiritual kingdom — the other-mind's power. A censer is nothing but a cup. This golden censer can be looked upon as the golden cup that is poured upon Babylon (Rev 14:7-10). Notice the golden censer of fire is poured out on the earth (Rev 8:5). Anything poured out of a cup or censer falls all at once. This pictures the fire of the lake of fire falling on the earth all at once. When the bombs go off there will be "thunderings, lightning, and an earthquake" as Revelation 8:5 shows and Revelation 11:19; 16:18, 20-21; Isa 29:6. The hail stones are merely caused by the unbelievable Last War.

pr375» Notice that Peter says on this day that, "the heaven being on fire shall be dissolved, and the elements shall melt with fervent heat" (2 Pet 3:12, 10). God has reserved a cause and effect law for this great Last War. If the elements of the sky are burning as Peter tells us on that day, then there must be great heat generated. There must be a certain temperature when reached that will cause the sky to be set on fire. In Revelation 16:21 it says the hail stones weigh as much as a talent, which is approximately 100 pounds. The great heat will cause matter to explode, "have you seen the treasures of the hail, which I have reserved against the time of trouble, against the day of battle and war?" (Job 38:22-23) No we have never seen it, but Revelation 16:21 describes it as does Ezekiel 38:22.

First Trumpet

pr376» Now notice what happened after the trumpet is blown, "and there followed hail and fire mingled with blood" (Rev 8:7). This hail is the same hail we just spoke about, and the fire causes the hail, and the fire will come from man's own weapons for God's wrath is man's wrath against himself as we've shown you in PR4.

pr377» Now what happens when one is in a lake of fire caused by man's wrath against himself? "Their flesh shall consume away while they stand upon their feet, and their eyes shall consume away in their holes, and their tongue shall consume away in their mouth" (Zech 14:12). "And their blood shall be poured out as dust, and their flesh as the dung" (Zeph 1:17). Some have accused the true God of doing such acts, but we see herein how these things will happen.

pr378» Further in Revelation 8:7 we see where one-third of the trees are to be burnt up and the grass also. Now trees are symbolic of kingdoms as well as of the people in these kingdoms (Isa 10:18-19). This is merely a symbolical way of describing the fact that one-third of those living before the day of wrath will die on that day (Rev 9:15, 18). Notice, "by these three was the third part of man killed, [1] by the fire, [2] and by the smoke, [3] and by the brimstone" (Rev 9:18).

pr379» Revelation 8:7 also says all the grass was burnt up. Thus this means that all the grass around where this war will be located will burn up (over one-fourth of the earth, Rev 6:8), and since grass is symbolic to people (Isa 40:6), then all the people in this area of the earth will burn up except those supernaturally saved (Matt 24:22).

Second Trumpet

pr380» Now the second trumpet sounds and we see a great mountain burning that is cast into the sea. Read Jeremiah 51:24-25 where it identifies this mountain as Babylon. Since we know it doesn't mean the old Babylon but the Babylon described in Revelation (Satan's kingdom), then we know Satan's kingdom will be destroyed by burning and then at the same time thrown into the sea. The "sea," is used interchangeably in the Old Testament with the pit — bottomless pit (see Ezek 27:32; 28:8). Actually the bottomless pit or lake of fire of Revelation 20:1-3, 10 is an antitypical event of what happened to the Pharaoh and his troops — the Red Sea buried them (Ex 14:27). The lake of fire will bury the antitypical Egypt, Babylon, and the Pharaoh.

pr381» Next we see a third part of the sea becomes blood (Rev 8:8-9). The higher meaning here again reiterates that one-third of all the angels are being destroyed (see next section).

Third Trumpet

pr382» Then when the third trumpet sounds we see a star falling to the earth. The higher meaning here pictures an angel falling to the earth, for stars are symbolic of angels (Rev 1:20). This angel is identified as Satan the Dragon who brings down one-third of the total angels (stars) to the earth (Rev 12:3-4, 9, 12). This is also pictured in Revelation 6:13 and in Isaiah 14:12ff.

pr383» Notice that this star called Wormwood fell on a third part of the rivers and that third part became wormwood. What does that mean? What is the higher or antitypical meaning? Moving or running water is symbolic to spirit (John 7:38-39). Thus, the star or angel called Wormwood (Satan) fell on a third of the rivers of water (spirit) and they became wormwood; they became Satan's angels (Rev 12:4). "And many men died of the waters [spirits of Satan] because they were made bitter" (v. 11).

pr384» Thus, now we know what the following verse means, "I will feed them, even this people, with wormwood [Satan], and give them water [spirit] of gall to drink" (Jer 9:15; 23:15). And now we know by putting Revelation 8:10-11 and Jeremiah 9:14 together what Peter meant when he said to Simon of Samaria, "for I perceive that you art in the gall of bitterness," that is, he was bitter with the Wormwood (Satan) that was inside him misleading him.

Fourth Trumpet

pr385» Then the fourth angel sounded the trumpet, and one-third of the sun, moon, and stars were smitten, and made dark. What is the higher meaning here? Now darkness is symbolic to Satan as light is symbolic to God (1 John 1:5) since Satan and God are opposite qualities as darkness is opposite to light (see Col 1:13). Thus, one-third of the sun and moon and stars were darkened by Satan. Now we're aware that one-third of the stars (angels) were darkened by Satan's way, but what does it mean when it says the sun and moon were darkened?

pr386» If you have read the paper on the symbolic meaning of the sun and moon you know they are symbolic of God and Jesus Christ the man. Now we know if a third of the sun (God) is darkened then we know a third of the moon will also be darkened, for the moon merely reflects the sun's light. Now at the beginning the stars (angels) were created by God. Since angels are made of spirit and God is spirit, the angels were thus made out of the material of God. One-third of the darkened angels were at one time a part of God's Spirit. And if you read the *God Papers* you will see that God doesn't consider himself complete until the end of creation when *all* things are gathered into Christ. This includes all the angels. Now since the sun is symbolic of Christ, what is meant by it being one-third darkened, is that, one-third of God (the completed God) is darkened. Not until these darkened angels are made light again will the Body of Christ be completed. In other words, the fourth trumpet merely reiterates the fact that one-third of the angels are of Satan, and through the knowledge about the sun's symbolic meaning, we know God considers one-third of his potential is also darkened.

Fifth Trumpet

pr387» Then the fifth trumpet sounds at this point (Rev 9:1), and we see a star fall to earth with the key of the bottomless pit. Stars are symbolic to angels, thus, the higher meaning here means that an angel came to earth with the key. Now this same event is shown in Revelation 20:1-3. This bottomless pit elsewhere in the Bible is called hell (cf Ezek 32:24, 27). The bottomless pit is hell, the grave. Who has the key to the bottomless pit, to hell? "I am he that lives, and was dead; and, behold, I am alive into the ages of ages, and have the keys of hell and of death" (Rev 1:18). God has the keys to the pit — to hell. We have already shown you that the seven angels are merely manifestations of Christ, so the angel with the key in Revelation 9:1 and 20:1 is Christ.

pr388» Revelation 9:2 shows the pit and smoke coming out. Now we know that God will not initiate the lake of fire, but those nations who will be fighting among themselves will initiate the fire. And since the weapons that could cause the heavens to burn and the elements to burn (2 Pet 3:10, 12) are atomic in nature, this Last War will begin and end with atomic weapons and other weapons flying everywhere. The deeds of this war will fall on man's own head (Obad 1:15). Yet this war is begun by the spiritual madness of Satan who knows his time is short: "Woe to the inhabiters of the earth and of the sea! for the devil is come down unto you, having great wrath, because he knows that he has but a short time" (Rev 12:12).

pr389» Satan and his angels through their influence in the minds of mankind will cause man to go mad at the end of this age. The smoke coming out of the pit (Rev 9:2) is the smoke from the aftermath of the atomic weapons. This is where the clouds of smoke come from that cover the stars (Isa 13:10; Ezek 32:7).

pr390» "The heathen are sunk down in the pit that *they* made ... Hell from beneath is moved for you [Satan, Babylon, Lucifer, see context] to meet you at your coming ... All they [nations] shall speak and say unto you [Satan], Art you also become weak as we? art you become like unto us? Your pomp is brought down to the grave, and the noise of your vials: the worm is spread under you, and the worms cover you. How art you fallen from heaven, O Lucifer, son of the morning ['darkness' — from Strong's # 7837 & 7835]! How art you cut down to the ground, which did weaken the nations!" (Psa 9:15; Isa 14:9-12) This pictures Satan after he is cast down to the earth (Rev 12:12), after his rulership is taken away. Remember all these things happen at once: the Last War (Matt 24:7; Dan 9:26-27), Satan's power being taken away (Rev 20:1-3), and the kingdom of God taking over (Rev 11:15-18).

pr391» "And out of the smoke came locusts *into* the earth [pit]" (Rev 9:3). The correct translation shows locusts passing away into the earth. Now these locusts are identified in Nahum 3:15-18 as the troops of the king of Assyria. This same king is the one described in Isaiah 10:5-19. This king prefigured the leader of the Beast of Revelation 13, and is also the false-prophet. This king is also a shadow of Satan himself (2 Thes 2:9). Thus, not only do these locusts indicate the troops of this Assyrian king, but also the troops of what this king represents on earth — Satan's troops, his angels. These locusts at once picture the Assyrian troops and Satan's angels. They are destroyed by the effects of the Last War. One effect of the Last War being the smoke.

pr392» Now Revelation 9:5 should be translated, "and to them [the locusts] it was given that they should not kill them [man], but that they [man] will be tormented five months: and their torment as the torment of a scorpion, when he strikes a man." This pictures man being tormented by the symbolic locusts (Satan's angels) for five months *before* the Last War. This can't be after the Last War because there will be no evil after this instant war. Man will be mentally tormented for five months before God returns. But, of course, since the garden of Eden man has been tormented by Satan (see "Old Mind" paper [NM 21]).

pr393» Verse six shows mankind seeking death, but afraid to kill himself. Why? The spirit of man that misleads mankind is a spirit of fear. Even though these spirits are making men miserable, men will be afraid to take their own lives, for they don't know that there is no hell-fire for themselves. There is a hell-fire for the spiritual evil angels, but man because of these confused spirits in their minds think that they themselves will be tormented in this fire (see the "Thousand Years and Beyond" paper [NM 15]).

pr394» Notice the crowns of these locusts' heads in Revelation 9:7. Compare this with Nahum 3:17.

pr395» Notice the proof that these locusts are symbolic of Satan's angels: "and they had a king over them, which is the angel of the bottomless pit, whose name in Hebrew is Abbaddon, but in the Greek tongue has his name Appollyon." These are two of the many names the Bible uses to describe Satan. Appollyon means destroyer. Satan is the destroyer of the world. His way is of destruction (Isa 14:12, 20).

Sixth Trumpet

pr396» Then comes the sixth trumpet (Rev 9:13-21). Now in verse 14 it speaks of four angels. Who or what are these four angels? Notice in Zechariah 6:5 it identifies four horses as four spirits or winds since the Hebrew word means both spirit and wind. These four winds or spirits are shown in Revelation 7:1, "the four winds of the earth." Here, they are being held back until the saints are sealed. These four winds are the four horses, which are the four Beasts, which are the kingdom of Satan. Thus, in Revelation 7:1 it pictures the kingdom of Satan (the four winds or spirits or horses or Beasts) being held back from destroying in the Last War until the saints are sealed. Yet since angels are spirits (Heb 1:7), we know the four angels of Revelation 9:14 are symbolic of the four spirits (winds) of Zechariah 6 and Revelation 7, or the four horses of Revelation 6. Therefore these four angels picture, in a way, what is being said in Revelation

7:1. These four angels of Satan's rulership are being held back from the end-of-the-age's wrath until the appointed time of wrath or judgment (Acts 17:31).

pr397» Now the Beasts of Daniel and/or Revelation specifically describe the kingdom of Satan that has or had rulership in or around Jerusalem. **Yet the whole world is a part of Satan's kingdom**.

pr398» Notice what Christ prophesies about Satan's kingdom at the end: "every kingdom divided against itself is brought to desolation; and a house divided against a house falls. If Satan also be divided against himself, how shall his kingdom stand?" (Luke 11:17, 18)

pr399» Next we see the four angels (the horses of Rev 6) being let loose, and a great army is allowed to cross the Euphrates river. This army was prepared for this battle for over a year (v. 15). It is by and with this army that a third of mankind and angelkind in the Last War will be destroyed or as good as destroyed. Who are these nations?

pr400» Ezekiel 38 and 39 picture these same nations as does Jeremiah 50 and 51, and Isaiah 13:6-22. These are the nations of the north, the Medes, Ma-gog, Meshech, etc. Somewhere today these nations or peoples exist. Along with these and other nations and peoples, are the ones who come from the east and north towards Jerusalem (Dan 11:44). These nations are a part of Satan's rulership. (In Biblical symbolism, the "east" represents the future — the direction of the Sun's coming day light; and the "north" represents the spiritual *left*, the spiritual evil side. See Hebrew words for "east" and "north" in the Lexicon.)

pr401» Notice what Ezekiel 38:10-11 says about these nations, "thus says the Lord GOD; It shall also come to pass, that at the same time [the 'latter years,' v. 8] shall things come into your mind [the mind of these national leaders], and you shall think an evil thought: and you shall say, I will go up to the *land* of unwalled villages [the Middle East, see v. 8]" (see also Jer 51:28). They will prepare to attack. They thought up this plan to attack one year, one month, one day, and one hour before they actually will attack (Rev 9:15). **In a Spiritual sense, the spiritual Beast is in the minds of Spiritual Jerusalem as the other-mind. See *Old Mind Paper*.** [NM 21]

pr402» This great army of the north (Ezek 38:15) will not only attack the *land* of the Middle East, but also the people of God's Church who will be within the strike of the army (Ezek 38:16; Mic 4:11; Jer 6:23; Isa 54:15). **Since in the Spiritual sense the land of Spiritual Israel is the whole earth [*Seed Paper*], then God's Church need not be located in the Middle East at the very End**. Actually this is a main reason this war will happen. Remember Satan's spiritual influence rules this world (Rev 13:2). But Satan will be committing cosmocide when he tries to stop the Church from being born. Revelation 12:2-4 pictures Satan trying to destroy the child that is about to be born. Isaiah 66:6-9 helps to identify this child as the born Church.

pr403» Thus, there are two reasons these nations will come against this land at the end:

- to spoil the rich Babylon (Jer 50:10)
- to try and destroy the Church at the same time (Rev 12:2-4; Isa 54:15).

pr404» Revelation 9:18 shows the destruction caused by the sides of Satan's kingdom coming against each other. Verse 20 says those not killed in these plagues did not repent or change their minds. But remember this is only the sixth trumpet, there is still one more. All these trumpets, seals, and vials happen at once. But after the completion of these, the spirit of man, the other-mind, will be locked up in the pit so that they will not mislead man again (Rev 20:1-4; Zech 13:2). These spirits in man's mind are what causes man to hate God's way of harmony even though God's way is the way of peace. Thus, after these spirits are taken out of man's mind, one knows "the kingdom of God is come upon you" (Luke 11:20).

pr405» Follow these verses to see exactly what will happen *after* the Last War: Revelation 20:1-3; Micah 7:16-17; Isaiah 52:14-15; Zephaniah 3:11, 15; Isaiah 60:2-4, 18; Isaiah 59:19; Isaiah 24:13-15; 17:7.

pr406» Chapter 10 to 11:13 of Revelation are inset or parenthetical chapters (see "Two Witnesses Paper" [PR8]).

Seventh Trumpet

pr407» The seventh trumpet (rev 11:15) shows the Church being born of God, and the kingdom of God taking over rulership (note, 1 Cor 15:52-55; 1 Thes 4:16-17; Rom 10:6-7). Notice at the sounding of the seventh trumpet the door of the temple is opened which, as we explain in the notes to this paper, is the door into the finished Spiritual temple (Rev 11:19). At that same time the earthquakes, thunder, and hail go off due to the atomic Last War.

pr408» Again we repeat, all the seals, trumpets, and vials happen all at once. They merely amplify this moment of time and tell a few events that lead up to them, like the northern army preparing to make war for a year (Rev 9:15).

Vials

pr409» Now let's quickly cover the vials of chapter 16. But instead of going over again what we have already put forth, let us just say the vials picture the damage done by the Last War — the blood, fire, etc. These verses picture evil spirits gathering the nations to fight this last battle. They are gathered at the "Armageddon" which was prefigured in the land of the Middle East many years ago. But the real Armageddon battle will be the final sacrifice:

- "And it shall come to pass in the day of the LORD's sacrifice, that I will punish the princes, and the king's [Satan's] children, and all such as are clothed with strange apparel. In the same day also will I punish all those that leap on the threshold, which fill their masters houses with violence and deceit" (Zeph 1:8-9).

pr410» This pictures the last great sacrifice on the brazen altar. The lake of fire is the antitypical meaning of the fire that always burned on this altar (Ex 38:1-5; Lev 6:13). The gathering of Satan's kingdoms (horns) towards Jerusalem is the antitypical meaning of the four horns around this brazen altar. This final sacrifice of the LORD is how the antitypical daily sacrifice is taken away. But as shown in PR4, it is actually Satan's sacrifice, for *his* ways cause trials and destruction. This is the *last* sacrifice for man at the hands of Satan's kingdom. The four horns of the altar represent the four kingdoms of Satan. The four kingdoms are described in Daniel 7.

What Is Important

pr411» It isn't really that important to know exactly where each army will be, or if such and such a nation mentioned in the Bible is modern day such and such. Why? It is because all nations will fight or be a casualty in the last war, so there is no need to identify them. All we need to know is that the seals, trumpets, and vials are the same event, an end-of-the-age war — the Last War. Much of Revelation describes and qualifies this Last War, and the events leading up to it, and the events right after it.

pr412» The important thing to know is that at the time of that war one-third of the people are killed (afterward one-third of the angels are locked up), one-fourth of the earth is destroyed, and Christ comes at that point to *save* the world (Matt 24:22). The Last War happens 1260 days *after* the Beast-man takes control of the Beast system (see "Beast-Man Paper" [PR2] and the "End of the Age" paper [PR7]). God's wrath is man's wrath on their *own* system.

Notes for PR5

Church In Symbolism

pr413» Now notice Revelation 15:8, where it says, "no man was able to enter into the temple, till the seven plagues of the seven angels were fulfilled." But we quoted before that the Church was the temple (Eph 2:19-22). What is Revelation 15:8 saying then? If there is a Church now on the earth, then men are already of, or in, the temple of God, yet Revelation 15:8 says no man can enter the Temple until the last plagues which are described in the 16th chapter of Revelation.

pr414» To clear this up we need to know that the Church is made up of Spiritually *begotten* people. At the last trumpet then they will be *born* of God (1 Cor 15:52-55). The Church can be looked upon as a people in the womb of its mother (the Church) who are growing into a born child of God. The Church is now in the process of being built, only when it is born will it be complete. Notice Isaiah 66:6-9 where it pictures a pregnant woman just before birth, and then giving birth. It indicates in verse eight that a whole nation was to be born at once. This nation is called the "holy nation" by Peter (1 Pet 2:9) after he called this same nation a "spiritual house" (v. 5). And he indicates in context of these verses that this nation, this spiritual house, is the Church. Thus, the Church is the nation to be born at once, and is now a begotten people in its mother's womb.

pr415» Notice that Paul calls "Jerusalem which is above ... the mother of us all" (Gal 4:26). What is this Jerusalem which is above? It is the "heavenly Jerusalem" which is the "church of the first-born" (Heb 12:22-23). And this "heavenly Jerusalem," or as Galatians calls it, the Jerusalem which is above (in heaven, thus the heavenly Jerusalem), is also described in Revelation 21:2, "New Jerusalem, coming down from God *out of heaven*, prepared as a bride adorned for her husband."

pr416» This pictures the heavenly Jerusalem coming down from heaven; it also calls this city the *bride*, or in verse nine the "Lamb's wife." Ephesians 5:22-33 says that wives or women are symbolic to the Church. Thus, here is another proof that the Church is a mother — the wife of the Lamb (Christ). But further, we see that it is the New Jerusalem, the temple, the house of God, the Lamb's wife, and the mother of us all. In other words, there are many names in the Bible that describe the same Church.

pr417» This same mother Church or wife Church is described in Revelation 12:1-2. Here it pictures it about to deliver its child. As we noted in Isaiah 66:6-9 this "child" of Revelation is the Church. Isaiah 66:7 calls this child a "man child." This same man child is shown in Revelation 12:5 (see also Isa 26:17-20). This "man child," pictures Christ's Spiritual Body (the Church) in its antitypical meaning. Thus again we see the begotten Church as a child in a woman's womb growing into a born child.

pr418» Yet we have shown God's temple as being symbolic to the Church. But note in Ephesians 2:21 that the Church is in the process of growing into a "holy temple." From the English translation in the *Interlinear Greek — English New Testament* (Zondervan Pub) verse 22 reads, "in whom also you are being built together for a habitation of God in Spirit." Also in this same translation it says the Church members "are being built up a house spiritual, a priesthood holy" (1 Pet 2:5). In other words, the temple (Church) is in the process of being built. It is not yet built, it is like a baby in a womb, it is growing into the finished product, the born Church.

pr419» Hence, the temple of Revelation 15:8 is the true temple (the *born* Church). This is the reward that Christ is to bring back to the earth, the Church (or more correctly the first-products of the Church). No person can enter this Spiritual temple, in the truest sense, until the plagues are poured out.

pr420» Thus, what Revelation 15:8 is saying is that no one will be born of God until after the last plagues. This is proof that God's kingdom does not take over until after the last plagues. Yet Revelation 11:15 says that after the seventh trumpet, the kingdom of God will take over rulership. And 1 Corinthians 15:52 shows after the seventh trumpet ("last trumpet"), the begotten Church will become the born Church. Of course, this is because the seven seals, trumpets, and plagues of Revelation are the same events. These are merely metonymical terms for the same events. And the description given is an amplification of one instant of time, for the verses we've shown to you previously prove the Last War happens all at once. Revelation merely amplifies that one point in time as well as gives information of the events up to that time, and after that Last War.

47. This 1260 days or 42 months rulership of the Beast System and Individual is just before Christ and his Saints take control of the whole world. (Dan 7:25-27,9-11; see Beast Papers PP2 and PP3)

Church During the 3 1/2 Years

48. Holy city shall they tread under foot **forty-two months** (Rev 11:2)

49. Holy people's power scattered for **a time, times, and a half** [3 ½ years] (Dan 12:7); woman or Church nourished for **a time, and times, and half a time** [3 ½ years] from the face of the serpent (Rev 12:14)

50. The woman or Church is fed [Spiritual food] for **1260 days** (Rev 12:7); the two witnesses teach in their **1260 days** (Rev 11:3)

At the very end, Beast fights against Christ and his Saints

51. **Make war against the saints** (Dan 7:21; 8:24; Rev 13:7)

52. Stand up and try to make war against the returning Christ (Dan 8:25; Rev 17:14; 19:19)

53. Sits in the temple and **calls himself God** (2 Thes 2:4; Ezek 28:2)

But

54. The **saints will prevail** (Dan 7:22, 27; Rev 11:18)

55. The Lamb or **Christ will overcome** (Dan 7:14; Rev 11:17; 17:14; 2 Thes 2:8)

1. Read our Prophecy Papers for more information not provided here; read the Greek and Hebrew scriptures if possible; Since the Beast-man is in the shadow of Satan, most scriptures that describe Satan will also describe the Beast-man.

© 1998 by Walter R. Dolen

PR6: God's Wrath: An Outline

Outline Review

pr421» **(1) There is one-half of a week (of years) remaining of Daniel's seventy weeks, which equals three and one-half years as explained previously in PR5.**

During these 3 ½ years:

- The physical Beast will rule a great part of the world; The spiritual Beast rules all the earth. (Rev 13:5; Dan 7:25; Rev 12:9)
- The Church will be in the spiritual wilderness. (Rev 12:6, 14)
- The Church will be in a spiritual trial or tribulation. (Dan 12:7, 10: 11:33-35; 7:25; Rev 12:17; 3:18; 11:2; see also the "Old Mind" paper [NM 21])
- The two witnesses will teach during their 1260 days. (Rev 11:3, 4; Zech 4:11-14)
- It will be a period of great tribulation for the whole world. (Isa 13:4-11; Matt 24:31; etc.)
- During this time the great false-prophet will say he is God (Rev 13:11-18; 2 Thes 2:3-9; Dan 7:25; Dan 8:11, 23-25; Dan 11:37).

pr422» **(2) Then at the *full* end of the 3 ½ years will come the Last War:**

- "and the end thereof with a flood, and unto the end of the war that makes desolation is determined" (Dan 9:26).
- "and until the end war to cut off the arrangement of destruction" (Dan 9:26; trans. from the Septuagint).

(A proof that this war comes at the *full* end of the last 3 ½ years comes from Daniel 9:27 in the word translated "consummation" in the KJV, which was translated from a Hebrew word meaning — **Full** or **Complete** end. Read last part of Daniel 9:26 & 27. These verses are speaking of the same time.)

pr423» **(3) The nations will be gathered at the end:**

- "All the nations of the earth be gathered together against it." (They will be gathered against Jerusalem, the physical and Spiritual one.) [Zech 12:3; Joel 3:2, 11, 9; Isaiah 13:4; 66:18; Zeph 2:1; 3:8; Mic 4:11-12; Matt 25:31-32; Rev 19:19]

- The modern day Gog, Tubal, Persia, Ethiopia, Phut, Gomer, Togarmah, and so forth will gather against Jerusalem. [Ezek 38:7-8, 15-16; Rev 20:8; 16:12; Rev 16:14-16; Jer 1:14; 50:9, 41; Jer 51:28; Isa 13:17; Jer 50:29; Jer 51:11; Dan 11:44]
- This is the gathering of the nations for the great last sacrifice — Jehovah's sacrifice. [Zeph 1:7-9; Ezek 39:17; Rev 19:17-18]
- Gathering together the tares that are to be burnt. [Matt 13:30, 40, 42; Isa 10:17; Isa 27:4]
- Gathering together of God's wheat; but the chaff of the wheat is burnt up. [Matt 3:12; Luke 3:17]
- The gathering of fish to cast into the furnace (fish=people, Matt 4:19; Hab 1:14). [Matt 13:47, 50]
- The gathering together of the guests for the wedding — both the good and the bad guests. [Matt 22:10]
- The nations will gather like a flood. [Isaiah 59:19; 17:12-13]

pr424» **(4) Then after the gathering of the nations, the Last War will begin and the nations will fight against each other; people against people, city against city:**

- "nation shall rise against nation." (Matt 24:7)
- "violence in the land, ruler against ruler." (Jer 51:46)
- "evil shall go forth from nation to nation" (Jer 25:32).
- Concerning spiritual Egypt (see Rev 11:8): "the Egyptians against the Egyptians: and they shall fight every one against his brother, and every one against his neighbor; city against city, and kingdom against kingdom" (Isa 19:2).
- "Every man's sword shall be against his brother" (Ezek 38:21).
- "I will overthrow the throne of kingdoms ... and their riders shall come down, every one by the sword of his brother" (Haggai 2:22).
- "and they shall lay hold every one on the hand of his neighbor, and his hand shall rise up against the hand of his neighbor" (Zech 14:13).
- "By the swords of the mighty will I cause your multitude to fall" (Ezek 32:12).
- The beast will destroy itself for the antitypical "whore" is the "woman" of Revelation 17, which is the great city (v. 18), which is the system of Babylon (Rev 14:8; 18:16), which is the antitypical Babylon (See Beast Papers [PR2 PR3], Rev 17:16-17).

pr425» **(5) Why will these nations fight against each other? Isn't this madness?** Wouldn't it be the end of mankind if all nations came against each other, especially with the modern weapons of mankind? Then the world must go mad at the end of the present age if these things are to happen.

- "In that day, says the LORD, I will smite every horse with astonishment, and his rider with MADNESS" (Zech 12:4).

- "Babylon has been a golden cup in the LORD's hand, that made all the earth drunken: the nations have drunken of her *wine*; therefore the nations are MAD" (Jer 51:7; see also Jer 25:15-16).

- "Babylon is fallen ... because she made all nations drink of the wine of the wrath of her fornication" (Rev 14:8; see also, Rev 16:19; 18:3). The higher meaning here is that the spiritual Babylon, that system of spiritual evil that lives in all mankind, has all the people drunk on its spiritual wine of confusion and evil.

pr426» What is the "Wine" of Wrath?

- "Stay yourselves ... and cry: they are drunken, but not on wine ... For the LORD has poured out upon you the *spirit of deep sleep*, and has closed your eyes" (Isaiah 29:9-10).

- It is "the *spirit* of the kings of the Medes" that will be raised up against modern day Babylon for the "vengeance of his temple." (Jer 51:11)

- This is the opposite wine or spirit that God's people are or will drink — the new wine. (Zech 9:17; Luke 5:37)

- The spirit of the Adversary will make the world go mad at the Last War. "For the devil is come down upon you, having great wrath, because he knows that he has but a short time" (Rev 12:12; see also, Isa 14:17, 12).

pr427» **(6) How long will the Last War last?**

Take the antitypical meaning of the following items for the answer:

- One day [Isa 10:17; Zech 3:9 Rev 18:8]
- one hour [Rev 18:10, 19]
- as an overrunning flood [Nah 1:8 & Dan 9:26]
- speedily or as a speedy riddance [Luke 18:8; Zeph 1:18]
- Babylon suddenly falls [Jer 51:8]
- suddenly [Isa 47:11; Eccl 9:12]
- at an instant, suddenly [Isa 29:5-6; 1 Thes 5:3; Psa 73:19]
- destroyed & devoured at once [Isa 42:14]
- swiftly, speedily [Joel 3:4; Mal 3:5]
- as in a moment [Psalms 73:19]

pr428» **(7) Who will be destroyed by the Last War?**

- The transgressors are destroyed *together*; The real transgressors are the spiritual evil minds. (Psa 37:38; Isa 1:28; see "Old Mind" paper [NM 21])

- In spiritual Babylon, "shall fall the slain of *all* the earth" (Jer 51:48-49). Remember all the nations will be gathered against each other at the Last War.

- At the same time Gog comes against "the *land* of Israel, says the Lord GOD, my fury shall come up in my face. For in my jealously and the fire of my wrath have I spoken, Surely in that day there shall be a great shaking [through the weapons of mankind] in the land of Israel" (Ezek 38:18-19; cf Zeph 3:8). But all the earth belongs to Spiritual Israel.. ("Seed Paper" [PR1]) Gog thus comes against *all* the land of Spiritual Jerusalem — the whole earth.

- "And the slain of the LORD shall be at that *day* from one end of the earth even unto the other end of the earth" (Jer 25:33).

pr429» **(8) Therefore all nations will have gathered, and one-third of all the transgressors will be destroyed at once (see PR5).**

Here follows is a list of some of the various nations to be destroyed as powers, as well as in population. For example only one-sixth of the modern Ma Gog, Meshech and Tubal will be saved after the Last War (Ezek 39:1-2). The Bible uses the original name of the families that grew into nations, but today these families or nations described in the Bible have different names, yet they are the same peoples the Bible is prophesying against.

- List of nations to be destroyed as powers and in population: [Zeph 2:9; Jer 25:17-29; Ezek 30:4-5; 32:22, 24, 26, 30, 31-32; Ezek 31:18, 14; 39:11; Joel 3:2, 12, 14; Isa 14:12, 21-22, 25; Isa 30:30-33]

Thus, all nations will be gathered and all destroyed as powers along with the invisible power behind these nations — the spiritual adversary, Satan. It will be an instantaneous Last War destruction.

pr430» **(9) Now if all nations fight against each other, and the war happens in an instant, then how else can it happen besides it being an Atomic Last War?** Atomic weapons will be used in this war along with other such destructive weapons.

pr431» **(10) When the nations come at once against the Beast he will panic (See, Jer 50:41-43; 51:28-29). AND:**

- "But tidings out of the East and out of the north shall trouble him: therefore he shall go forth with great fury to destroy, and utterly to sweep away many" (Dan 11:44).

But in this great madness the Beast will destroy itself (Rev 17:16-17). All these nations will destroy themselves. This is God's righteous end-of-the-age judgment on the nations of this age (see, Psa 9:15-16):

- "For the day of the LORD is near upon all heathen: as you have done, it shall be done unto you: Your reward shall return upon your own head." (Obadiah 1:15, see Joel 3:4)

pr432» **(11) But there will be another reason besides the nations mad plan (Ezek 38:10-12; Isa 13:17) initiated by the spiritual mind of wrath in their minds. There is the spiritual reason:**

- It is Satan's wrath against God's people (Rev 12:12, 2, 4).

pr433» Not only are the nations gathered against the antitypical Babylon (the Beast), but the Bible emphatically says the nations are also gathered against the Church or the people of God. This is the spiritual reason the mad spirits of Satan gather the nations to fight (Rev 16:12-16; Jer 51:11; Isa 19:2, 3, 14; and Rev 20:8-9):

- Read Jeremiah 6:22-29. Note that the "daughter of Zion" is the Church (Heb 12:22).
- Read Revelation 19:19; 17:14; 20:9. Note respectively in each verse: "his army" with verse 14 and 8; "and they that are with him" and "the camp of the saints."
- God in Isaiah 29:8 describes what will become of the dream of the nations (the subconscious dream of the satanic spirits in their minds) "that fight against mount Zion." Again, the higher meaning for Zion is God's Church (Heb 12:22).
- The nations will gather against Jerusalem, and will be destroyed "in that day." (Zech 12:2, 2, 4, 8, 9) Those of the city of Jerusalem will be "as God" for then they will be God's sons and daughters. Remember the higher meaning for Jerusalem is God's Church or people (Heb 12:22 and the section on "New Jerusalem" in [NM 18]).
- This is the "day of trouble" for God's people (Hab 3:16; Psa 102:2, 13-17; Dan 12:1; Isa 33:2; Isa 26:16, 17-20; Jer 30:6-8; remember the higher meaning of Israel is God's Church, Rev 7:4; Gal 6:16).
- But, the Lord "shall defend them" and Zion (God's Church) will be cheerful with its new wine. (Zech 9:9 Zech 9:14-17; see also Isa 33:3; 34:8; Isa 31:4-5)

pr434» Here are other verses that show the nations gathering against the Church:

- Read Isaiah 54:15, notice that the barren woman is the barren woman that Paul speaks about in Gal 4:26-27.
- Read Ezekiel 38:16 and compare it with Revelation 20:9. Remember the higher meaning of "my people Israel" is the saints or the Church, Rev 20:9; Rev 7:4; Gal 6:16.

- Read Micah 4:11, 13; Isaiah 10:32. Remember "Zion" is the Church. See Hebrews 12:22.
- Read Isaiah 37:3, 11-12 and notice the talk by the Assyrian king against the fact that God's Church will be Born of God. This Assyrian king is representative of the end-of-the-age's false-prophet.

pr435» Notice God through his word asks the rhetorical question:

- "We [the Church, Rev 12:2] have been with child, we have been in pain, we have as it were brought forth wind; we have not worked any deliverance in the earth" (Isa 26:18).
- "Shall I bring to the birth, and not cause to bring forth: says the LORD" (Isa 66:9).

pr436» Notice the Church's reaction to the blasphemy of the false-prophet (Isa 37:3, 11-12) against the fact that the Church will bring forth. Read Isaiah 37:22-23 and you will see Faith in action:

- KJV Isaiah 37:22 This *is* the word which the LORD hath spoken concerning him; The virgin, the daughter of Zion, hath despised thee, *and* laughed thee to scorn; the daughter of Jerusalem hath shaken her head at thee. 23 Whom hast thou reproached and blasphemed? and against whom hast thou exalted *thy* voice, and lifted up thine eyes on high? *even* against the Holy One of Israel.

pr437» God through his word answers the negative talk by the false-prophet and His own rhetorical question of Isaiah 66:9:

- God will bring forth his people, they will be born of God all at once. That is, the "first fruits" will be born all at once; the rest will be born of God later (Isa 45:8; 66:8; Rev 11:15 with 1 Cor 15:52-55 & 1 Thes 4:16-17; etc.).

pr438» Notice just how close God's Church is to being destroyed:

- The "children of Israel" (the Church) "were *ready* to perish in the land of Assyria." Note the context — "in that day" and "trumpet shall be blown" (Isa 27:13). The land of Assyria was the land of physical Israel's enemy at that time. The antitypical "land of Assyria" for the antitypical Israel is the land of their enemy (Satan) — the whole earth.
- "The sinner of Zion [one-half of those at the end of this age who think they are of the true physical organized Church] are afraid; fearfulness has surprised the hypocrites. WHO AMONG US SHALL DWELL WITH THE DEVOURING FIRE?" (Isa 33:14; note Psa 1:5)
- "Fear, and the pit, and the snare, are upon you, O inhabitant of the earth. And it shall come to pass, that *he who flees from the noise of fear shall fall into the pit.*" (Isa 24:17-18; note Luke 17:31-33; & 2 Chron 20:13-17)

pr439» In other words, just as the Church is ready to be physically destroyed by the flames of the Atomic Last War, God will defend it and will save and free it. This is salvation. They will be born of God. They will thus not be hurt by the fire of the Last War. But those among them who *say* they were in the Church will fear and thus begin to run. Yet the war begins and ends speedily and they will die in the lake of fire. This is what Paul was physically speaking about when he said:

- "Every man's work shall be made manifest: for the day shall declare it, because it shall try every man's work of what sort it is. If any man's work abide which he has built thereupon, he shall receive a reward. If any man's work shall be burned, he shall suffer loss: but he himself shall be saved, yet so as by fire" (1 Cor 4:13-15). This last part speaks of the agelasting fire for the satanic angels which is their fire baptism, and the agelasting death baptism for the humans who die in this fire. (see, "Thousand Years" paper [NM 15])

pr440» Because the Last War happens at once and the atomic fire at once, those in the Church killed by this fire will not know it, for:

- "In a *moment*, in the twinkling of an eye, at the last trump: for the trumpet shall sound, and the dead shall be raised incorruptible [immortal], and shall be changed ... Death is swallowed up in victory" (1 Cor 15:52, 54).

pr441» The Church will die by the fire for only as long as an instant (see Isa 54:8; 10:24-25), then they will become infused to the Spiritual and will be lifted into the clouds (1 Thes 4:16-17) to meet Christ to bring him down to earth (Rom 10:6) to rule on the earth (Rev 5:10).

Notice how in Matthew it describes this:

- "For nation shall rise against nation ... All these are the beginning of travail" (Matt 24:6-7).

pr442» This pictures the beginning of the instant Atomic Last War. It is the beginning of the Church's travail. Isaiah finishes the picture:

- "for as soon as Zion travailed she brought forth her children" (Isa 66:8). YET:
- "*Before* she travailed, she brought forth; before her *pain* came, she was delivered of a man child" (Isa 66:7).

pr443» Thus, at the very beginning of the travail, which is the Last War (Matt 24:6-7), just before the pain or hurt, but *as* the fire is destroying her, she is born of God. Remember that Atomic weapons go off in a flash; all this happens in an *instant* (note Psa 58:9-10).

pr444» This brings memories back as to what happened when the physical Israel was escaping Egypt. Just as the Pharaoh's troops were about to reach the people of Israel, the water of the Red Sea destroyed the Pharaoh's troops and saved Israel (Ex 14:10, 13-14, 21-23, 27-30). Notice Amos 9:5; 8:8; Isaiah 17:13-14; Daniel 9:26.

pr445» **(12) And from this Last War the earth shall be moved with a GREAT earthquake:**

- Jeremiah 10:10; 49:21: 50:46; Isaiah 13:13; 29:6; Ezekiel 31:16; 38:19, 20; Joel 2:10; 3:16; Haggai 2:21 Zech 14:5 Revelation 16:18; 11:19, 13; 8:5; 6:14; especially see Isaiah 24:18, 20

pr446» And there are many scriptures that show the destruction of the Last War, called the lake of fire. We'll only give a few more:

- 2 Peter 3:10, 12; Zeph 1:18; 3:8; Mal 4:1-2; Isaiah 34:3; 29:6; Zech 14:12; Ezek 38:22

pr447» **(13) At the very moment of the Last War, God's kingdom or Spiritual rulership will take over (Rev 11:15-19).** And after this instant war, and the taking over of the world by the rulership of God, then evil will *not* rise a second time:

- I will smite my hands together and I will cause my fury to rest. [Ezek 21:17]
- they will not learn war again [Isa 2:4; Mic 4:3]
- violence no more [Isaiah 60:18]
- affliction not to rise a second time [Nah 1:9]
- we shall see no more evil [Zeph 3:15]
- the hail will sweep away the lies [Isaiah 28:17]
- they shall *not* hurt nor destroy in *all* God's holy mountain or kingdom [Isaiah 11:9]
- no oppressor shall pass through them any more [Zech 9:8]
- God's kingdom and peace will not depart or be removed [Isa 54:10]

PR7: End of the Age

If we won't know the Day, Why Watch?
As in Noah's Day
End on a Holy Feast Day
Feasts of Israel Pre-Figured
Which Year?

End of the Old Age; Beginning of the New Age

pr448» The disciples came to Christ in private and asked, "tell us, when shall these things be [the destruction of Jerusalem]? and what shall be the sign of your coming, and of the end of the world [*age*]?" (Matt 24:3) The disciples asked Christ when the age would end, and when his return would be. Christ then gave them some signs of his coming (Matt 24:4-44).

Father Only Knows the Date?

pr449» But notice with these signs, Christ said, "but of that day and hour [of his return] knows no man, no, not the angels of heaven, but my Father only" (Matt 24:36). And again he said, "therefore be you also ready: for in such an hour as you think not the Son of man comes" (Matt 24:44).

We Will Know the Date

pr450» From the two just quoted verses and other verses people conclude that no one will know the date of Christ's return. But this overlooks many other verses that tell us we will know the date of His return. Those who say we do not know, or will never know the date of His return are overlooking scripture that proves we (meaning the Church) will know the date. *But the Church will only come to know the date for sure some 3 ½ years before the date.*

pr451» We'll show several reasons why Matthew 24:36 and 24:44 are taken out of context with other scriptures that say we will know the date of the end of the age.

Principles of Biblical Study

pr452» First we must know a very important principle on ascertaining the doctrines of the Bible: "Whom shall he teach knowledge? And whom shall he make to understand doctrine? Them that are weaned from the milk, and drawn from the breasts. For precept must be upon precept, precept upon precept; line upon line, line upon line; here a little, and there a little" (Isa 28:9-10).

pr453» To understand doctrine one must study all the details of the doctrine found throughout the Bible. You must take a line here, and a line there from the whole Bible and put it together in order to understand it. But shall one just take any line here, and any line there, to ascertain or figure out doctrine? No, they should take the lines pertaining to each doctrine. But further they should examine *all* the scriptures on any one subject before putting the verses together. And the only way to do this is to study the whole Bible. If we want to know what the Bible says about the nature of God, we must study every scripture pertaining to God. If we want to know what the Bible says about the return of Jesus Christ, we must study every scripture pertaining to His return.

Christ Given All The Power

pr454» In order to understand the mistaken notion that we will not know the date, we want you to note the following fact:

- When Christ spoke about only his Father knowing the date (Matt 24:36), he was still a man not yet resurrected to God. If you understand who Christ is now, you will understand how significant this fact is in understanding Christ's words (see *God Papers*). But even if one does not understand who Christ is now, or does not want to believe it; he will have a hard time discounting a statement made by Christ after he was resurrected to God: "All power is given unto me [Christ] in heaven and in earth" (Matt 28:18; see Luke 10:21-22).

pr455» Christ has been given *all* the power of his Father. If Christ has all the Spiritual power of his Father, then he must also know the date.

Christians to Receive Power

pr456» Notice in Acts 1:7-8, Christ was speaking to the apostles after his resurrection to the Father, "And he said unto them, It is not for you to know the times or the seasons, which the Father has put in his own power." But Christ was given all his Father's power (Matt 28:18), therefore Christ has the power to know the times and the seasons — to know when the end of the age is. To continue in Acts 1:7-8: "But you shall receive power after that the Holy Spirit is come upon you." On the Pentecost the power was given to the disciples to know (Acts 2), for at that time they received the Holy Spirit. Therefore the apostles could know the date after they received the power of the Spirit.

Christians to Receive Knowledge

pr457» Notice, "I have yet many things to say unto you, but you cannot bear them now. Howbeit when this, the Spirit of truth, is come, it will guide you into *all* truth ... it will show you things to come. This [the Spirit of truth] shall glorify me: for it shall receive of mine, and show it unto you. All things that the Father has are mine: Therefore said I, that it [the Spirit of truth] shall take of mine, and show it unto you" (John 16:12-15).

pr458» These verses clearly say that the Spirit will show the apostles all that is Christ's. The Father had the power to know the times (Acts 1:7), but Christ was given all the power of the Father (Matt 28:18), for "all things that the Father has are mine" said Christ (John 16:15). Through the Spirit and scripture Christ will show us about the things to come (John 16:13).

Church Knows Hidden Secrets

pr459» *Notice the scriptures about the Church knowing the hidden secrets.* The Church will know because the Spirit shall reveal it through the scriptures:

- "For nothing is secret, that shall not be made manifested; neither any thing hid, that shall not be known and come abroad" (Luke 8:17).

- "In that hour Jesus rejoiced in Spirit, and said, I thank you, O Father, Lord of heaven and earth, that you have hid these things from the wise and prudent, and have revealed them unto babes: even so, Father; for so it seemed good in your sight. ALL THINGS are delivered to me of my Father: and no man knows who the Son is, but the Father; and who the Father is, but the Son, and he to whom the Son will reveal Him" (Luke 10:21-22).

- "Fear them not therefore: for there is nothing covered, that shall not be revealed; and hid, that shall not be known" (Matt 10:26).

- "For there is nothing hid, which shall not be manifested; neither was any thing kept secret, but that it should come abroad. If any man have ears to hear, let him hear" (Mark 4:22-23). This indicates that the secrets will be known.

- "Behold, the former things are come to pass, and new things do I declare: *before* they spring forth I tell you of them" (Isa 42:9).

- "I have much to say to you, more than you can now bear. But when he, the Spirit of truth, comes, he will guide you into all truth. He will not speak of his own; he will speak only what he hears, and he will tell you what is yet to come. He will bring glory to me by taking from what is mine and making it known to you. All that belongs to the Father is mine. That is why I said the Spirit will take from what is mine and make it known to you" (John 16:12-15, NIV).

- "But the Counselor, the Holy Spirit, whom the Father will send in my NAME, *will teach you all things* and remind you of everything I have said to you" (John 14:26, NIV; see 1 John 2:27). The verb translated in the English as, "I have said," is an aorist verb, which is a verb of action, not of time. Thus, this Spirit will remind ("will put into the mind" — Greek future verb) Christians of what Christ says (or said, or will say). As John 16:12-15 indicates, Christ did not at that time give all the truth to them, but said that in the future the Spirit of truth would lead them into all the truth. In the book of Acts it shows Christ revealing new truth to them (Acts 15:7 cf 10:28 & 10:1-33 & 11:7ff; Acts chap 15 — the teaching that physical circumcision was not needed; etc.). And the one who comes in the Spirit of Elijah will eventually lead the Church into all the truth (see "Two Witnesses" paper [PR8]).

Spirit Reveals Hidden Wisdom and Knowledge

Spirit Reveals

pr460» The secrets will be revealed through the Spirit (John 16:12-15). And, "but we [of the Church] speak the wisdom of God in a mystery, even hidden wisdom, which God ordained before the world unto our glory ... But God has revealed them [the hidden wisdom] unto us by his Spirit: for the Spirit searches all things, yea, the deep things of God ... Which things also we speak, not in words which man's wisdom teaches, but which the Holy Spirit teaches; comparing spiritual things with spiritual" (1 Cor 2:7, 10, 13).

Times known

pr461» One of the things that the Spirit will teach is the time of the end of the age. In Acts 1:7 it speaks of the power to know "the times and the seasons" and this power the Father has. But then in the very next verse (Acts 1:8) it says, "you shall receive power." They were to receive the power of the Father — His Spirit. It is through this power of the Spirit that ALL THINGS would be revealed because what the Father had was given to the Son (Matt 28:18; John 16:15; etc.). And the Son was to show these things to his servants (John 16:15, 13; Matt 11:27; Luke 10:22; 8:17).

pr462» The New Testament Church did know the typical end of the age: "but of the times and the seasons, brethren, you have no need that I write unto you" (1 Thes 5:1). Why? "And that, knowing the time" (Rom 13:11). They knew the times. This doesn't mean they knew the date of Christ's return, although they could have known it even then. More than likely they knew that this was the evil age and that the new age was fast approaching. But further they knew that there was an antitypical rest or Sabbath (Heb 4:1-10). And they knew God's days are counted as 1,000 years (2 Pet 3:8). Also they knew the typical sabbath rest was on the seventh day of the week. Thus they could have easily have figured that the antitypical rest or sabbath was the seventh 1,000 year "day." And through the chronology of the Bible they could see that Christ appeared near the 4,000th year of man. Thus, they could have figured up that the date of Christ's return was still about 2,000 years off (see *Chronology Papers*).

Daniel's Vision

pr463» Notice what Daniel was told about the prophecies given him, "but you, O Daniel, shut up the words, and seal the book, even to the time of the end" (Dan 12:4).

pr464» Daniel's prophecy is locked up until the time of the end of the age of evil. Thus at the time of the end of the age is when the appointed time of the end of the age will be revealed. All secrets are to be made known before they happen per the verses we have already quoted. And at the time of the end is when Daniel's book will be opened completely, for at the time of the end is when *all things* shall be restored (Mal 4:5; Amos 3:7; Matt 17:11; see "Two Witnesses" paper [PR8]).

Mistakes of Others' Interpretation

pr465» We will return to Daniel in a moment after we go over a couple of parables. These parables are put forth by some when they attempt to prove that we will not know the date of Christ's physical return. We will show that these parables are taken out of context.

pr466» First before we go over these parables note the following facts:

- What Christ said in Matthew 24 is also written about in Mark and Luke.

- The parable he spoke in Matt 24:44-51 was uttered by Christ *before* he repeated it to the disciples on the occasion mentioned in Matthew 24. (Luke 12:40-48) Thus at the time it was repeated to the disciples, the disciples had already heard it. We will explain why this is important in a moment.

- There is evidence in studying Matthew, Mark, Luke, and John that Christ repeated the same parables or teaching almost everywhere he went. When an account of any parable is given by one writer, it may be retold only in part. **We must compare each parable or teaching with all accounts of the same parable in order to understand the full extent of the words Christ used to explain these parables.** For example, Matthew in writing about a parable may have left out a certain sentence that Christ spoke pertaining to the parable, while Luke in his account may mention this missing sentence. Therefore we must put both accounts of Matthew and Luke together in order to understand what Christ said. If we don't do this we, in effect, are taking Christ's words out of context.

pr467» Now let's look at what is written in Matthew 24:37-51. It is very important that we comprehend what we are about to study. These verses, if taken alone, are out of context with what Christ said. Christ spoke these parables on many occasions, like any minister today repeats and repeats things, so Christ in his ministry repeated his parables.

pr468» Further in any one book on the sayings of Christ, each author gives the story from a different view point, and at times leaves out important sayings of Christ. But each thing each author (Matt, Mark, Luke, and John) says is true, yet to find out all the things Christ spoke of concerning a parable, one must compare all the books that mention the parable to get the full information. We need the full information because we don't want to take Christ's words out of context.

If we won't know what day the Lord comes back, why watch?

pr469» This is the Basic question of which we will now answer. First lets look at Matthew 24:37-51:

- Mat 24:37 As it was in the days of Noah, so it will be at the coming of the Son of Man. [38] For in the days before the flood, people were eating and drinking, marrying and giving in marriage, up to the day Noah entered the ark; [39] and they knew nothing about what would happen until the flood came and took them all away. That is how it will be at the coming of the Son of Man. [40] Two men will be in the field; one will be taken and the other left. [41] Two women will be grinding with a hand mill; one will be taken and the other left. [42] "Therefore keep watch, because you do not know on what day your Lord will come. [43] But understand this: If the owner of the house had known at what time of night the thief was coming, he would have kept watch and would not have let his house be broken into. [44] So you also must be ready, because the Son of Man will come at an hour when you do not expect him. [45] "Who then is the faithful and wise servant, whom the master has put in charge of the servants in his household to give them their food at the proper time? [46] It will be good for that servant whose master finds him doing so when he returns. [47] I tell you the truth, he will put him in charge of all his possessions. [48] But suppose that servant is wicked and says to himself, 'My master is staying away a long time,' [49] and he then begins to beat his fellow servants and to eat and drink with drunkards. [50] The master of that servant will come on a day when he does not expect him and at an hour he is not aware of. [51] He will cut him to pieces and assign him a place with the hypocrites, where there will be weeping and gnashing of teeth.

Correct the Translation

pr470» Matthew 24:37-51 basically shows us that as in the days of Noah, so will be the days before the return of Christ — people will be engrossed in the every day things of life and will not be looking and noticing the times (notice Mark 13:33-34; Luke 21:34-35). Then in verse 42 Christ said, "*watch therefore because you do not know on what day your Lord will come.*" Let's translate this verse directly from the Greek text, using the Greek Lexicon published by Zondervan, and Thayer's Lexicon:

- The word "watch" is in the second person plural. Therefore should have been translated, "You be watchful," or "you be awake," or "you be attentive."
- The word translated "because" in the NIV or "for" in the KJV can just as well be translated, "that." In fact in the *New International Version* (NIV) of the Bible, out of 1298 times this Greek word (*hoti*) was translated, it was translated "that" more often than any other English word: 492 times

translated "that"; 205 times translated "because"; and 145 times translated "for" (*The Niv Exhaustive Concordance*, Greek word #4022, p. 1766).

- The word translated "hour" in the KJV should have been translated "day" and is translated "day" in the NIV. See footnote *f* for Matt 24:42 in the *Interlinear Greek New Testament* by G.R. Berry, Published by Zondervan in 1969.

Therefore a correct translation of Matthew 24:42 from the Greek is:

- "you be watchful therefore: that you do not know what day your Lord will come."

As in Noah's Day so at the Coming of the Lord

pr471» Christ was warning that in the time of Noah before the flood people behaved as always until the flood took them away, and so will it be at the end of the age: "and they knew nothing about what would happen until the flood came and took them all away. That is how it will be at the coming of the Son of Man" (24:39). He said at His return it would be the same with people not recognizing the times. He warns them not to be like those in Noah's day: "you be watchful therefore: that *you* do not know what day your Lord will come."

pr472» It was because Noah *knew* what time the flood would come that he prepared the ark. Christ was merely telling them to be careful so that they won't be like those of the flood who did not prepare themselves for the flood like Noah did. *He wasn't saying that all would not know the time of his coming, but he said that they should not be in the position of not knowing the time of his coming because then they would be like those dying from the flood.*

pr473» After this Christ went on and told about how happy will be the servant who is doing His work when He comes, and the future weeping of the unfaithful one or ones who are not doing God's work, but eating and drinking. The parallel here is that Noah was the faithful servant who knew the time of the flood and prepared the ark, but those who did not know, but kept on as always, were destroyed by the flood.

Wicked Servant Will Not Know the Time

pr474» Christ wasn't saying His true servants would not know the date, but that the unfaithful ones, or one, would "say *in his heart*, My lord delays his coming" (Matt 24:48). Inside his mind, the unfaithful servant will not believe the date or time of Christ's coming like those who did not believe Noah's warnings of the flood. "The master of that servant [wicked or unfaithful one] will come on a day when he [the wicked one] does not expect him [Lord] and at an hour he is not aware of" (Mat 24:50).

pr475» Matthew 24:44 should be correctly translated as, "and because of this [V. 43] you be ready: that in such an hour as you suppose not, the Son of man will come." In other words, be careful that *you* don't suppose wrongly about the time of His coming. Why? You will be like those who were destroyed by the flood, if you do not know the time.

Christians Not Asleep

pr476» Now we will show you an important verse that qualifies these sayings of Christ. If you look in Robertson's, *Harmony of the Gospels*, you see that Christ said some more things after he spoke what was recorded in Matthew 24:42. After Christ warned them about being watchful for his return, Christ adds, "lest coming suddenly he [Christ] find you *sleeping*" (Mark 13:36).

Christians not Asleep

pr477» But notice Paul's words about true Christians:

- "But of the times and seasons, brethren, you have no need that I write unto you. For yourselves know perfectly that the day of the Lord so comes as a thief in the night. For when they [non-Christians] shall say, Peace and safety, then sudden destruction comes upon them [like the flood came on those who did not believe Noah], as travail upon a woman with child; and they shall not escape [like those of the flood did not escape]. **But you, brethren, are not in darkness, that the day should overtake you as a thief.** You are all the children of light, and the children of the day: we are not of the night, nor of darkness. Therefore let us not sleep, as do others; but let us watch and be sober" (1 Thes 5:1-6).

pr478» If we are of the day, if we are of the children of light, if we are faithful servants; *then* we will not sleep and be drunk with the world's way. We will know the times so that we will not be destroyed like those of the flood.

All Must Watch

pr479» After Christ said be watchful "lest coming suddenly he find *you* sleeping," he said, "and what I say unto you I say unto ALL, watch" (Mark 13:37). Christ was not only speaking to his apostles at that time, but he was speaking to *all*, to all mankind. All mankind must be watchful lest they be asleep when Christ physically returns and the flood of it all takes them away to destruction.

pr480» Notice the confirmation on our last statement. Christ in Luke 12:37-40 is again speaking about watching. He was speaking to the disciples. "Then Peter said unto him, Lord, speakest you this parable unto us, or even to *all*?" As Mark 13:37 said, "what I say unto you I say unto *all*, watch."

Thus a close study of what we have put forward proves the true Christians will know the time of the end of the age, but others will not perceive the time.

Times of the Gentiles

pr481» In Luke's account of what Christ told his disciples about the time of the end of the age, Christ said Jerusalem would be "trodden down of the Gentiles, *until the times of the Gentiles be fulfilled*" (Luke 21:24). And Paul said that physical Israel would be blinded to the truth, "*until the fullness of the Gentiles be come in*" (Rom 11:25). This physical blindness of physical Israel also applies to all the other peoples, because they do not have the New Mind.

pr482» What are the times of the Gentiles? In context of Luke's writings, Christ will come right after the fullness of the times of the Gentiles (Luke 21:24-27). In the truest sense of Paul's writing, Israel's blindness will not cease until Christ physically returns. Therefore the times of the Gentiles must be fulfilled before Christ returns, then Christ shall immediately return.

pr483» What are the times of the Gentiles, and when will they be fulfilled? When we answer this question we will know when Christ shall return.

End of the Times on a Feast Day

pr484» In Colossians 2:16-17 we read, "Let no man therefore judge you in food, or in drink, or in respect of a *holyday, or of the new moon, or of the sabbath days: which are a foreshadow of things to come*." The holydays Paul was speaking of are enumerated in the Old Testament. These holydays are foreshadows of things to come. Notice the pattern of some holydays or ceremonies:

Festivals of Israel Pre-Figured the Real Events

1. Sabbath

Type:	Six days of work; one day of rest (Lev 23:3; Gen 2:1-3)
Anti-type:	Six 1000 year-days, then a Sabbath of rest (2 Pet 3:8; Heb 4:1-10; Rev 20:4; NM 16)

2. Passover

Type:	Passover lamb (Lev 23:5; Exo 12:5-6)
Anti-type:	Christ the real Passover Lamb of God (John 1:29; 1 Cor 5:7)

3. Sheaf of First Fruits

Type:	Sheaf of barley was waved before the BeComingOne to be accepted for the people *after* the weekly Sabbath (Lev 23:10-11; "on the day after the Sabbath" - Lev 23:11)
Anti-type:	Christ ascended to his Father on Sunday morning after the Sabbath. (Col 1:15, 18; 1 Cor 15:20, 23; CP 4; NM 16)

4. Pentecost

Type:	Feast of Weeks after Wheat Harvest (Lev 23:15-22)
Anti-type:	Not fulfilled perfectly yet, only in an imperfect way when the New Testament Church was given the Spirit on the first Pentecost after Christ went to his Father at the time of the sheaf of first fruits (Acts 2; NM 16).

pr485» The first, second, third, and fourth ceremonies or holydays we cover in *New Mind Papers*, part 15 and 16 which are mentioned in Leviticus, chapter 23, and other places in the Bible. The second and third ceremonies have all come true antitypically (see "God's Appointed Times" paper [NM 16]). The first holyday was the Sabbath. It will be fulfilled in the seventh 1000 year period (see "God's Appointed Times" paper [NM 16]). The 4th festival is the Feast of Pentecost. This occurred typically after the harvest of first fruits. The next resurrection will be the resurrection of fruits as explained in NM16. The 2nd and 3rd feasts perfectly foreshadows their antitypical fulfillment. *In fact on the very day on which the typical events were celebrated, is when the antitypical event occurred.* For example the foreshadowed Passover lamb sacrifices were performed on the 14th of the first month of the Hebrew's calendar. Christ the real Passover died also on the 14th of the first month. See *Chronology Papers* CP4 for more information on this Passover.

pr486» The next festival that hasn't yet been fulfilled perfectly in an antitypical way is the Feast of Pentecost. The next big prophesied event is the return of Christ and the resurrection of the saints. The foreshadowed festival of the Pentecost happened after the harvest of wheat. Thus, Christ's return, the antitypical event of the Feast of Pentecost, will happen on the day of the Pentecost in the Hebrew's calendar.

pr487» It should also be noted that the Sabbath holyday described in Lev 23:3 has not yet come true in its Spiritual or antitypical sense. As shown in the "God's Appointed Times" paper [NM 16] and the Thousand Years and Beyond" paper [NM 15], the physical Sabbath represents the 1000 year Sabbath.

pr488» Thus, so far we have learned that the DATE of the return of Christ, which is the beginning of the rule of the kingdom of God on earth, which is the end of the old age, which is the beginning of the NEW age, which is the beginning of the 1000 year Sabbath, will occur on the Pentecost.

Which Year?

pr489» We know that the fulfillment of the next feast day, Feast of Pentecost, will happen on the very day the Bible scripture tells us it will happen on. See NM16 for details. But we do not know which *year*.

pr490» There is one way to ascertain the DATE:

- "Concerning the coming of our Lord Jesus Christ and our being gathered to him ... that day will not come until the rebellion [apostasy] occurs and the man of lawlessness is revealed, the man doomed to destruction" (2 Thes 2:1-4, NIV).

pr491» The coming of Christ will *not* occur until a rebellion occurs and the manifestation of the man of sin. There is a dual sense here. The antitype of the rebellion is the final war of Satan's angels against God's angels (see "God's Wrath" paper). The type is the apostasy of those who think they are in the Church (see "Great Falling Away" paper [PR10]). In context this man of sin is the mean horn of the Beast (see "Beast-System Paper" [PR2]). The two senses of the man of sin are: (1) his first manifestation at the 1290/1260 day periods; (2) the truest sense is when he declares his godhood (see "Beast-Man Paper" [PR3]). Thus, the coming of Christ will only occur after the apostasy and the manifestation of the Beast person and system. From the "Beast-System Paper" [PR2] we see this Beast system will last for 1260 days after 3 of its ten "kings" are subdued. ***Therefore we know the DATE of the coming of the NEW age exactly 1260 days before that date.*** We will recognize the 1260th day *before* Christ's return by the events of that day: That is, on that day the ten nation Beast will become a seven nation Beast (see "Beast-System Paper" [PR2]).

pr492» What this means at this time is that we do not yet for sure know the *year*, but we do know the day of the month. We also know through chronology that the seventh 1000 year period is near (see *Chronology Papers*). By using astronomical computer programs we can ascertain with reasonable accuracy future dates when the Pentecost of the Hebrew Calendar will occur. We use the observational calendar, not the modern calculated calendar, because in Christ's time and before His time dates were ascertained primarily by observation and only secondarily by calculation (see *Chronology Papers*). Today, following these premises various dates are possible. One thing that makes this difficult is that the new moon or new month starts when we *see* the first crescent of moon, not how we calculate it now. No matter how far fetched it may sound, the earth and moon through some astro-catastrophe could change their path and thus make our present calculations wrong. We will wait to see the events that will happen on the 1290th and 1260th day before we attempt to speak about the future.

pr493» **We are not setting any date here**. Through scripture we are getting close to ascertaining a date. But only when the 1260th day manifests itself will we know for certain. Any date must be tentative until the 1260th day manifests itself.

pr494» **Note**: Like others who have tried to determine the date of Jesus Christ's return, we have speculated on certain dates, hoping for the early return of our Lord. But even in this speculation we emphasized that it was only tentative, that we must wait for the 1260th day to manifest itself (5-9-97, WRD).

PR8: Two Witnesses
Elijah
Two Olive Trees
Anointed Ones
Who is the Other Witness?
Notes: 30 Years and John

pr495» At the end of the age before Christ's physical return someone shall come and restore all things (Matt 17:10-11). John the Baptist was merely the typical Elijah, but there shall be an antitypical Elijah who shall restore all things. He comes "*before* the great and dreadful day of the LORD" (Mal 4:5). Therefore before he comes the Truth shall not be full in the Church. But when he comes he shall restore all things, yet they will do "unto him whatsoever they listed, as it is written of him" (Mark 9:13). Elijah was rejected in the scripture by physical Israel, the true Elijah will also be rejected before Christ returns by those who will eventually become a part of Spiritual Israel. He will endure and restore the Truth, the Spiritual sacrifice of the Spiritual altar, to Spiritual Israel, which is the Church (1 Kings 18:30 with Heb 13:10; Matt 17:10-11). Spiritual Israel, is the Israel of God, which is the Church (see "Seed Paper" [PR1]).

Elijah will come

pr496» But who are the two witnesses who "shall prophesy a thousand two hundred and threescore days" (Rev 11:3). Although many have identified one of the two witnesses, as he who is to come in the spirit of Elijah, as promised by Malachi 4:5-6, most don't know who the other witness is or, that is, what the second witness will represent Spiritually from the Old Testament. Some believe they will be Elijah and Elisha. Now is the time of the end of the old age, and somewhere on this earth the two witnesses are alive. Herein we will identify *not* the names of the two witnesses, but what Spirit they will or are coming in, that is, what two Old Testament people the two modern day witnesses will fulfill. One of these two witnesses is Elijah, not the Elijah of the Old Testament, but a person who will do the major things that the Elijah of the Old Testament did. This person will be the antitypical Elijah.

pr497» Let's prove that one of the two witnesses is Elijah, and let's identify the other witness, and at the same time we'll break the symbols of Revelation chapter 11.

Two Olive Trees / Two Witnesses

pr498» Notice, "these are the two olive trees, and the two candlesticks standing before the God of the earth" (Rev 11:4). The two witnesses are called the two olive trees.

pr499» "And two olive trees by it, one upon the right side of the bowl, and the other upon the left side thereof ... What are these two olive trees upon the right side of the candlestick and upon the left side thereof ... What be these two olive branches which through the two golden pipes empty the golden oil out of themselves? ... Then said he, These are the two anointed ones, that stand till the Lord of the whole earth" (Zech 4:3, 11, 12, 14).

pr500» These two stand on the right and left of the candlestick. But the Church is the candlestick (Rev 1:20). And the Church is the body of Christ (1 Cor 12:12). Notice that Christ is in the midst of this same symbolic candlestick (Rev 1:13; 2:1). Thus, these two stand on the right and left of Christ, they "stand till the Lord of the whole earth" (Zech 4:14).

pr501» Further they stand "immediately preceding the God of the earth" (Rev 11:4). These two teach for 3 ½ years immediately preceding the return of Christ (Rev 11:3,7,11,12,14,15).

Purpose of the Two

pr502» What exactly is the purpose of having these two witnesses? There are at least two reasons:

- "At the mouth of two witnesses, or three witnesses, shall he that is worthy of death be put to death; but at the mouth of one witness he shall not be put to death" (Deut 17:6). In other words, the way of man/Satan will be destroyed only if there are at least two witnesses to speak out against man's way.

- "And he shall confirm the covenant with many for one week" (Dan 9:27). Here, it speaks about Christ confirming the new covenant for the last prophetic week (seven years) of Daniel's 70 prophetic weeks (See "Last War and God's Wrath" paper [PR5]). But Christ has only taught for 3 ½ years to confirm the covenant, not the full seven years (see *Chronology Papers*). But it is through the two witnesses that Christ will do this. This is the second main reason for the two witnesses — to fulfill the last 3 ½ years of the 7 years that Christ was to confirm the covenant. These two "stand till the Lord of the whole earth," as agents of Christ (Zech 4:14).

Anointed Ones

pr503» Next notice these two are the "anointed ones." But from the Hebrew, it should read — the two sons of the oil. And from the Septuagint it reads — the two sons of the fatness. Now the anointed one is Christ. "Christ" is a translation from a Greek word that means, *anointed*. The two witnesses are the sons of the anointed one through the Spirit in them (Rom 8:16). Yet not only are they sons in this sense, but they are commissioned like sons who take the place of their father while he is away. Christ will be the Father when He returns (Isa 9:6), and these two are His sons who act as His agents while He is away, until He comes.

Power of the Two

pr504» Now "if any man will hurt them, fire proceeds out of their mouth, and devours their enemies" (Rev 11:5). Now this is symbolical, as is much of the book of Revelation. What is the symbolic meaning of fire?

- "the tongue is a fire" (James 3:6)
- God's word is like fire (Jer 23:29)
- God's tongue is a devouring fire (Isa 30:27)
- there is a fire of God's mouth (2 Sam 22)

pr505» Thus, the fire that comes out of these two agents of Christ is God's word. Any one who tries to hurt them will be devoured by the fire of the truth that comes from their mouth.

pr506» Further Revelation 11:5 says that any who harms them will be likewise harmed. These two are eventually killed near the end of the 3 ½ years (3 ½ days before Christ returns) by the Beast of Revelation (Rev 11:7), but the Beast in return is killed (Rev 19:19-20).

pr507» Next they have power to smite the earth with plagues, etc (Rev 11:6). But as Christ did the will of his Father (John 14:31; 12:49; 6:38), so too will these two do *only* the will of God. And the will of the God is manifested in the Bible. The plagues shown in the Bible are what they have power over. Or more correctly, they will tell the world what is to happen before it happens and they will ask for the will of God to be done (1 John 5:14).

Rain

pr508» Notice that they have "power to shut heaven, that it rain not in the days of their prophecy." Does this mean it will not rain for 3 ½ years? No! God tells us to look to the higher meaning (Phil 3:18-19; Col 3:1-2). Revelation is filled with symbolism. The "rain" in this verse is symbolic of a higher meaning. This event happened typically in the days of Elijah: "Elijah was a man subject to like passions as we are, and he prayed earnestly that it not rain: and it rained not on the earth [land of Israel] by the space of three years six months" (James 5:17). This will happen in its antitypical or Spiritual fulfillment during the last 3 ½ years of man/Satan's misrule. Notice that "rain" is symbolic of God's word (see Isa 55:10-11; Deut 32:2). Christ said that "in the days of Elijah, when the heaven was shut up three years and six months ... great *famine* was throughout all the land" (Luke 4:25). It so happens that the higher meaning of "famine" is the famine "of hearing the words of the LORD" (Amos 8:11). Thus, there will be a famine of God's true word during this 3 ½ years, except for the two witnesses' teachings (Rev 11:6,3). "There shall not be dew nor rain these years, but according to my [Elijah's] word" (1 Kings 17:1).

Elijah is One of the Witnesses

pr509» Since what is to happen when the two witnesses teach (famine of God's word, except for the witnesses' teachings), has happened before typically with Elijah, and since Elijah is to come before the day of the LORD (Mal 4:5); then one of the two witnesses must be Elijah.

Who Is the Other Witness?

pr510» We want you to note that these two stand before the Lord (Zech 4:14), they are on the right and left side of the candlestick, which is the Church, which is the body of Christ. Therefore, they stand on the right and left side of Christ (Zech 4:11; Rev 1:20; 1 Cor 12:12). And also they are the two "anointed ones."

Two at Christ's Ascension

pr511» Now notice Acts 1:9-11, from the New International Version: "After he said this, he was taken up before their very eyes, and a cloud hid him from their sight. They were looking intently up into the sky as he was going, when suddenly two men dressed in white stood beside them. 'Men of Galilee,' they said, 'why do you stand here looking into the sky? This same Jesus, who has been taken from you into heaven, will come back in the same way you have seen him go into heaven.'"

pr512» Who were these two men? These men were in bright-white clothes, and they said Christ would come in the same manner as the people saw him go up into heaven. When Christ went up these two men were there. When he comes again, he will come down when these two men are there. Who were these two men in bright-white clothes?

pr513» "Truly I say unto you, There be some standing here, which shall not taste of death, till they see the Son of man coming in his kingdom" (Matt 16:28). Now the kingdom of God in its truest sense has not yet come, so what did Christ mean by this statement? [Note: The kingdom of God has come in one sense. That is, the Spirit of the kingdom has come into man through Christ.]

Two at Transfiguration

pr514» "And after six days Jesus takes Peter, James, and John his brother, and brings them up into a high mountain apart, and was transfigured before them: and his face did shine as the sun, and his raiment was white [or as bright] as the light. And, behold! there appeared unto them *Moses* and *Elijah* talking with him" (Matt 17:1-3).

pr515» Thus, none of the disciples of Christ saw the kingdom of God coming literally, but they saw it by the means of the transfiguration. But what were they to see? — "the Son of man coming in his kingdom." And what did they see? They saw Christ with Moses and Elijah.

Scripture Together

pr516» What did the two men say when Jesus went into heaven? (Acts 1:9-11) They said he would come in a like manner. That is, he will come with the two men being present. And at the transfiguration of his coming to his kingdom Moses and Elijah were beside him.

pr517» Now notice Revelation 11:12. After the two witnesses were killed (v.7) their bodies laid around for 3 ½ days (v. 9). Then *after* these 3 ½ days they then were resurrected (v. 11), "and they ascended up to heaven in a cloud, and their enemies beheld them" (v. 12).

pr518» This isn't any special resurrection. "For the Lord himself shall descend from heaven with a shout ... and with the trump of God: and the dead in Christ shall rise first" (1 Thes 4:16).

pr519» Revelation 11:11-12 pictures the resurrection of the dead. The witnesses went up into a cloud "and their enemies beheld them." That is, they beheld Christ *and* the two witnesses.

pr520» And how was Christ's coming shown in the transfiguration? He was with *Moses* and *Elijah*.

pr521» Who stands by the Lord? The two olive trees, or the two witnesses stand by the Lord (Zech 4:14, 11).

pr522» Who was mentioned with Elijah in the prophecy of Malachi 4:5? "Remember you the law of *Moses* my servant" (Mal 4:4).

Moses and Elijah

pr523» Through comparing what has been shown you, how could the two witnesses be anyone else other than the two who will come in the antitype of Moses and Elijah? There are no other persons even implied besides Moses and Elijah. The Bible seems to point out the two witnesses as coming in the Spirit or antitype of Moses and Elijah.

pr524» This makes sense, for the typical Moses led the typical Israel out of the typical Egypt. Today, the antitypical Moses will lead the antitypical Israel (the Church, Gal 6:16; Rev 7:4) out of the antitypical Egypt or Satan's kingdom (see Rev 11:8; and "Last War and God's Wrath" paper [PR5]).

pr525» And the antitypical Elijah will come to challenge antitypical Israel (those who *say* they are in the Church) who will have "ministers" who will be between two opinions (Baal's & God's, 1 Kings 18:21-22), and this antitypical Elijah will "slay" these ministers with the sword of God, which is God's word (1 Kings 18:40). Thus, the antitypical Elijah will repair the altar (1 Kings 18:30), and restore all truth (Matt 17:11). This will help fulfill Daniel's word that at the end of the age "knowledge shall be increased" (Dan 12:4). **Note:** We know that the truest sense of the antitypical Israel is that all people ever born will eventually be in the antitypical Israel, the full Church or Body of Christ (see "All Saved" paper [NM 13], etc.). And we know that there are groups of people who *say* they are the Church who may only have a minority with the Spirit. Thus, there are two senses to the antitypical Elijah's challenge: (1), He will challenge all the people of the world at the end of the old age, who are between opinions on who or what is the true God; and (2), in this challenge of all the people he will challenge groups (churches) who say they are in the Church. But the real Church is the remnant of Israel.

pr526» What is another proof that the antitypical Elijah will challenge the *antitypical* Israel at the end of the age and not just the typical Israel?

pr527» First, we are to look to the higher meanings of the Bible (see "Duality Paper" [BP4]). Since we know the antitypical Elijah will come and do similar things that the typical Elijah did, then if the typical Elijah challenged the typical Israel's religion, the antitypical Elijah must challenge the antitypical Israel's religious belief: all religious belief in the world.

Further Proof

pr528» Notice further proof in Revelation, chapters two and three. In these chapters Christ the God speaks not only to each of the seven churches, but also to *all* the churches — that includes the Philadelphia church (Rev 3:7-13). Revelation speaks of the Church and "them that hold the doctrines of Balaam, who taught Balak to cast a stumbling block before the children of Israel, to eat things sacrificed unto idols, and to commit fornication" (Rev 2:14).

pr529» The higher meaning here is spiritual fornication with modern idols and doctrines. This event happened while the typical Moses was leading Israel to the promised land (Num ch 22-23). This again will happen, but this time to the antitypical Israel as Revelation 2:14 says.

pr530» Further proof is in Revelation 2:20. Note "Jezebel" in this verse. Her kind of fornication is what the typical Elijah went up against (1 Kings 18:17; 19:2; etc.). The antitypical Elijah will go against the spiritual fornication of Jezebel. But notice not all of the people who say they are in the Church will have fallen into spiritual fornication (Rev 2:14, 24). God "will fight against them with the sword of" his "mouth" (Rev 2:16). God will fight through his prophet, the antitypical Elijah (cf Rev 2:16 with 1 Kings 18:40; "sword" = God's Word, Eph 6:17).

The Two Witnesses Are Coming In The Spirit Or Antitypical Sense of Moses And Elijah.

pr531» Elijah will come at the end of the age to rebuke the world and those who *say* they are in the Church with God's word! Moses and Elijah will become the two witnesses in the 3 ½ years right before the Messiah returns with His peace and harmony.

pr532» *Elijah* means: "God [Eli] (is) Yehowah [Jah]" or "God (is) He (Who) Will-Be," or "God (is) (the) BeComingOne" since Yehowah or Jehowah means, "He (Who) Will-Be," or the "BeComing-One."

pr533» *Moses* means: "drawn from the water."

Notes for PR8

30 Years

pr534» Now the sons of Kohath had to be 30 years old to do the work of the tabernacle (Num 4:3-4), for they took care of the holy things (Num 4:4; 3:30-31). Antitypically, Jesus Christ who is in charge of the holy things (the Church) was not set aside to *begin* his Spiritual work until he was 30 years old (Luke 3:21-23).

pr535» Now John was born six months before Christ (Luke 1:36, 26-66; see *Unger's Bible Dict.* under "John the Baptist"). John was in the wilderness teaching and preparing the ways before Christ's coming (Luke 1:80, 76-77). John began openly preaching when he was 30 years old (Luke 3:1-2), just like Christ began to preach at about 30 years old. Since John was 6 months older than Christ, then John's work lasted for 6 months before Christ came to him to be baptized. During these 6 months, John preached about the kingdom of God (Matt 3:2). Then Christ took over preaching the kingdom (Mark 1:14-15). Since John's commission was to prepare the people of Israel *before* Christ came, then when Christ came his official commission was over. Therefore since the commission of the typical John was *before* Christ came to teach Israel about the kingdom of God, then the antitypical John (Elijah) will teach before Jesus Christ's return to set up the kingdom of God.

PR9: Seven Churches of Revelation

Speaks to the End Time

Days at Hand When Book Fully Opened

pr536» As all the Bible is dual so too are chapters 2 and 3 of Revelation. The book of Revelation is "the Revelation of Jesus Christ, which God gave unto him, to show unto his servants things which must shortly come to pass" (Rev 1:1). These things mentioned in the book have not come true in the truest sense. Christ has not returned, Satan has not been locked up, etc. It further says happy is "he that reads, and they that hear the words of this prophecy" (v. 3). This doesn't mean merely hearing it physically, but hearing it Spiritually, for there are people who only hear physically (Mark 4:11-12). Yet there are some who have a Spiritual ear to hear (Rev 2:7; Matt 13:16). Furthermore Revelation 1:3 speaks of those who hear, and at the time that they hear: "the time is at hand." And in Ezekiel 12:22-23 it speaks of the days or time being at hand, "and the effect of every vision." When Revelation was written the true day of the Lord was not at hand. Therefore at the time it was written they didn't understand the book of Revelation in its truest sense. It is only when the days are at hand that the whole book of Revelation shall be opened up fully.

Book to All the Churches in Christ

pr537» Typically John was told to "write a book, and send it unto the seven churches which are in Asia; unto Ephesus, and unto Smyrna, and unto Pergamos, and unto Thyatira, and unto Sardis, and unto Philadelphia, and unto Laodicea" (Rev 1:11). Notice this *one* book that was to go to these seven churches in Asia in the order written. Hence this one book was carried first to Ephesus, then to Smyrna, and so forth until it came to the Laodicean church. But moreover notice that in each message to each church it says the book spoke to the churches (Rev 2:7, 11, 17, 29; 3:6, 13, 22). The book didn't just speak to one church, but to all the churches. Therefore not only does this book speak to each church, but speaks to all the churches that are in Christ.

Book Speaks to the End Time and Thereafter

pr538» The things written about in this book John wrote were the things that were in his time, "and the things which shall be hereafter" (Rev 1:19). Concerning the seven churches, this indicates the churches as they were at John's time, and the things that were to come concerning the Church. The book spoke of the state of the churches of Christ at that time and what was to come.

pr539» Antitypically, we are in the time when the book is opened fully, and the effect of every vision is to come true soon. **Therefore antitypically the book of Revelation now is speaking of the present state of the churches**, and "the things which shall be hereafter." The book will be perfectly fulfilled shortly. All the things mentioned about the seven churches concern the present Church of God at the time the book was opened up, and shortly thereafter.

Chapters Two and Three Speak of the Condition of Today's Church

[section written on April 4th, 1971; revised January 23, 1998 {some singular words changed to plural}]

pr540» At this writing there are false apostles in with those of the true Church, or those who say they have a commission by God to perform ("two witnesses"). But some in the Church "found them liars" (Rev 2:2).

1. Some have fallen from their love of the first, and are asked to turn, yet at the same time they hate the false doctrines of the Church. These will endure, and labor through the NAME of Christ, for they have the Spirit of Christ inside him (Rev 2:4, 5, 6, 3).
2. These in the Church are relatively poor physically, but rich Spiritually (Rev 2:9).
3. The Church will go through a trial; some will be put in prison (Rev 2:10).
4. The Church is dwelling or will dwell where Satan's throne is, or power is. The modern day Antipas will be killed where Satan dwells (Rev 2:13).
5. The present Church holds false doctrines (Rev 2:14-15).
6. But they will be reproved soon after they have been given a period to change their minds (Rev 2:16, 21, 3:3).
7. Those who continue in the false doctrines will die the death, the agelasting death (Rev 2:23, 18-23).
8. Some in the Church do not hold in their minds these false doctrines (Rev 2:24).
9. At this time the present Church has a name that lives, but is dead Spiritually. They have "dead" leaders, biased behavior, etc (Rev 3:1).
10. Those of the Church are asked to "strengthen the things which remain, that were about to die: for I have not found your works complete before God. Remember therefore how you have received and heard, and hold fast." The Church will be reproved, it is asked to remember how they received this truth, to hold it, and to strengthen it (Rev 3:2, 3).

11. Again it says some in the present Church are Spiritually in Christ (Rev 3:4).

12. Now here it shows the door being opened to the one who shall reprove the Church. This one has not denied Christ's NAME (Rev 3:7-8).

13. The Church will have a little while strength. Thus they will receive a little while power (Rev 3:8).

14. The scripture about the Laodicean Church pictures those now in the Church, physically, who are comparatively rich physically but not Spiritually. Those with false assurance in goods will be reproved, for as many as God loves, he rebukes (Rev 3:14-19).

15. The door to the Church is now being knocked on. (Rev 3:20)

16. Those who overcome will be saved (Rev 3:21).

PR10: Great Falling Away
Forty Days
Tithe of God's People

pr541» In order to find truth in the Bible we look for patterns; we look in a Spiritual way for Spiritual patterns (See *Duality Paper*). Paul found patterns in the Bible and manifested them to his physical churches through his letters (Epistles). Throughout our papers we do our best to manifest the patterns found in the Bible. Before the day of the Lord there is to be a great falling away (2 Thes 2:3, 1 Tim 4:1). What does this mean? If we are alive at the end, will we recognize this falling away or departure from the faith?

- "For the time will come when they will not permit [bear] sound doctrine, but they will heap up to themselves teachers who tickle the ear according to their own lusts. And they will turn away their ear from the truth and will be turned aside to myths" (2 Tim 4:3-4).

- "Now the Spirit speaks expressly, that in the latter times some shall depart from the faith, giving heed to seducing spirits, and doctrines of devils; Speaking lies in hypocrisy..." (1 Tim 4:1-2).

- "Concerning the coming of our Lord Jesus Christ and our being gathered to him... Don't let anyone deceive you in any way, for that day will not come until the rebellion occurs [falling away] and the man of lawlessness is revealed, the man doomed to destruction" (2 Thes 2:1, 3).

This lawless man is the Beast man, the man who will rule the Beast system, and is in a shadow of Satan. Satan will be inside this lawless man misleading him during the last 1260 days (See *Beast Papers*, PR2, PR3). But what about the "falling away" or the "rebellion?"

pr542» Those who say they are in the Church at the end (but are not) will not permit or will have cast aside sound doctrine, and will be or will have fallen away to myths. A myth is a belief that is not true. Pertaining to Biblical doctrine, a myth is a belief in something not Biblical, something not found in the Bible. The so-called doctrine about the "Trinity" is an example of something not found in the Bible and something that is impossible (See *God Papers*, Part 1). Now, what is going to happen at or near the end? At the end of the age before Christ's physical return someone will come and restore all things (Matt 17:10-11) through the power of the Spirit (John 14:16-17, 26). In a way the scriptures in John, Chapter 14, concerning the "Spirit of Truth" applied to Paul, and in a certain degree applies to all those with the Spirit, according to the power given them, but also this scripture applies to the Spiritual Elijah. There will be an antitypical and Spiritual Elijah who will restore all things. He comes "before the great and dreadful day of the lord" (Mal 4:5). Therefore before he comes the Truth shall not be full in the

Church or anywhere on earth. But when he comes he shall restore all things, yet they will do "unto him whatsoever they listed, as it is written of him" (Mark 9:13). At first the physical Elijah was rejected in the scripture by physical Israel; the Spiritual Elijah will also be rejected. Yet he will endure and restore the Truth, the Spiritual sacrifice of the Spiritual altar, to Spiritual Israel, which is the Church (1 Kings 18:30 with Heb 13:10; Matt 17:10-11; see New Mind Papers). Thus when Elijah comes "they will not permit" or bear or admit or hold up or conceive his sound doctrine (2 Tim 4:3; Strong's #430 from #2192). Yet the Bible says he will overcome them and restore all the truth to the Spiritual Church and teach the truth to all the earth as one of the two witnesses (See *Two Witnesses*).

Antitypical Ezekiel

pr543» Remember we look for patterns in the Bible (see *Duality Paper*). Notice in Ezekiel, chapters two to four, there is a prophecy that has happened typically, but not antitypically. In chapter 2 God speaks to the Son of man and sends him to Israel. God tells him not to be afraid of their words (v. 6), tells him to speak God's words even if they forbear (v. 7), tells him to eat the book of words he has been given (Ezek 2:8-10; 3:1-3; see Rev 10:8-11). He was to go to the house of Israel and give them the words of the book whether they hear or not (Ezek 3:1-11). He was restricted not to go out among them, and he would not reprove them at first (Ezek 3:25-27). Spiritually speaking, Israel is the Church. This speaks of someone who will restore the truth, but at first they would not Spiritually hear him. Today, we only see some of the true doctrines of the Spiritual Church through the writings of Paul, James, Peter, John, and the others of the New Testament. Most of these were letters. Paul in person, surely, had more detailed information regarding doctrine. If we had doctrinal papers written by Paul, there would be much less disagreement among those who call themselves Christians. (Of course, this could have allowed more of those who say they are Christians, but don't have the Spirit, to fool others who do have the Spirit.) Yet since Paul was not the Spiritual Elijah, he may not have held all the truth that God will allow us to learn before Christ's return.

Great Falling Away

pr544» Elijah was also to go to Israel, but Israel would not Spiritually hear him, and for a while would not answer him (1 Kings 18:21). The Son of man (Ezekiel) was to speak to Israel "whether they will hear, or whether they will forbear." Also the Son of man was to shut himself within his house (3:24), while he sieged Jerusalem (the Church) and prophesied against it (Ezek 4:3, 7). But he would not reprove it at first (Ezek 3:26). In prophecy, Ezekiel and Elijah's stories point to the soon coming events at the end-of-the-age, much as different physical persons and events of the Old Testament pointed to Jesus Christ. If you look at the scripture that pointed to the first coming of Christ, you can see why physical Israel did not recognize Christ's first coming. These scriptures are spread throughout the Old Testament and sometimes only one part of a scripture pointed to the first coming, while the other part pointed to his second coming. This was confusing to those without the Spirit. It is easy for us now to understand these scriptures because they were fulfilled by Christ, and because we have the Spirit.

390 & 40 Days

pr545» The antitypical Elijah-Ezekiel will 'siege' the antitypical Jerusalem (Ezek 4:2,7), the Church, for two periods of 390 and 40 days (Ezek 4:4-9), whether they listen to the words of the siege or not (Ezek 3:27). During the 390 day period he was to eat a grain diet of about ten ounces and a liquid of about four cups, from time to time. But he was to have another period of 40 days:

- "and when you have completed these [390 days] you shall lie down on your right side and bear *a second time* the iniquity of the house of Judah, **forty days**, a day for each year, I assign you" (Ezek 4:6, literal translation).

pr546» He already bore the iniquity for 390 days (Ezek 4:4-5). But now he must for the *second time* ("again") bear or put-up with the iniquity. The people of Israel would not listen to Ezekiel for the 390 days and Ezekiel would have to endure them for another 40 days. These typical or physical events may have happened one right after another, but this doesn't mean the antitypical events will happen likewise. This is much like ambiguous scriptures that pointed to Christ: one part of the scripture may have pertained to Christ's first coming; the other to His second coming (Dan 9:26-27). At this time these scriptures are not clear.

Forty Days /Forty Years

pr547» Before the day of the Lord there is to be a great falling away (2 Thes 2:3, 1 Tim 4:1). This "falling away" begins after the siege, after the "40 days." The antitypical Elijah's mouth and power to *reprove* is closed during the period (Ezek 3:25-26; 4:8), but his mouth will be opened at the end (Ezek 9:6; 24:21, 24-27; 33:21-22; 29:21). After the "siege" of forty days he will overcome and begin to restore the truth to the Church/Israel. Remember also that Moses after **forty days** came down from mount Sinai, where he received the ten commandments (Ex 34:28), and then he began teaching Israel the law. And remember that after Christ's water baptized he had a 40 day period of trial. After Christ's 40 day trial he began to teach Israel (Luke 3:22; 4:1-2, 13-15). Remember that Elijah had a period of forty days before he went out and before he had his 7,000 in Israel (1 Kings 19:8-19). These forty day periods are also connected in someway to a forty *year* period: "a day for each year" (Ezek 4:6). Moses received the physical Ten Commandments for Israel from the angel of God twice during two *forty day* periods (Ex 24:18; 32:15-19; 34:27-28; Deut 9:18-10:10) at the beginning of the *forty year* period of Israel and Moses' wandering in the wilderness (Ex 20:1ff); Israel died by multitudes during the forty years because of their rebellion:

> "Your sons shall be shepherds for forty years in the wilderness, and they will suffer for your unfaithfulness, until your corpses lie in the wilderness. According to the number of days which you spied out the land, forty days, for every day you shall bear your guilt a year, forty years, and you will know my opposition." (Num 14:33-34)

Moses reiterated the Law at the very end of the forty years (Deut 5:1ff), and Israel went into the promised land after their **forty years** in the wilderness. Notice how forty days are connected to forty years. So it will be with the antitypical Moses, he will receive the commandments (Spiritual law and truth) during a forty day period. This forty day period will be somehow connected to a forty year period because a day is counted as a year and the forty years are connected to the wondering of Israel in the wilderness. Today the whole world is a wilderness and those who will belong to the Spiritual Israel (Church) will have gone through their own forty years of wondering near the end-of-the-age in order to fulfill the type and antitype of scripture. After a "forty day" period the antitype Moses and Elijah will begin to teach Spiritual Israel the truth. But many will not want to admit the sound doctrine (2 Tim 4:3) and will fall away (1 Tim 4:1), and begin to persecute the true Christians (Luke 21:12, 16-17; Matt 24:10) after Elijah is revealed (Matt 11:12-14). Therefore after the siege by the antitypical Elijah-Ezekiel, then will occur the "falling away."

One-Third

pr548» At the end of the prophesying siege by the typical Ezekiel notice what happened: "when the days of the siege are fulfilled," then a third part will fall by the sword [the word of God, Eph 6:17], and another third by pestilence and famine [the effects of the sword and trials thereof] will be consumed (Ezek 5:2, 12). These are the two-thirds who are to fall away: "and it shall come to pass, that in all the land, says the LORD, two parts therein shall be cut off and die, but the third shall be left therein" (Zech 13:8). Two-thirds "leave" or are cut off from the Church/Jerusalem. They are cut off because, "they went out from us, but they were not of us; for if they had been of us, they would have continued with us" (1 John 2:19).

pr549» Notice what Zechariah says about the one-third that is left: "And I will bring the third part through the fire, and will refine them as silver is refined, and will try them as gold is tried" (Zech 13:9; see Ezek 5:3-4). Malachi shows this same refining (Mal 3:3). This refining is a "trial of your faith" (1 Pet 1:7; 1 Cor 3:12-14). Also Revelation 3:18 pictures trial or refining by fire of the Church. (There is a higher meaning here concerning Satan's angels and God's angels: the one-third and two-thirds of the angels versus two-thirds and the other one-third of mankind. See *God Papers* [GP7 & GP8]).

Tithe of God's People

pr550» Immediately at Christ's return one-tenth of Jerusalem (the Church) will fall (Rev 11:13). That is, one-tenth who will be cut off are those who *say* they are in the Church before the "falling away." Seven thousand were killed (Rev 11:13). But Elijah is to have 7,000 when he comes (Rom 11:2-4): he is one of the two witnesses. Furthermore, one-half of the Church (Jerusalem) was not cut off from the city while the other half are sent away from the city (Zech 14:2). Thus, those cut from the city and sent away from the city are the 50 percent of those who say they are in the Church (just before Christ returns physically), but actually do not have the Spirit (Oil) and thus are sent into the fire (Matt 25:1-12; 7:23; 13:41-42).

pr551» Putting this together, therefore there will be 14,000 (7,000 & 7,000) or so who will be physically in the Church at the very end, but only one-half of them will Spiritually be in the Church. These are the 7,000 for Elijah, "the residue of the people shall not be cut off from the city" (Zech 14:2).

pr552» Revelation 11:13 says that those who fell were one-tenth of the city. This one-tenth are the tithe of those in the physical Church near the end of the old age when the end-time events begin to come to pass.

- All tithes of herd and flock, every tenth one that passes under the shepherd's staff, shall be holy to the LORD (Lev 27:32).

Antitypical John

pr553» John the Baptist is a type of the Elijah (Matt 11:12-14; Luke 1:16-17). As John cried in the wilderness to make ready, for the time is at hand, so will the antitypical Elijah. As John did this until his time for publicly taking office, or his manifestation to Israel, so too shall Elijah until he publicly takes office or his manifestation to the Spiritual Israel (Matt 3:1-13; Luke 3:4; 1:80, "showing" is translated from a Greek word meaning: to openly take an office; or manifestation; or showing forth).

pr554» While John was in the wilderness his food was wild honey, which antitypically means God's word (Psa 19:9-10; 81:16; 119:103). This is the angel's food that Elijah ate (1 Kings 19:5-7; Psa 78:24-25; John 6:32, 63).

pr555» But after Elijah's time in the wilderness or as we have seen after the antitypical "390 day" period and the "40 day" period, then he will take office. As John was to prepare a people to make straight the way of God, so too the antitypical Elijah (Luke 1:16-17, 76-77, 3:4-5). He teaches that *all* will see the salvation of God (Luke 3:6; 16:16). And as John taught Israel six months before Christ and His 3 ½ years so too will the antitypical John (Elijah) teach before the 3 ½ years mentioned in the book of Revelation.

Two-thirds of Mankind Cut Off

pr556» What will happen to the Church first will also happen to the whole world, for the end-time destruction will begin with God's sanctuary (Ezek 9:6; 1-11; 24:21). A still higher meaning is that the two-thirds cut off are the two-thirds of mankind who were cut off from the Body of Christ during the old age of Satan. (See *God Papers* [GP7])

pr557» [**Comment**: Before I ran across this pattern in the Bible in 1971, I thought of true Christians being numbered in the millions near the end of the age. But if this paper's rendition of the "falling away" is close to the truth, then there are only thousands in the Church near the end. I have searched far and wide for a physical Church of God that held numerous Spiritual Christians, and I have yet to find one. This paper speaks about a physical church(es) counted as Spiritual Jerusalem (the Church), but only about one-tenth of it are real Christians. The Bible speaks about three groups or three orders being resurrected from the dead (1 Cor 15:20-28):

- the first was Christ;
- the second the 144,000 (Rev 7:4), the sealed servants of God;
- the third the "great multitude, which no man could number, of all nations..." (Rev 7:9).

The 144,000 is a very small number to come out of the billions of people who have ever lived on the earth for the first six thousand years of man's history. So maybe 7,000 plus would be about the right number to exist near the end. Too small for me, but what is the purpose of the 144,000 anyway? God made them kings and priests: and they shall reign on the earth (Rev 5:9-10). The kings, queens, and priests of this old age are the type of the antitype. These old kings and queens ruled ruthlessly. Those born of God from this evil age will rule as kings and queens during the 1000 years, and will rule with love. The 144,000 is about the right number of people to help rule billions on the earth during the 1000 years. So maybe the 7,000 as a group is not so few after all. This 7,000 is one-tenth of another group(s) who say they are Christians. But who is this group(s) of 70,000? Time will tell. Hopefully, the time is short. Remember, we don't fear the end, because this is when our Messiah comes to save the world, and then and only then will peace come to the earth.]

[**Note**: This paper was first written in 1971]

PR11: Information on the Beast and his Name

Christ came in his Father's Name
Antichrist comes in his Father's name
Beast as Superman?
Deadly Wound
How do you calculate the number of the Beast?
Things to know when Calculating the Number of the Beast
Tables on Calculating the Number
666 Web Page
More on Calculating the Number
Antichrist exists in the last 3 ½ Years

How important is a name?

pr558» **Importance of God's Name.** God's Name is very important. Even one of the ten commandments warns against taking his Name in vain (Ex 20:7; Deut 5:11). In the first part of the God Papers (GP1: "Great Significance of the NAME") we point out from the Bible how important God considers his Name. If you haven't studied this section, you should study it, so you can better understand how important God considers his Name to be (See GP1c).

Christ came in his Father's Name

pr559» **Christ's Name and Person Denied.** "I have come in my Father's **Name,** and you do not accept me; if another comes in his own **Name,** you will accept him" (John 5:43).

Not only has the world not accepted the true Messiah, it has also rejected his Name. As shown in the first part of the God Papers, God's Name as revealed by God in Exodus 3:14 is the "BeComingOne" or "YHWH" or "He (who) Will-Be," or in his own words, "I will be." His Name is not the "Lord," or "I am" as commonly misrepresented in today's Bibles. Just two verses above Exodus 3:14 in Exodus 3:12 the *same* Hebrew word that many use to "prove" that God's Name means "I am" is translated as "I will be." This same Hebrew word appears in about 42 verses in the Bible, where it is mostly translated as "I will be" ("I will be" in GP1). I will be or He will be is God's Name, not I am.

Last Antichrist comes in his Father's Name

pr560» We know that there will have been many antichrists before the real and last Antichrist comes (1John 2:18). Christ came in his Father's Name and was rejected, but Satan will come inside a man and be identified by the number of this man's name (Rev 13:18, 11) and yet he will be accepted and followed by the world (Rev 13:8, 3). Even though the Beast's identity will be obvious (he has the number of the Beast; he is connected to the ten/seven nation league), he will be accepted and followed, and his identity as the Beast-man will be denied by his followers who will claim he is a leader doing "good" for the world. As Satan pretends to be a minister of light, "even Satan disguises himself as an angel of light" (2 Cor 11:14), so will the Beast-man appear to those without the New Mind to be "good." He looks like a "lamb," but in reality Satan the dragon speaks and acts through him (Rev 13:11). Although he is the real Antichrist and real false-prophet those of the world willingly believe his lies and are deceived (Rev 19:20; 2 Thes 2:9-12).

pr561» **The number of the Beast helps to identify him**. By carefully comparing scriptures of Daniel and Revelations we know that there is an *individual* Beast with Satan inside of him influencing his activities, and there is a *system* of the Beast that starts out with ten nations in some kind of league (See PR2 & PR3). It is the individual Beast that has a name that can be figured or calculated to be six hundred and sixty-six (Rev 13:18). But in order for this man to be the Beast-man he must also be the voice or leader of a group of nations that starts out with ten nations, then later the group will only have seven nations because three of them will have been destroyed (PR2 & PR3). We have identified a leader of a great nation who has the number of the Beast (see Numerical Value Chart below). He now has many of the qualities of the Beast, but not all of them (Beast Character web page). For example he is not yet a lover of military force as the Beast-man will be. He is also not yet connected to any ten nation group. But we know from prophesy that this Beast-man will be connected with the system of the Beast for a 1260 to1290 day or 3 and ½ year period (Rev 13:5; Dan 7:25; PR2 & PR3). This period has not yet started so we cannot call this man the Beast-man yet (written 11-28-1998). It may turn out to be another man, but the fact that his name equals six hundred and sixty-six in *both* of the Biblical languages makes it seem likely that he will become that Beast-man. We will continue to watch this.

Beast as Superhuman?

pr562» **Miracles**. Now some may think that the man with the number cannot be the last Antichrist because he is not superhuman. But the Beast-man will **not** be superhuman or actually perform real miracles:

> "**lying wonders**... God shall send to them [who worship the Beast] strong delusion, **that they should believe a lie**... and **deceived them** that dwell on the earth by these [lying] miracles" (2 Thes 2:9, 11; Rev 13:14)

pr563» Satan cannot preform real miracles or resurrect himself from the dead, for only God has the power of resurrection from death (John 5:26; 11:25), and He will **not** give that power to Satan for any reason or for any period. That is why Satan deceives the world with **lying** wonders or miracles. Satan cannot preform real miracles.

pr564» The man we have identified with the number is not **now** the Beast-man (11-28-98). He will only be the Beast-man when he enters the 1290-1260 day period. But we will know this ahead of time, for God promised to show his servants ahead of time (Isa 42:9 Luke 8:17; 10:21-22; Mark 4:22-23).

Deadly Wound

pr565» Some say that the Antichrist (that is, Beast-man; that is, false-prophet; that is, Anti-Messiah) must be superhuman since he recovers from a deadly wound (Rev 13:3, 12). But the scripture speaks of the Beast "as if" or "like" it was wounded to death[1] (Rev 13:3). The scripture is not speaking of a literal death of a person and then a resurrection thereafter. You may say that there are two "deadly wounds": one for the Beast-man; one for the Beast-system.

There is a "deadly wound" to the *system* of the Beast:

pr566» The following section is from Beast-system Paper [PR2]:

Deadly Wound. Notice that in Revelation 13:3 that a head was as wounded to death, but its deadly wound was healed. This deadly wound will happen to the seventh mountain or kingdom of Revelation 17 with its ten horns or nations. And this "deadly wound" will subdue three of the ten horns (nations) of this seventh kingdom ("mountain") which is the ten-nation Beast (Dan 7:24). Thus, the eighth mountain or kingdom is the *healed* Beast of Revelation 13:3. It had ten horns, but three nations ("horns") will be subdued by the mean horn (Dan 7:20, 24).

In other words, "the Beast that *was* [the ten-nation Beast], and *is not* [the ten-nation Beast], even he is the eighth, and is out of the seven, and goes to perdition" (Rev 17:11). This Beast *was* [the ten-nation Beast], and *is not* [the beast with ten horns or nations], and *yet is* [the beast, but with only seven nations]. The "deadly wound" destroys the kingdom that *was* by subduing three nations ("kings"); the healing of this deadly wound creates a kingdom with seven nations as opposed to ten nations as before. The seven-nation Beast "is not" like the ten-nation Beast, "yet is" the same beast, but with three nations subdued.

(The above section is from Beast-system Paper [PR2])

---

[1] USA President Trump's bullet to his head (ear) was within an inch of killing him (July 13, 2024) is an example of such a wound.

There must also be a "deadly wound" for the Beast-man.

pr567» The fact that the "deadly wound" happens to *one* of the Beast's heads, and the fact that Beast-man only has one head, means the "deadly wound" refers to the system of the Beast, and that it is only a "deadly wound" to the Beast-man in the sense that part of the Beast-man's power base was destroyed or wounded as just explained above. It is after the "deadly wound" that the mouth or voice of the system of the Beast speaks for the system for 42 months (Rev 13:3-5).

Superhuman: To Summarize

pr568» Satan and his followers cannot perform real miracles. Some of the things he will do, like make fire come down from heaven (atomic bombs), are wonders and may have seemed miraculous to John in his vision, but they are the wonders that any nuclear-armed power can perform.

How to Calculate the Number of the Beast

Calculate from Hebrew or Greek or Both?

pr569» Now some say that only the Greek language of the Bible can be used to calculate the number of the Beast, since the book of Revelation was written in Greek, or, that is, appears to have been written in Greek by John. But was it? There is some evidence that at least part of the New Testament of the Bible may have been first written in Hebrew and then translated into Greek after the Hebrew nation was destroyed by the Romans. After all, were not the first leaders of the Church Jewish or Hebrew? Even Paul was a Hebrew.

pr570» In the fourth century, Jerome in his *Concerning Illustrious Men* wrote about the book of Matthew being first written in the Hebrew language and only later translated to Greek. (See part 1 of the *God Papers* for more information on this.) Although Jerome spoke specifically about the book of Matthew, the book of Revelation and other books, such as Mark, may have also been written first in Hebrew. The book of Revelation has been called "the most Hebraistic in thought and language of all the New Testament books" (*Hermeneutics of the New Testament*, by A. Immer, 1873, pp. 132-144; taken from p. 126 of *Biblical Hermeneutics*, Milton S. Terry). Because the Catholic Church has done its best to rid Christianity of anything Jewish, it is almost impossible now to know how many books in the New Testament were first written in Hebrew, or first written in Greek and then translated into Hebrew for the Jewish Christians to read. So it is thus very significant that the man with the number has the number in *both* languages, especially since both languages have different values for their letters, and especially since Hebrew has no numerical values for its vowels since vowels were not written. But there are those falsely saying[1] that there are many leaders with the number 666, and thus helping to blind the world because of their lies (2Thes 2:11-12). Also the modern "rapture" myth helps to blind people. Most modern rapture believers will not recognize the Beast or acknowledge him because they mistakenly think that they will be raptured before the Beast comes. Since they are not raptured they, of course, discount anyone with the number.

Things to know when Calculating the Number of the Beast

666. "This calls for wisdom: let anyone with understanding calculate the number of the beast, for it is the **number of a man. Its number is six hundred sixty-six**." (Revelation 13:18)

Not a number of a title, nor of a computer, nor an address. Scripture says the number of the Beast is the number of a man, not a system, not money, not a computer system, not a title, not a law, not an address, not anything but the number of a male human being. The book of Revelation was speaking about calculating or adding up the numbers of a man's name.

Irenaeus. Almost 1900 years ago Irenaeus in his *Against Heresies* told fellow believers that the number of the Antichrist was six hundred and sixty-six, and that it was figured by knowing the value of each letter of the name, "since [Greek] numbers also are expressed by letters."

Calculate number of the name by adding the numerical values of each letter of the name. Unlike modern languages which use the Arabic numerical system (0, 1, 2, 3, 4, 5, 6, 7, 8, 9), languages around the time of the book of Revelation and before, either spelled out the numbers or used letters that had numerical values. Each letter in Hebrew (except vowels) or Greek has a numerical value. Latin has its Roman numeral system. So by calculating or adding up the numerical values of the letters of a person's name, you will get the number of his name.

Not three sixes in a row. The number of the Beast-man is six hundred sixty six and it is not just three 6s in a row (6+6+6=18), but six hundred sixty-six. Three sixes in a row is not the number of the Beast-man.

Not the gematria system. We are not speaking about gematria. Gematria was a part of the Jewish mysticism which dealt with mystical aspects of words' numerical value. The Truth of the Bible is not found by mysticism. People are using the word "gematria" when they should be using the phrase, "numerical value."

---

[1] There are Internet sites where people claim that numerous individuals and leaders not only have the number 666 in Hebrew and Greek, but also in English, yet English has no numerical value for its letters. When you look at their material, the names are manipulated to fit the number of the Beast, it is undocumented, inaccurate, and often simply made-up to fit their own wishes – in other words worthless.

Use your own mind and study the following tables:

Hebrew Alphabet with numerical values			English Transliteration values		Greek Alphabet with numerical values		
letter sign	letter name	num. value	Hebrew	Greek	letter sign	letter name	num. value
א	aleph	1	guttural	a	α	alpha	1
ב	beth	2	b (bh)	b	β	beta	2
ג	gimel	3	g (gh)	g	γ	gamma	3
ד	daleth	4	d (dh)	d	δ	delta	4
ה	he	5	h	e	ε	epsilon	5
ו	waw	6	w	w [old usage]	ς	digamma or stigma	6
ז	zayin	7	z	z	ζ	zeta	7
ח	cheth	8	h	e	η	eta	8
ט	teth	9	t	th	θ	theta	9
י	yod	10	y (j)	i (j or y)	ι	iota	10
כ	kaph	20	k (c)	k (c)	κ	kappa	20
ל	lamed	30	L	L	λ	lambda	30
מ	mem	40	m	m	μ	mu	40
נ	nun	50	n	n	ν	nu	50
ס	samekh	60	s	x	ξ	xi	60
ע	ayin	70	guttural	o (short)	ο	omicron	70
פ	pe	80	p	p	π	pi	80
צ	sadi	90	s		-	koppa	90
ק	koph	100	q	r	ρ	rho	100
ר	resh	200	r	s	σ	sigma	200
ש	shin	300	s (sh)	t	τ	tau	300
ת	taw	400	t (th)	y, u	υ	upsilon	400
				ph	φ	phi	500

				kh (ch)	χ	chi	600
				ps	ψ	psi	700
				o (long)	ω	omega	800
				-		sampi	900

Transliterating from English to Hebrew or Greek

Hebrew

(Remember the Hebrew language did not have any numerical value for its vowels. When writing they wrote only the consonants, not the vowels.)

```
William  =   6 + 30 + 30 + 40            =          106
J        =  10                           =           10
Clinton  =  20 + 30 + 50 + 400 + 50  =            +550
                                                   666
```

Greek

(Remember the "ia" in William is a diphthong and the second vowel of a diphthong is not usually pronounced in Greek, thus we do not transliterate it from English to Greek.)

```
William  =   6 + 10 + 30 + 30 + 10 + 40           =    126
J        =  10                                    =     10
Clinton  =  20 + 30 + 10 + 50 + 300 + 70 + 50  =     +530
                                                      666
```

English

(Remember that the English language does not have any numerical values for its letters. English uses the Arabic numeral system: 0, 1, 2, 3, 4, 5, 6, 7, 8, 9)

```
William  = 0 + 0 + 0 + 0 + 0 + 0 + 0     =     000
J        = 0                             =      00
Clinton  = 0 + 0 + 0 + 0 + 0 + 0 + 0     =    +000
                                               000
```

Note: When proper nouns are transliterated from Hebrew to English the "yad" or "y" [׳] is traditionally translated as "J." For example Yehu is translated as Jehu, Yirmeyah as Jeremiah, or Yeshua as Jeshua. The same is true in transliteration in reverse. Therefore our Jesus becomes Yeshua or Yehosua, our Jeremiah becomes Yirmeyah and our Jehu becomes Yehu. When we transliterate "Jesus" into Greek we get "Iesous" or into Hebrew we get Yehosua (Jehoshua or Joshua). Therefore the "J" in English is transliterated to the "i" in Greek, and vice versa when translating the other way.

This example in no way is saying that Clinton is or will be the Beast man.

Copy of 666 web page below:

666 = Number of the Beast

William J. Clinton has the number of the Beast [1]

"This calls for wisdom: let anyone with understanding calculate the **number of the beast**, for it is **the number of a man**. Its number is **six hundred sixty-six**." (Revelation 13:18) Thus the number of the Beast is the number of a man, not a system, not money, not a computer, not a title, not anything but the number of a male human being. Each letter in Hebrew (except vowels) or Greek has a numerical value.

The official name and signature of the president of the United States is: William J. Clinton
But you think, he cannot be since he is not supernatural or ...

William J. Clinton's name = 666 in Hebrew and Greek
even though the numerical value of letters is different in each language

In Hebrew, William J. Clinton = 666					In Greek, William J. Clinton = 666				
English	Hebrew	Hebrew Name	Transliteration and/or Pronunciation	Num. Value	English	Greek	Greek Name	Transliteration and/or Pronunciation	Num. Value
W =	ו	Waw	W	6	W =	ς	Digamma	W	6
i =			n/a	0	i =	ι	Iota	i	10
l =	ל	Lamed	L	30	l =	λ	Lambda	L	30
l =	ל	Lamed	L	30	l =	λ	Lamdba	L	30
i =			n/a	0	i =	ι	Iota	i	10
a =			n/a	0	a =	α	Alpha	closed vowel	0
m =	מ	Mem	M	40	m =	μ	Mu	M	40
J =	י	Yod	Y (J)	10	J =	ι	Iota	i (J or y)	10
C =	כ	Kaph	K	20	C =	κ	Kappa	K	20
l =	ל	Lamed	L	30	l =	λ	Lambda	L	30
i =			n/a		i =	ι	Iota	i	10
n =	נ	Nun	N	50	n =	ν	Nu	N	50
t =	ת	Taw	T	400	t =	τ	Tau	T	300
o =			n/a		o =	ο	Omicron	O	70
n =	נ	Nun	N	50	n =	ν	Nu	N	50
			=	666				=	666

Numerical Values
Click on "Num. Value" above the numerical value column to see source of information. Click here for more information.
Notes: Hebrew had no written vowel letters; The English letter "J" in such names as "Jesus" or "Jehovah" or "Jerusalem" is transliterated to a Hebrew "y" or vice versa; this information first calculated/published by WRD to the web on Dec 8-9, 1997

This table and other links of interest can be found: http://becomingone.org/666.htm

Numerical Values
Click on "Num. Value" above the numerical value column to see source of information. Click here for more information.
Notes: The old Greek letter digamma had the sound of an English "w." (see Dict.) English names beginning with "J" such as "Jesus" or "Jesse" or "Judah" are transliterated to an "I", the Greek letter Iota. First calculated on Aug 26, 1998 by WRD; published on Aug 29, 1998 by WRD

http://becomingone.org/666/   6/22/00 11:09:45 AM

These two pages are an example of how to calculate the number of the Beast man; this is in no way saying Clinton was or is the Beast man. As of today we do not know who the Beast man is.

INFORMATION ON THE BEAST AND HIS NAME

666 = Number of the Beast

Note: Click on "Num. Value" above either the Hebrew or Greek column to see the source for numerical value.

Footnotes:

1. Although having the number of the Beast does not in itself mean Clinton is/will be the Beast-man or the last anti-Christ, the Beast will have the number six hundred sixty-six (666) when he comes, and will be a great liar. [Dan 8:25; "When he lies, he speaks his native language, for he is a liar and the father of lies." (John 8:44)] No leader has had a name that equals six hundred sixty-six (666) in **both** languages of the Bible, Hebrew and Greek. This may be "impossible," since both languages have different numerical-letter values, but Clinton has the number nevertheless. Will Clinton become the Beast-man of Revelation? If he joins himself to a ten-nation group, he will be on his way to fulfilling prophecy. Do not be fooled by others, English and most languages do **not** have numerical values for each letter, but Hebrew (except its vowels) and Greek do, and a few letters of Latin do.

False Argument: Clinton is not supernatural therefore he is not or will not become the Beast-man (or the last anti-Christ). This argument is based on a misreading of scripture. Satan and his children do not have power to perform real miracles; all Satan's miracles are false or faked. Satan only has power over death, evil, and lying. The real Beast-man will blaspheme, lie, cheat, kill, deceive, and fake being "good."

"C" = "k" sound. In English, the sound of "c" is the sound of "k" before all consonants. (*Webster's New World Dictionary*)

"J" & "Y": The letter "J" in most proper names starting with "J" in English Bibles is transliterated from the Hebrew "Y". The English letter "J" in such names as "Jesus" or "Jehovah" or "Jerusalem" is transliterated to a Hebrew, "y" or vice versa;

No Vowels: Hebrew had no written vowel letters, and thus no numerical value for them.

Digamma or stigma: This old Greek letter had the sound of an English "w." (see the 1966 *Unabridged Edition of the Random House Dictionary*, 1966, under the letter "W" and under "digamma." See also A.T. Robertson in his *A Grammar of the Greek New Testament*, p. 209; *The Exact Sciences in Antiquity*, O. Neugebauer, p. 25 under "ad9") This Greek letter was dropped and is no longer used except in charts that represent the numerical values of Greek letters. See "beast links" below for more detail.

Closed Vowel: "A *diphthong* is a combination of two vowels in a single syllable. The second letter of a diphthong is always a close[d] vowel. The first letter is always an open vowel except in the case of *yi* [*ypsilon, iota*]." (*New Testament Greek for Beginners*, MacMillan-1945, by J. Gresham Machen) "The Greeks resisted the idea of one vowel following another ... When the verb starts with a vowel, instead of adding another vowel [to change its "tense"], that vowel becomes long." (Edward W. Goodrich, *Hebrew and Greek*)

Iota sometimes has the force of the consonants *j* (*y*). (*A Grammar of the Greek New Testament In light of Historical Research*, by A.T. Robertson, p.198.) English names beginning with "J" such as "Jesus" or "Jesse" or "Judah" are transliterated into an "I", the Greek letter *iota*.

See more about calculating the number and other attempts in history to find the one with the number.
See our original table as published on December 8, 1997.

Other Beast Links:

Character of the Beast | Check List to identify the Beast | Beast-man (last anti-Christ) | Ten Nation Beast | Beast Chart | God's Name versus the Beast's Name | Beast of Revelation and Daniel

Copyright ©1997, 1998 by Walter R. Dolen

Home Page

The following taken from *Gesenius' Hebrew Grammar*, Edited by E. Kautzsch and A.E. Cowley, from page 26:

26   *The Individual Sounds and Characters*   [§ 5 b]

b   2. The Alphabet consists, like all Semitic alphabets, solely of consonants, twenty-two in number, some of which, however, have also a kind of vocalic power (§ 7 b). The following Table shows their form, names, pronunciation, and numerical value (see *k*):—

FORM.	NAME.	PRONUNCIATION.	NUMERICAL VALUE.
א	ʼĀlĕph	ʼ *spiritus lenis*	1
ב	Bêth	b (bh, but see § 6 n)	2
ג	Gîmĕl (Gîml)	g (gh, ,, ,, ,,)	3
ד	Dālĕth	d (dh, ,, ,, ,,)	4
ה	Hē	h	5
ו	Wāw (Wāu)	w (u)[1]	6
ז	Záyin	z, as in English (soft *s*)	7
ח	Ḥêth	ḥ, a strong guttural	8
ט	Ṭêth	ṭ, emphatic t	9
י	Yôd	y (i)[1]	10
כ, final ך	Kaph	k (kh, but see § 6 n)	20
ל	Lāmĕd	l	30
מ, final ם	Mêm	m	40
נ, final ן	Nûn	n	50
ס	Sāmĕkh	s	60
ע	ʽAyin	ʽ a peculiar guttural (see below)	70
פ, final ף	Pê	p (f, see § 6 n)	80
צ, final ץ	Ṣādê	ṣ, emphatic s	90
ק	Qôf	q, a strong k[2] formed at the back of the palate	100
ר	Rêš	r	200
שׁ	Šîn	š	} 300
שׂ	Śîn[3]	ś, pronounced sh	
ת	Tāw (Tāu)	t (th, but see § 6 n)	400

[1] Philippi, 'Die Aussprache der semit. Consonanten ו und י,' in *ZDMG.* 1886, p. 639 ff., 1897, p. 66 ff., adduces reasons in detail for the opinion that 'the Semitic ו and י are certainly by usage consonants, although by nature they are vowels, viz. *u* and *i*, and consequently are consonantal vowels'; cf. § 8 m.

[2] As a representation of this sound the Latin *q* is very suitable, since it occupies in the alphabet the place of the Semitic ק (Greek κόππα).

[3] Nestle (*Actes du onzième Congrès ... des Orientalistes*, 1897, iv. 113 ff.) has shown that the original order was שׂ, שׁ.

Following taken from the University of Chicago's *A Manual of Style*:

NUMBERS

9.118 Numbers, when not written out, are represented in ordinary Greek text by the letters of the alphabet, supplemented by three special characters, ϛ' = 6, ϙ' = 90, and ϡ' = 900. The diacritical mark resembling an acute accent distinguishes the letters as numerals, and is added to a sign standing alone or to the last sign in a series, 111 = ρια'. For thousands, the foregoing signs are used with a different diacritical mark: ͵α = 1,000, ͵αρια' = 1,111, ͵βσκβ' = 2,222. The entire series of Greek numerals is shown in table 9.3.

Editing and Composing Classical Greek / 9.124

9.121 If a consonant is doubled, or if a mute is followed by its corresponding aspirate, divide after the first consonant:

    ἀπ-φύs   Ἀτ-θίs   Βακ-χίs   ἔγ-χοs

9.122 If the combination of two or more consonants begins with a liquid (λ, ρ) or a nasal (μ, ν), divide after the liquid or nasal:

    ἄλ-σοs   ἀρ-γόs   ἄμ-φω   ἄν-θοs

    (But, before μν: μέ-μνημαι)

TABLE 9.3: GREEK NUMERALS

#		#	
1	α'	24	κδ'
2	β'	30	λ'
3	γ'	40	μ'
4	δ'	50	ν'
5	ε'	60	ξ'
6	ϛ'	70	ο'
7	ζ'	80	π'
8	η'	90	ϙ'
9	θ'	100	ρ'
10	ι'	200	σ'
11	ια'	300	τ'
12	ιβ'	400	υ'
13	ιγ'	500	φ'
14	ιδ'	600	χ'
15	ιε'	700	ψ'
16	ιϛ'	800	ω'
17	ιζ'	900	ϡ'
18	ιη'	1,000	͵α
19	ιθ'	2,000	͵β
20	κ'	3,000	͵γ
21	κα'	4,000	͵δ
22	κβ'	5,000	͵ε
23	κγ'		

9.123 The division comes before all other combinations of two or more consonants:

    πρᾶ-γμα   ἀ-κμή   ἀ-φνω   ἔ-τνοs   ἄ-στρον

9.124 Compound words are divided into their original parts; within each part the foregoing rules apply. The most common type of compound word begins with a preposition:

    ἀμφ-   ἀν-   ἀπ-   ὑπ-   ἐξ-έβαλον
    ἀφ-   ἐφ-   ὑφ-   κατ-   καθ-ίστημι

Following taken from "History of Mathematics," by D.E. Smith, pp 51-52

As seen above, the Greeks had twenty-four letters in their common Ionic alphabet, but for a more satisfactory system of numerals they needed twenty-seven letters. They therefore added the three forms F or Ϛ (the old digamma), ϙ or sometimes Ϙ (the Phœnician *koph*), and ⅄² (perhaps the Phœnician

[1] S. Reinach, *loc. cit.*, p. 220.
[2] A modern name for the character is *sampi* (σαν+πι, *san'pi*), suggested because of its resemblance to π in its 15th century form. The form in the 2d century was ⅄, and it may go back to the Ϡ (s), which was used from the 5th to the 2d century B.C. See Roberts, *loc. cit.*, p. 10.

52   READING AND WRITING NUMBERS

shin or tsadé), after which they arranged their system as follows:

Units	A	B	Γ	Δ	E	F	Z	H	Θ
	1	2	3	4	5	6	7	8	9
Tens	I	K	Λ	M	N	Ξ	O	Π	ϙ
	10	20	30	40	50	60	70	80	90
Hundreds	P	Σ	T	Y	Φ	X	Ψ	Ω	⅄
	100	200	300	400	500	600	700	800	900

To distinguish the numerals from letters, a bar was commonly written over each number, as in the case of Ā, although in the Middle Ages the letter was occasionally written as if lying on its side, as in the case of ⋖.

INFORMATION ON THE BEAST AND HIS NAME

Note below Revelation 13:18 pertaining to the <u>man with the number</u> from the following book *Interlinear Literal Translation of the Greek New Testament*, by George Ricker Berry. The Greek texts either had the letters with the numerical values that added up to *six hundred sixty-six* See (1st arrow below), or the Greek **words** for *six hundred sixty-six* written out long hand (see 2nd arrow below).

More on calculating the number of the Beast

pr571» Let me show you how to calculate the number by first using some examples from Ethelbert W. Bullinger in his book, *Numbers in Scripture*, with my comments. The following numbered items are Bullinger's points with my comments after each item:

> **1. Six hundred and sixty six is "the number of a name"** (Rev 13:17-18).
>
> **My Comment:** True, six hundred sixty-six is the number of the name of the Beast. Bullinger later mistakenly speaks about 6s or three 6s. In the Greek texts it did **not** have three symbols each with the value of six (6+6+6=18), but it had either the letters with the numerical value that added up to *six hundred sixty-six* or the Greek **words** for *six hundred sixty-six* written out long hand (See previous page).

> **2. When the *name* of Antichrist is known** its gematria [numerical value] will doubtless be found to be the number 666.
>
> **My Comment:** Correct, if he means six hundred sixty-six and not just three consecutive 6s in a row. He misuses the word "gematria" here.

3. Many names may be found, the numerical value of whose letters amount to 666. We have a list of about forty such *gematria*. Most of them are ridiculous, inasmuch as instead of the *gematria* being confined to Hebrew and Greek (which have no Arabic [1, 2, 3, ...] or other special signs for *figures*), the principle is extended to names in English, French, and other modern languages, on the assumption that they would have been spelt in exactly the same way; whereas we know that names both of persons and places are not simply transliterated in various languages.* It is absurd therefore to attempt to take words from the modern European languages which use Arabic figures.

> (*Take "Venice". This is the English spelling. But the French is Venise; the German is Venedig; while the Italian is Venezia.)

My Comment: Bullinger uses the word "gematria" here instead of "numerical value." But since "gematria" has to do with cultism, we do not use that term in our papers, since the Bible's truth is not found using cultish systems. What Bullinger seems to do is superficially limit the Beast-man to being either a Hebrew or a Greek while mixing up the principle of transliteration. What Revelation says is that you can calculate or add up the number of the Beast's name (Rev 13:18). The two main languages of the Bible are Hebrew and Greek. In both Hebrew and Greek, letters have numerical values (See Heb-Gk or below). It would make sense to limit the figuring of the number of the name to the Hebrew or Grecian numerical values. And it would make sense that if a person has an English name, that you would transliterate that English name to Hebrew or Greek, and then use the respective Hebrew or Greek numerical values for each transliterated name to figure or calculate the number of the name. You don't transliterate an English name into French and then use the French letters to again transliterate it into Hebrew or Greek, but you transliterate it directly from its own language into Hebrew or Greek. Otherwise it would be pointless or even deceptive. And you don't prove anything by saying that you can transliterate a city's name into many different spellings. This is irrelevant. First of all, we are looking for a name of a male person not a city's name. Second, we use the way the person spells his own name, especially if it is some kind of official name or legal name. We use the man with the number's official and legal name (as spelled by him) as a head of state. We are not going to superficially limit the Beast-man's identity to only those with Hebrew or Greek names, and we are not going to be distracted by the irrelevant fact that any name will appear with different spellings in different languages or cultures.

> **4. Gematria is not *a means* by which the name is to be discovered**; but it will be a *test* and a *proof* by which the name may be identified after the person is revealed.
>
> **My Comment:** We identify the Beast-man by the number of his name, by his character, and by his connection to a ten nation league.

> **5. But 666 was the *secret symbol* of the ancient pagan mysteries** connected with the worship of the Devil. It is today the secret connecting link between those ancient mysteries and their modern revival in Spiritualism, Theosophy, etc.
>
> **My Comment:** I don't know if this is true, but it is not important anyway since the Bible manifests to us that the number of the Beast (six hundred sixty-six) identifies the Beast, and that this Beast-man is a shadow of Satan who speaks for Satan the Dragon.

Method at Least 18 Centuries Old

pr572» The method we use to figure the number of the man with the number is at least 18 centuries old. The oldest record we have of anyone explaining the correct method of calculating the number was from Irenaeus, Bishop of Lyons, and a so-called father of the Church. He wrote over 18 centuries ago. The following is from Irenaeus' Against Heresies, Book 5, chapter 30, paragraph 1:

> "Such, then, being the state of the case, and this number being found in all the most approved and ancient copies(3) [of the Apocalypse], and those men who saw John face to face bearing their testimony [to it]; while reason also leads us to conclude that the number of the name of the beast, [if reckoned] according to the Greek mode of calculation by the [value of] the letters contained in it, will amount to six hundred and sixty and six;"
>
> [St. Irenaeus biography online at the New Advent Catholic Supersite. He lived in the second century.]

Irenaeus wasn't speaking about a street address, or a number of a law, or the number of letters in some person's name. He said you calculated the value of the name by adding up the value of each letter in the name. And the amount you must come to is six hundred and sixty-six, not 18 (6 + 6 + 6).

Evidence of Alphabetic-Number Systems goes Back to BC

Hebrew's system can be traced back to at least 2nd Century BC

pr573» Gesenius, in his *Hebrew Grammar*, in § 5k, tells us that there is evidence that the consonants were used as numerical signs back to the second century BC, because this usage was found on Maccabean coins and consonants were also commonly employed for marking the numbers of chapters and verses in editions of the Bible. Also you will find evidence of Hebrew letters having numerical value in such books as, *History of Mathematics*, by D.E. Smith (pp. 53).

Greek's system can be traced back to about the 8th century BC

pr574» You can find some historical evidence for the Greek alphabet being used as numbers in such books as, *History of Mathematics*, by D.E. Smith (pp. 49-53), and in *The Exact Sciences in Antiquity*, by O. Neugebauer (pp. 9-11), and *A Manual of Style*, 12th Edition, by University of Chicago Press (pp. 232-233). According to Dr. Neugebauer, "Considerations of this type [the method Neugebauer wrote about] allow us to date the origin of the Greek alphabetic number system to about the 8th century B.C."

No English system exists

The English language does not have numerical values for its letters. You don't find it in English dictionaries, you don't find it in English grammars, you don't find it taught in public schools, but you will find it on the Internet and among those who have some religious or occult need to have it so, thus they have made it up out of thin air.

pr575» **To summarize:** We calculate the number of the Beast's name by transliteration. That is, we take the man's name as spelled in his own country, transliterate it to Hebrew or Greek, and then calculate the numerical value of the name. We calculate the number of the man with the number using the numerical values for each letter.

Antichrist exists in the last 3 ½ Years

Not Seven Years

pr576» Concerning the seventieth week of Daniel's prophecy, there are about as many interpretations as there are theologians. Some say the Beast will make an agreement for seven years and at the end of the of period the Beast will be destroyed. But the scripture does not speak of making a new agreement, but of strengthening a covenant or agreement. (Of course the Beast-man may make a seven year agreement, but this does not fulfill scripture, since the scripture was speaking about confirming a covenant.) Some have the Beast ruling for seven years, but the scripture speaks of only 42 months or 3 ½ years (Rev 13:5). The fact remains that the Antichrist rules as the Beast in the last 3 ½ years. The Beast could well rule as something else besides the Beast-man before the 3 ½ year period, but the Bible is only telling us about the Beast-man in his 3 ½ year rulership as the Beast.

> "Dan 9:26 After the sixty-two weeks, an anointed one shall be cut off and shall have nothing, and the troops of the prince who is to come shall destroy the city and the sanctuary. Its end shall come with a flood, and to the end there shall be war. Desolations are decreed. 27 He shall make a strong covenant with many for one week, and for half of the week he shall make sacrifice and offering cease; and in their place shall be an abomination that desolates, until the decreed end is poured out upon the desolator" (Dan 9:26-27).

pr577» To many today the last Antichrist will make a seven year agreement in the end of time, just before Christ returns. Others believe these seven years pertain to the Messiah. Such books as the *The Millennium Bible* by William E. Biederwolf show the various interpretations of Daniel 9:24-27 over the years (see below). As Biederwolf's book showed, in the past some attributed the seven years to the last Antichrist; others attributed the seven years to Christ. In the Prophecy Papers we explain our position on the seven year period mentioned in Daniel 9:24-27. This scripture refers to the Messiah and the Anti-Messiah. We attribute these verses to both the Messiah and the last Anti-Messiah for reasons also mentioned in the God Papers.

pr578» As shown in the Prophecy Papers in the last 3 ½ years the Beast will rule and the two witnesses will teach. The Messiah was to confirm the covenant for seven years but he was cut off in the middle of the seven years, after the first 3 ½ years. The two witnesses will finish this confirmation of the covenant during the last 3 ½ years of the seven year period. The Beast-man may make an agreement at the start of the last 3 ½ year period. But after the 3 ½ year period, the Beast-man will be cut off and the real Messiah will return to take power. Thus the Beast will rule for only 3 ½ years (42 months, Rev 13:5) not seven years. This 3 ½ year period is the period the two witnesses will teach (Rev 11:2). The last 3 ½ years is the 1290/1260 day period mentioned in the book of Daniel and the book of Revelation (PR2).

For your information the following is from The Millennium Bible (*Second Coming Bible*) by William E. Biederwolf (ex President of Lake School of Theology):

DANIEL

destruction of Jerusalem by the Romans. (Au. Pu. Rei. Hav. and the majority of the older orthodox school.)

3. Those who give it an eschatological meaning directly, the periods of time being taken symbolically,—seven weeks till Christ; sixty-two weeks till the apostacy of the times of the Antichrist, and one week (divided into two times three and one-half), the rise and fall of Antichrist. (K. Kl. Ley.)

"*Seven weeks, and three-score and two weeks*",—With very few exceptions expositors take these two periods together, making sixty-nine weeks or 483 years. If you separate them you leave the last clause without any governing preposition. The fact that the sixty-two weeks are repeated in the next verse with the article "*the*" does not make them any more of an independent period than they otherwise would be, coming after the seven weeks. The abrupt pause before "*it shall be built*", etc., is just what you would expect, being a resumption of the former statement that Jerusalem should be rebuilt. Neither is there sufficient evidence, as Zoeckler claims, for believing that the writer wants to make the building commence at the beginning of the sixty-two weeks. But we would expect the building to begin at once, at the beginning of the seven weeks (forty-nine years) for this was the very *terminus a quo* of the entire prophecy. Then the forty-nine years were after all historically the building period.

The expositors are conveniently divided into Messianic and anti-Messianic.

I. THE ANTI-MESSIANIC.
  1. The destructive rationalistic class:
     (a) Daniel made a prediction never fulfilled. (Eckermann.)
     (b) Verses 25-27 are a gloss of some later rabbi. (Lowenheim.)
     (c) The weeks are ordinary weeks (490 days) and extend from the time of the vision to the time of Cyrus.
  2. The more considerate class, who as a rule refer the fulfillment of the prophecy to the time of Antiochus Epiphanes. Of a score of interpretations we give a few, all of which break down historically.
     (a) Zoeckler and Farrar start with Jeremiah's prophecy and make the "*anointed one*" to be Cyrus at the end of seven weeks. But Cyrus became king and issued his edict B. C. 536. They make the "*anointed one cut off*" in verse 26 to be Onias III. who was murdered B. C. 171. Count back from B. C. 171 and the Cyrus date is missed sixty-nine years and the Jeremiah prophecy date as many.
     It misses the dates of the four decrees on an average of 150 years.
     Keil, arguing against starting with the prophecy of Jeremiah, well says, "All such references to Jeremiah are excluded by the fact that the angel names the commandment for the restoration of Jerusalem as the *terminus a quo* (the starting point) for the seventy weeks and could thus only mean a word of God, the going forth of which was somewhere determined or could be determined just as the appearance of the

DANIEL

anointed prince is named as the termination of the seventy weeks."

(b) Bleek and Maurice start with the prophecy of Jeremiah but refer the *"anointed one cut off"* to Philopator (Seleucis IV). But heathen kings can scarcely be said to be anointed. However Philapator was murdered B. C. 176 and counting back 483 years (seven weeks plus sixty-two weeks), we have B. C. 659, missing the Jeremiah dates by sixty years.

(c) Bertholdt makes the *"anointed one cut off"* refer to Alexander the Great. But he died B. C. 323 and no count can even approximate the Cyrus date (B. C. 536) or the Destruction of Jerusalem date (B. C. 588) with which he begins.

(d) Ewald starts with destruction of Jerusalem (B. C. 588) and makes the *"anointed one cut off"* to be Philopator, B. C. 175. But there is a shortage here of seventy years. Ewald says it was formerly in the text but has been lost.

(e) Hitzig and Lengerke start with the B. C. 588 date for both the forty-nine years and the 434 years (seven weeks and sixty-two weeks), paralleling the periods. Hitzig makes the *"cutting off"* refer to Onias III, B. C. 171, but counting back 434 years brings us to B. C. 605. Lengerke makes the *"cutting off"* refer to Philopator, B. C. 175, but counting back 434 years we have B. C. 609, thus missing the B. C. 588 date in both cases. *It would seem that historically the reference of this vision to the time of Antiochus Epiphanes is hardly justifiable.*

II. THE MESSIANIC.

1. Those who hold the vision to be only typically Messianic:

   (a) Kranichfeld reckons the forty-nine years from the destruction of Jerusalem, B. C. 588, which brings him to Cyrus, the anointed prince, which he takes to be B. C. 539, and from here he reckons 434 years to Christ, missing it 100 years, which period he says was unnoticed by the prophet in harmony with the law of perspective vision.

   (b) Some make the *"anointed one cut off"* to be Onias III (typical of Christ) from whose death, B. C. 171, they count back 434 years (sixty-two weeks) to B. C. 605. They then add one week (seven years) to B. C. 171, bringing it to B. C. 164, and then they transpose the seven weeks (forty-nine years) and add them to B. C. 164, or rather leave a hiatus between B. C. 164 and the first preaching of the Gospel in the time of Christ and the Apostles, from which latter time the seven weeks, a mystical period, begins and lasts until the second coming and judgment of the world. (Fu. Del. Hof. and Wies.)

2. Those who hold that the vision is directly Messianic:

   (1) Christian expositors of older times.

   (a) Africanus reckons from the twentieth year of Artaxerxes (B. C. 445) to the death of Christ. (He reckoned on

DANIEL

Jewish lunar years, making only 465 solar years.) (Jer. Chr. Aug. Isi. Bed. Theo.)

(b) Hippolytus reckons from the decree of Cyrus, B. C. 536, sixty-nine weeks (483 years) to the birth of Christ, making the periods mystical, and refers the last mystical week to the time of the Antichrist in the final end.

(2) Christian expositors of recent times.

(a) The majority reckon from the decree of Artaxerxes in the twentieth year of his reign, B. C. 445 (Neh. 1.1; 2.1) and count 483 years to Christ's baptism, A. D. 28. To get this latter date they make the twentieth year of Artaxerxes B. C. 455 instead of B. C. 445. (Hav. Hen. Der. Less. Scholl.)

(b) Klieforth reckons from the edict of Cyrus, B. C. 536, and counts sixty-nine mystical weeks to the birth of Christ.

(c) Some reckon from the decree given by Artaxerxes in the seventh year of his reign, B. C. 457 (Ez. 7.8) and count 483 years to Christ's baptism in A. D. 26. (Pu. Au. Bla.)

(d) Some take the reckoning of Africanus as above. B. C. 445 to A. D. 32 is 476 years, or 173,740 days. This plus 116 days for leap years makes 173,856 days. The exact date of the crucifixion was April 6 (A. D. 32), and the exact date of the edict was March 14 (B. C. 445), giving twenty-four days more, which added to 173,856 makes 173,880 days. This is exactly 483 times 360 days (a prophetic year). (Gab. *Sir Robert Anderson.*)

In harmony with the direct Messianic interpretation of the prophecy "the *anointed one*" of verses 25 and 26 are the same person, i. e., Christ. (K. Pu. Au. Kl. Hav. Hen. Hof. Del.)

Of those who make the baptism of Christ the *terminus ad quem* of the sixty-nine weeks, most of the older and many of the later expositors make the "one week" (the last week—seven years) follow immediately, the crucifixion (the "cutting off") taking place at the end of three and one-half years (in the midst of the week) which put an end to O. T. sacrifices. The rest of the last week they leave indefinitely with no precise chronological determination, referring it to the founding of Christianity through the preaching of the Apostles.

Of those who make the crucifixion the *terminus ad quem*, some add next a hiatus of 2000 years and make the last week the period of the final Antichrist. (Gab. Sco. Mor. Tor. Mack.)

Klieforth, who holds the mystical theory, reckons the seven weeks from the edict of Cyrus to the advent of Christ, the sixty-two weeks from the advent of Christ to the Antichrist week which is the last week, the "one week".

"*built again even in troublous times*"—This occurs under Nehemiah

221

DANIEL

and Ezra, the enemies of God's people causing them much trouble. Historically the reconstruction period cannot be extended throughout the entire sixty-nine weeks, as some (F. Zo.) have interpreted. The temple was built as early as B. C. 515. (See Neh. 6.15 and Ez. 6.15.)

"The seventy weeks are divided into seven (forty-nine years); sixty-two (434 years), and one (seven years). In the seven weeks (forty-nine years) Jerusalem was to be rebuilt 'in troublous times'. This was fulfilled as Ezra and Nehemiah record. Sixty-two weeks (434 years) thereafter Messiah was to come. This was fulfilled in the birth of Christ." (Scofield.)

Ver. 26. *"and shall have nothing"*,—All Hebrew scholars agree with this reading. The meaning is that He shall then possess nothing; He shall not possess the kingdom or be the acknowledged King; He shall be deprived of everything. (C. Eb. Kr. Kl. Ju. Gab. Mor. Sco.)

The following are some of the numerous other renderings:
1. "not for himself", i. e., not for His own sake will Christ die, but for humanity. (V. Ros. Wil. Hav. Bul)
2. "shall have no adherents". (Au. Gro. Marginal reading.)
3. "there shall be none to help him". (Vat.)
4. "there shall be nothing to Him", i. e., the city, the sanctuary and the Jewish people shall be His no more. (Pu.)
5. "it shall not be to him", i. e., His place as Messiah—He has lost it. (K.)

Hengstenberg adopts the fourth reading but makes it mean that the earthly kingdom for which the Jews had hoped shall come to nought.

All of the above five renderings together with that of our text refer *"the anointed one"* to Christ. Those who refer *"the anointed one"* to Onias or Philopator or Alexander translate, "he shall have no successor".

"the prince that shall come",—To whom does this refer? (See explanation under verse 27.)

"and the end thereof", etc.,—According to our text this must be taken as the end of the city and the sanctuary (F. Au. Del. Hav. Hit. Gei. Len.), but it may quite as properly be rendered *"and his end"* and refer to the prince that shall come, the final Antichrist. (K. Kl. Kr. Zo. Hof. Wie. Gab. Sco. Mor. Tor. Treg.)

"and even unto the end shall be war",—Unto what end?
1. The end of the city and the sanctuary. (Au. Hav.)
2. The end of the prince, i. e., until he is destroyed. (Wie. as well as all who take the prince to be Antiochus Epiphanes.)
3. The end of all things. (Kl.)
4. The end generally, i. e., the end of the last week, whether it be viewed as then in progress or as a week yet to come in the future. (K. Hen. Len. Hit.) This last is without doubt correct.

Scofield says, "The crucifixion is the first event of verse 26. The second event is the destruction of the city, fulfilled A. D. 70. Then "unto the end", a period not fixed, but which has already lasted 2000 years. To Daniel was revealed only that wars and desolations should continue (Matt. 24.6-14). The New Testament reveals that which was hidden from the Old Testament prophets (Eph. 3.1-10) that during this period should

222

DANIEL

be accomplished the mysteries of the kingdom of heaven (Matt. 13.1-50), and the outcalling of the Church (Rom. 11.25). When the Church age will end and the 'seventieth week' begin, is nowhere revealed. Its duration can be but seven years; to make it more violates the principle of interpretation already confirmed by fulfillment."

"desolations are determined",—According to our text these words are to be joined to the preceding clause with a semicolon and are to be taken as an explanatory clause. (Kl. Kr.)

Many prefer the reading of the Authorized Version, "and unto the end of the war desolations are determined". (So. Fu. Ew. Hof. Ros. Vul. Sept.)

Another reading and one which we prefer is, *"and even unto the end shall be war, the determined desolations"*. The "determined desolations" are by this rendering taken in apposition with the word "war". (Au. Hit. Wie. Mau. Len. Hav.)

"determined",—i. e., decreed by God.

Ver. 27. *"make a firm covenant"*,—Many authorities take the word *"week"* to be the subject of this sentence, and explain the expression as follows:

1. The one week shall make the Old Testament covenant (adherence to the faith in Jehovah and to the theocratic law) hard (grievous) for many. (Hit.)
2. The one week shall confirm many in the covenant through tribulation and the trial of their faith. (Hof. Ros.)
3. The one week shall confirm a covenant to many through the seductive arts of Antiochus Epiphanes. (Len.)
4. The one week (especially by the death of the Messiah) shall lead to the conclusion of a new, strong and firm covenant with many. (Au. Hen. Hav.)

We prefer with our text to make *"he"* the subject of the sentence.

It would seem that *"he"* here must refer to the same person as does *"the prince that shall come"* in verse 26, and the reference in verse 26 must therefore be determined by the content of this verse 27 as well as by its own content.

It would seem evident therefore that *"the prince that shall come"* and the *"he"* cannot refer to Antiochus Epiphanes (Zo. Fa.), because, as Strong remarks, "the language was not fulfilled in any sense by Antiochus who aimed at the suppression of Jehovah's worship and virtually left the city and the sanctuary untouched"; nor can it refer to Christ, the Messiah (F. C. Rob. Wil. Str.) because it was not His people (verse 26) that destroyed the city and the sanctuary, nor is it without extreme difficulty that we can think of Him making a covenant for a week (seven years). His was an *"everlasting covenant"*. Once more, it can hardly refer to Titus (F. Bl. Ew. Len. Jos. Str.), because while verse 26 might be true of him, verse 27 can in no sense be said to be so. It would seem therefore that the reference in both verses must be to the Antichrist who is yet to come. (K. Kl. Kr. Sco. Mor. Gab. Wie. Hof.)

"many",—In the original the article *"the"* is found. Zoeckler and his class of interpreters make these to be the apostatizing Jews in the time

DANIEL

of Antiochus Epiphanes, but Keil well remarks that the mass of the Jews did not apostatize in his time, which this expression, by the use of the definite article *"the"* seems to make clear was the case. The reference, of course, consistent with our former explanation must refer to the Jews of the times of the final Antichrist. As Keil says, "That ungodly prince shall impose upon the mass of the people a strong covenant that they should follow him and give themselves to him as their God."

It must be noticed that, if *"the prince that shall come"* be taken as the Antichrist, it is not the Antichrist who destroys *"the city and the sanctuary"*, but the people of the Antichrist; that is, as Morgan says, "the people who are guided by the same principle of government that eventually characterizes the rule of the Antichrist".

Now, according to our explanation thus far, two distinct periods of time are referred to in the passages immediately before us. If we translate with our text, *"the end thereof"* in verse 26, and refer this to the end of the city and the sanctuary, then the end time in which the final Antichrist appears begins with verse 27, but if with Morgan and others we translate *"his end"* in verse 26, and refer this to the Antichrist himself, then the prophecy passes immediately after the semicolon on to events at the close of this age, when the Prince himself, the final Antichrist, shall be manifested. Then, as Morgan says, "The semicolon of Daniel is the coma which follows Isaiah's 'acceptable year of the Lord'."

"and in the midst of the week he", etc.,—The subject is of course the same throughout the verse. Says Scofield, "He will covenant with the Jews to restore their temple sacrifices for one week (seven years), but in the middle of that time, after three and one-half years, he will break the covenant and fulfill Dan. 12.11; II Thess. 2.3,4. Between the sixty-ninth week, after which the Messiah was cut off, and the seventieth week, within which the 'little horn' of Dan. 7 will run his awful course, intervenes this entire Church-age. Verse 27 deals with the last three and one-half years of the seven, which are identical with the 'great Tribulation', 'the time of trouble'; the hour of temptation; Matt. 24.15-28; Dan. 12.1; Rev. 3.10."

Those who refer the subject of this verse to Christ, the Messiah, maintain that the reference is to His perfect expiatory sacrifice on the Cross whereby He did forever away with the Levitical sacrifices. (F. Au, Str. Hav. Hen.) These authorities maintain, therefore, that half of Daniel's missing week has already gone in the three and one-half years of our Lord's earthly ministry. But the clear and distinct division of *"weeks"* in verses 26 and 27 rather argue against this view and lead us to believe that the whole of the missing week is still in the future.

"upon the wing of abominations shall one come that maketh desolate",—*"abominations"* mean "horrible things" and from the religious standpoint, "abominable idolatries".

"wing" is a literal translation. The word is equivalent to "screen, protection, covering, roof". It carries in it the idea of extension and so may be applied to the wing of a building. Some render it "pinnacle", but Bleek and Keil argue rather conclusively that the idea of extension which inheres in the word is always extension horizontally and never vertically. The idea of "pinnacle" may be gotten from one of its primal meanings.

DANIEL

i. e., "roof", and so by the rule of Synecdoche (a part being taken for the whole) the "wing" (extension) or the "roof" (pinnacle) may be applied to the entire building and so read "temple". The ancient versions all agreed in this. The Maccabean book, the most ancient translation of the words, so renders, as do also the most ancient translations, the Septuagint and the Vulgate. The literal reading would then be, "Upon the temple shall come the abominations of the one that maketh desolate", or "Upon the temple shall come the abominations of desolation", according as we translate "desolator" or "desolation". If the rendering "desolation" be adopted, this word would be considered as an apposition to "abominations", it being really a genitive of description.

Others translate, "Under the pinnacle of abominations comes the one temple where abominable idols were placed." (D. Oe. Os. Bul. Ges.) The last of these authorities translates with the margin of the Authorized Version, "On the pinnacle (of the temple) are the abominations of the one that maketh desolate". Jesus said, "When you see the abomination of desolation spoken of by Daniel". He quoted from the Vulgate and He also knew Hebrew and this lends pretty good evidence that the Vulgate translation is a good one. It would appear, however, that the only grammatically possible translation is that of our text.

Others translate, "Upon the pinnacle of abominations comes the one that maketh desolate". (K. Kl. Kr. Mau. Rei. Hen. Len.) The first three of these authorities makes the desolator to be the future Antichrist coming on the wings of idolatry, the power that moves and carries him over the earth. Still others translate, "On account of the pinnacle, or frightful height of abominations there shall come one that maketh desolate", thus giving the moral ground why in God's providence the desolator came. (F. Pu. Au. Eu. Gab.) Gaebelein translates, "On account of the protection of abominations there shall come one who maketh desolate".

Hitzig renders it, "Upon the extreme point of the abominations desolation shall come". This translation is much like that of our text, but by the "extreme point" he means the idol altar put up by Antiochus Epiphanes.

These different translations practically come to the same thing in their meaning; it was because of the idolatrous abominations that the desolator, or desolation, was to come upon the city and the sanctuary.

"even unto the full end",—Zoeckler says the expression for "full end" is an exact reproduction of Isa. 10.23; 28.22, and means "consumption", utter extinction, and he translates the last word of the verse "desolator", referring it to Antiochus Epiphanes. Fausset and Tregellius translate with Zoeckler but while Fausset refers the word to Titus as a type of the final Antichrist, Tregellius refers it to the final Antichrist directly. The word in question, however, is passive and so means "desolate", and means, we presume, the people who are made desolate.

CHAPTER TEN

14 Now I am come to make thee understand what shall befall thy people in the latter days; for the vision is yet for many days.

225

Index

1150 days. . . . . PR 2:18 | Pg 58
1260 days. . . . . PR 2:6 | Pg 46,
                                 PR 7:11 | Pg 133,
                                 PR 11:2 | Pg 156
   3 1/2 years. . . . . PR 11:18 | Pg 172
   two witnesses. . . . . PR 5:10 | Pg 90
1290 Days. . . . . PR 2:17 | Pg 57,
                                 PR 11:2 | Pg 156
1335th Day. . . . . PR 2:18 | Pg 58
144,000. . . . . PR 10:6 | Pg 152
2300 Evenings and Mornings
                                 PR 2:18 | Pg 58
3 1/2 years. . . . . PR 5:10 | Pg 90,
PR 5:15 | Pg 95, PR 6:1 | Pg 115, PR 8:2 |Pg 136

   1260 days. . . . . PR 11:18 | Pg 172
30 Years. . . . . PR 8:8 | Pg 142
390 & 40 Days. . . . . PR 10:3 | Pg 149
40 days. . . . . PR 10:3 | Pg 149
483 years. . . . . PR 5:9 | Pg 89
483 Years or 69 weeks. . . . . . PR 5:9 | Pg 89
666
   666 web page. . . . . PR 11:8 | Pg 162
   and Irenaeus. . . . . . . PR 11:16 | Pg 170
   calculating it. . . . . PR 11:4 | Pg 158
   how to calculate the number
                               PR 11:4 | Pg 158
   man with the number. . . . PR 3:2 | Pg 62
   number of the Beast. . . PR 11:2 | Pg 156
69 weeks. . . . PR 3:5 | Pg 65, PR 5:9 | Pg 89
7 years
   cut in half. . . . . PR 5:10 | Pg 90
70 weeks. . . . PR 3:5 | Pg 65, PR 5:9 | Pg 89
70 years. . . . . PR 5:8 | Pg 88
abomination of desolation. . PR 2:16 | Pg 56,
                                 PR 3:1 | Pg 61
Abraham. . . . . PR 1:2 | Pg 14
Angel and Angels of Revelation
                               PR 5:15 | Pg 95
angels of Revelation. . . . . . . PR 5:15 | Pg 95
anger
   from God. . . . . PR 4:9 | Pg 79
Anger of the Lord. . . . . PR 4:9 | Pg 79
Anointed Ones. . . . . PR 8:3 | Pg 137
   two witnesses. . . . . PR 8:3 | Pg 137
Anti-Christ
   comes in his father's name
                            PR 11:2 | Pg 156
   known as other names. . PR 3:4 | Pg 64
   time of 3 1/2 years. . PR 11:18 | Pg 172

Anti-Christ comes in his Father's name
                        PR 11:2 | Pg 156
Anti-Christ exists in the last 3 ½ Years
                       PR 11:18 | Pg 172
Antitypical John. . . . . PR 10:5 | Pg 151
Aorist Verbs. . . . . PR 5:1 | Pg 81
asleep
   Christians not. . . . . PR 7:8 | Pg 130
atomic weapons
   and Beast-man. . . . . . PR 11:4 | Pg 158
Babylon. . . PR 2:11 | Pg 51, PR 5:6 | Pg 86
   first Beast. . . . . PR 2:11 | Pg 51
Band of Iron and Brass. . . . . . PR 3:8 | Pg 68
  PR 2:1 | Pg 41, PR 3:1 | Pg 61, PR 11:2 |Pg 156
Beast
   as superhuman?. . . . . . PR 11:2 | Pg 156
   end-of-the-age. . . . . . . PR 2:6 | Pg 46,
                            PR 11:4 | Pg 158
   identity of fourth. . . . . . . PR 2:9 | Pg 49
   lying wonders of. . . . . . PR 11:2 | Pg 156
   man. . . . . PR 3:1 | Pg 61
   minds, inside of. . . . . . PR 5:29 | Pg 109
   other names of. . . . . PR 5:6 | Pg 86
   system. . . . . PR 3:1 | Pg 61
   voice of the system. . . . PR 11:4 | Pg 158
Beast Paper. . . . . PR 2:1 | Pg 41
Beast Set Up?
   when. . . . . PR 2:15 | Pg 55
Beast-man. . . . . PR 3:1 | Pg 61
   666 web page. . . . . PR 11:8 | Pg 162
   in the temple. . . . . PR 3:3 | Pg 63
   not a superman. . . . . . . PR 11:2 | Pg 156
   other names for. . . . . PR 3:3 | Pg 63
Beasts
   identification. . . . . PR 2:7 | Pg 47
   identity. . . . . PR 2:9 | Pg 49
Bible
   difficult on purpose?. . . . . PR 4:2 | Pg 72
   interpretation. . . . . PR 5:4 | Pg 84,
                            PR 7:5 | Pg 127
   interpretation of Rev. . . . PR 5:16 | Pg 96
   study, principle of. . . . . . PR 7:1 | Pg 123
Branch. . . . . PR 1:18 | Pg 30
brazen altar
   four horns. . . . . PR 5:22 | Pg 102
Bullinger
   Numbers in Scripture
                          PR 11:14 | Pg 168
Chaldeans
   Ur. . . . . PR 1:22 | Pg 34
Chaldeans Language. . . . . . . PR 1:26 | Pg 38

Christ
- Branch, King, Savior... PR 1:19 | Pg 31
- Came in Father's Name
  .... PR 11:1 | Pg 155
- false-Christ............ PR 3:1 | Pg 61
- mediator............. PR 1:20 | Pg 32
- power, given all....... PR 7:2 | Pg 124
- return, His........... PR 7:1 | Pg 123
- saves mankind......... PR 4:3 | Pg 73

Christ Comes to Save Mankind
.... PR 4:3 | Pg 73

Christ Given All The Power
- knows the date........ PR 7:2 | Pg 124

Christ Is The Stone.......... PR 2:8 | Pg 48
Christ The Mediator........ PR 1:20 | Pg 32
Christ versus Satan......... PR 1:19 | Pg 31
- David versus Saul...... PR 1:19 | Pg 31

Christ: The Branch, The King, The Savior
.... PR 1:19 | Pg 31

Christians
- asleep, not............ PR 7:8 | Pg 130
- know the times........ PR 7:4 | Pg 126
- knowledge, to receive... PR 7:2 | Pg 124
- power, to receive...... PR 7:2 | Pg 124
- secrets known by...... PR 7:3 | Pg 125

Christians Not Asleep....... PR 7:8 | Pg 130

Christians to Receive Knowledge
.... PR 7:2 | Pg 124

Christians to Receive Power
.... PR 7:2 | Pg 124

Christ's Ascension
- two others at.......... PR 8:4 | Pg 138

Church
- hidden secrets......... PR 7:3 | Pg 125
- symbolism.......... PR 5:32 | Pg 112

Church In Symbolism...... PR 5:32 | Pg 112
Church in the 1260 Days..... PR 3:6 | Pg 66

Church Knows Hidden Secrets
.... PR 7:3 | Pg 125

Church of Satan............ PR 5:6 | Pg 86

Conditions
- of promises........... PR 1:17 | Pg 29
- promises............. PR 1:17 | Pg 29

crowns
- seven................ PR 2:4 | Pg 44
- ten.................. PR 2:4 | Pg 44

Cyrus.................... PR 5:7 | Pg 87
Daniel.................... PR 3:8 | Pg 68
- vision, his............ PR 7:4 | Pg 126

Daniel's Vision............ PR 7:4 | Pg 126
David..................... PR 1:7 | Pg 19
David versus Saul.......... PR 1:19 | Pg 31
- Christ versus Satan..... PR 1:19 | Pg 31

day of the Lord............. PR 5:3 | Pg 83
Day of Trouble............ PR 5:13 | Pg 93
Deadly Wound............ PR 2:5 | Pg 45,
            PR 11:3 | Pg 157
- of the Beast.......... PR 11:3 | Pg 157

destruction
- from God?............. PR 4:8 | Pg 78

Destruction Comes From God Himself?
.... PR 4:8 | Pg 78

Ebla tablets................ PR 1:25 | Pg 37

Egypt
- great city............... PR 5:6 | Pg 86

Eighth Head................ PR 2:5 | Pg 45
Eighth Head?................ PR 2:5 | Pg 45
Elijah.................... PR 8:5 | Pg 139
- comes................ PR 8:1 | Pg 135
- witnesses, one of the two
.... PR 8:4 | Pg 138

Elijah is One Witnesses..... PR 8:4 | Pg 138
Elijah will come........... PR 8:1 | Pg 135
Elijah-Ezekiel............. PR 10:3 | Pg 149

end of the times
- feast day............. PR 7:9 | Pg 131

End of the Times on a Feast Day
.... PR 7:9 | Pg 131

end of the world............ PR 7:1 | Pg 123
- Christians know....... PR 7:4 | Pg 126
- feast day............. PR 7:9 | Pg 131
- Sabbath day.......... PR 7:11 | Pg 133
- year?................. PR 7:11 | Pg 133

end time
- Christians know....... PR 7:4 | Pg 126

Ephraim................... PR 1:5 | Pg 17

evil
- none after Kingdom starts
.... PR 5:18 | Pg 98

Ezekiel
- antitypical........... PR 10:2 | Pg 148

Falling Away............. PR 10:1 | Pg 147

false-prophet
- anti-Christ............ PR 3:3 | Pg 63

Father Only Knows the Date?
.... PR 7:1 | Pg 123

feast day
- end of the times........ PR 7:9 | Pg 131

First End-of-the-age Beast.... PR 2:6 | Pg 46
first seal................. PR 5:22 | Pg 102
Forty Days............... PR 10:3 | Pg 149
Four Beasts................ PR 2:2 | Pg 42

Four Beasts = Four Kingdoms
.... PR 2:2 | Pg 42

Four Beasts or Kingdoms..... PR 2:7 | Pg 47

four horns
- brazen altar.......... PR 5:22 | Pg 102

Four Horns of Brazen Altar
.... PR 5:22 | Pg 102

four horses............... PR 5:20 | Pg 100
- four winds........... PR 5:22 | Pg 102

four winds
- four horses.......... PR 5:22 | Pg 102

Four Winds; Four Horses... PR 5:22 | Pg 102
Fourth Beast................ PR 2:9 | Pg 49
- identity............... PR 2:9 | Pg 49

INDEX

gematria. . . . . PR 11:14 | Pg 168
Gentiles
    times of. . . . . PR 7:9 | Pg 131
Goat, Ram
    meaning of. . . . . PR 2:9 | Pg 49
God
    anger. . . . . PR 4:9 | Pg 79
    destruction from. . . . . PR 4:8 | Pg 78
    destuction comes from?. . PR 4:8 | Pg 78
    power over world's kingdoms
    . . . . PR 5:21 | Pg 101
God Repay Their Deeds?. . . . . PR 4:4 | Pg 74
God's Throne. . . . . PR 5:16 | Pg 96
God's wrath
    definition. . . . . PR 4:1 | Pg 71
    outline review. . . . . PR 6:1 | Pg 115
    what is it?. . . . . PR 4:5 | Pg 75
God's Wrath: An Outline. . . . PR 6:1 | Pg 115
God's Power Over the World's Kingdoms
    . . . . PR 5:21 | Pg 101
God's Throne. . . . . PR 5:16 | Pg 96
God's Wrath
    definition. . . . . PR 4:1 | Pg 71
great city. . . . . PR 5:5 | Pg 85
Greece
    third Beast. . . . . PR 2:11 | Pg 51
Greece With Four heads. . . . . PR 2:11 | Pg 51
Greek culture. . . . . PR 2:11 | Pg 51
head
    seventh. . . . . PR 2:3 | Pg 43
heads
    seven. . . . . PR 2:3 | Pg 43
hidden secrets
    known by Christians. . . . PR 7:3 | Pg 125
Horn. . . . . PR 2:12 | Pg 52
    mean & base. . . . . PR 2:12 | Pg 52
Identity of the Fourth Beast
    . . . . PR 2:14 | Pg 54
Image of the Beast. . . . . PR 2:6 | Pg 46
Individual Beast. . . . . PR 3:1 | Pg 61
interpretation
    principle of. . . . . PR 5:6 | Pg 86
Irenaeus
    and 666. . . . . PR 11:16 | Pg 170
Isaac. . . . . PR 1:3 | Pg 15
Israel and Judah
    split. . . . . PR 1:10 | Pg 22
Israel and Judah Split. . . . . . . PR 1:10 | Pg 22
Israel Scattered. . . . . PR 1:10 | Pg 22
Jacob. . . . . PR 1:4 | Pg 16
Jacob (Israel. . . . . PR 1:4 | Pg 16
Jacob's Name Changed. . . . . PR 1:4 | Pg 16
Jeroboam. . . . . PR 1:9 | Pg 21
Jews. . . . . PR 1:20 | Pg 32
Jews and Israel = Christian. . . PR 1:21 | Pg 33
John. . . . . PR 8:8 | Pg 142
    antitypical. . . . . PR 10:5 | Pg 151
Joseph. . . . . PR 1:5 | Pg 17

Joshua. . . . . PR 1:6 | Pg 18
Judah. . . . . PR 1:5 | Pg 17
    scepter. . . . . PR 1:16 | Pg 28
Judah and the Scepter. . . . . . PR 1:16 | Pg 28
Judah Scattered. . . . . PR 1:11 | Pg 23
Judges. . . . . PR 1:6 | Pg 18
judgment
    righteous. . . . . PR 4:3 | Pg 73
King, the
    Christ. . . . . PR 1:19 | Pg 31
Kingdom of Satan. . . . . PR 3:9 | Pg 69
Kingdom of the Enemy. . . . . PR 3:8 | Pg 68
Kings of the North and South
    . . . . PR 2:14 | Pg 54
land of Israel
    whole world. . . . . PR 5:29 | Pg 109
language
    Chaldean. . . . . PR 1:26 | Pg 38
Last Days Before Christ Rules
    . . . . PR 2:6 | Pg 46
last war. . . . . PR 5:12 | Pg 92
    how long?. . . . . PR 5:13 | Pg 93
    pattern. . . . . PR 5:13 | Pg 93
little horn. . . . . PR 3:2 | Pg 62
    unity power. . . . . PR 2:12 | Pg 52
Lord
    day of. . . . . PR 5:3 | Pg 83
love is. . . . . PR 4:2 | Pg 72
man
    Christ saves. . . . . PR 4:3 | Pg 73
man with the number. . . . . . . PR 3:2 | Pg 62
Manasseh. . . . . PR 1:5 | Pg 17
mark of the Beast. . . . . PR 3:6 | Pg 66
Matthew 24:37-51. . . . . PR 7:6 | Pg 128
Mean and Base Horn. . . . . . PR 2:12 | Pg 52
Meaning
    higher. . . . . PR 5:4 | Pg 84
Media-Persia. . . . . PR 2:11 | Pg 51
    second Beast. . . . . PR 2:11 | Pg 51
Metonymical Names
    fo the Beast-man. . . . . . . PR 3:3 | Pg 63
    of Satan's kingdom. . . . . PR 5:6 | Pg 86
metonyms. . . . . PR 5:6 | Pg 86
miracles. . . . . PR 11:2 | Pg 156
Moses. . . . . PR 1:6 | Pg 18, PR 8:5 | Pg 139
    forty days. . . . . PR 10:3 | Pg 149
Moses and Elijah. . . . . PR 8:5 | Pg 139
name
    Anti-Christ comes in the name of 666
    . . . . PR 11:2 | Pg 156
    Christ came in Father's Name
    . . . . PR 11:1 | Pg 155
Name of the Beast. . . . . PR 11:1 | Pg 155
nations
    all destroyed. . . . . PR 5:12 | Pg 92
Nations Destroyed. . . . . PR 5:12 | Pg 92
nations will be gathered. . . . . PR 6:1 | Pg 115
Nebuchadnezzar. . . . . PR 2:8 | Pg 48

Index

until the Stone. . . . . PR 2:8 | Pg 48
New Age.. . . . . PR 7:1 | Pg 123
Nisan
    first of. . . . . PR 7:11 | Pg 133
north and south
    kings. . . . . PR 2:14 | Pg 54
number of the Beast. . . . . . . PR 11:2 | Pg 156
    666. . . . . PR 11:2 | Pg 156
    how to calculate. . . . . . PR 11:4 | Pg 158
Old Wars as Pattern of the Last War
    . . . . PR 5:12 | Pg 92
One-Third. . . . . PR 10:4 | Pg 150
Pattern of the Last War. . . . . . PR 5:13 | Pg 93
plagues. . . . . PR 5:17 | Pg 97
power
    Christians to receive. . . . PR 7:2 | Pg 124
    two witnesses, of the.. . . PR 8:3 | Pg 137
Promises. . . . . PR 1:15 | Pg 27
    conditions. . . . . PR 1:17 | Pg 29
    David, to. . . . . PR 1:16 | Pg 28
    physical.. . . . . PR 1:6 | Pg 18
Promises and Prophecies. . . . . PR 1:1 | Pg 13
Promises That Did and Did Not Come True
    . . . . PR 1:11 | Pg 23
Promises to David. . . . . PR 1:16 | Pg 28
Promises To The Seed. . . . . . PR 1:13 | Pg 25
prophecy
    fulfillment. . . . . PR 1:6 | Pg 18
    Israel. . . . . PR 1:1 | Pg 13
rain
    higher meaning. . . . . PR 8:3 | Pg 137
Ram, Goat.. . . . . PR 2:9 | Pg 49
    meaning of. . . . . PR 2:9 | Pg 49
Righteous Judgment. . . . . PR 4:3 | Pg 73
Roman Empire. . . . . PR 2:12 | Pg 52
Sabbath
    first of Nisan. . . . . PR 7:11 | Pg 133
Sacrifice. . . . . PR 2:15 | Pg 55
    daily. . . . . PR 2:15 | Pg 55
Samuel. . . . . PR 1:6 | Pg 18
Satan versus Christ
    Saul versus David. . . . . . PR 1:19 | Pg 31
Satan's kingdom
    whole world. . . . . PR 5:29 | Pg 109
Saul. PR 1:7 | Pg 19
seal
    fifth. . . . . PR 5:23 | Pg 103
    first. . . . . PR 5:20 | Pg 100, PR 5:22 | Pg 102
    fourth. . . . . PR 5:23 | Pg 103
    seventh. . . . . PR 5:24 | Pg 104
    sixth. . . . . PR 5:23 | Pg 103
    third. . . . . PR 5:22 | Pg 102
seal second. . . . . PR 5:22 | Pg 102
seals. . . . PR 5:17 | Pg 97, PR 5:20 | Pg 100
Second Beast. . . . . PR 2:11 | Pg 51
secrets
    Spirit reveals.. . . . . PR 7:4 | Pg 126
Seed. PR 1:13 | Pg 25
Seed Paper. . . . . PR 1:1 | Pg 13
Seven Churches. . . . . PR 9:1 | Pg 143
Seven Heads. . . . . PR 2:3 | Pg 43
seven years
    cut in half. . . . . PR 5:10 | Pg 90
seventh head
    Beast. . . . . PR 2:3 | Pg 43
    who or what. . . . . PR 2:12 | Pg 52
Seventh Head With Ten Horns
    . . . . PR 2:3 | Pg 43
Seventh Head?. . . . . PR 2:12 | Pg 52
seventh seal. . . . . PR 5:24 | Pg 104
seventh trumpet. . . . . PR 5:30 | Pg 110
seventy weeks
    seventy years. . . . . PR 5:7 | Pg 87
Seventy Years
    antitypical. . . . . PR 5:8 | Pg 88
    antitypical meaning. . . . . PR 5:8 | Pg 88
    seventy weeks. . . . . PR 5:7 | Pg 87
Seventy Years And Seventy Weeks
    . . . . PR 5:7 | Pg 87
siege. . . . . PR 10:3 | Pg 149
Simultaneous Events. . . . . PR 5:2 | Pg 82
six heads. . . . . PR 2:12 | Pg 52
Sodom. . . . . PR 5:6 | Pg 86
Solomon. . . . . PR 1:8 | Pg 20
Spirit
    reveals secrets. . . . . PR 7:4 | Pg 126
Spirit Reveals Hidden Wisdom
    . . . . PR 7:4 | Pg 126
Spiritual False-Prophet, The Anti-Christ
    . . . . PR 3:3 | Pg 63
Spiritual Influence
    Satan's.. . . . . PR 4:6 | Pg 76
Spiritual Jews. . . . . PR 1:20 | Pg 32
Spiritual Promises of God. . . PR 1:13 | Pg 25
Spiritual Seed of Abraham. . . PR 1:20 | Pg 32
Spiritual Virgins. . . . . PR 1:20 | Pg 32
superhuman
    Beast?. . . . . PR 11:2 | Pg 156
System of the Beast. . . . . PR 2:1 | Pg 41
System versus Man-Beast.. . . . PR 3:1 | Pg 61
ten crowns. . . . . PR 2:4 | Pg 44
Ten Horns = Ten Kingdoms or Nations
    . . . . PR 2:4 | Pg 44
Ten to Seven.. . . . . PR 2:4 | Pg 44
Third Beast. . . . . PR 2:11 | Pg 51
three orders. . . . . PR 1:22 | Pg 34
throne
    God's. . . . . PR 5:16 | Pg 96
times
    know by Christians. . . . . PR 7:4 | Pg 126
    last. . . . . PR 7:1 | Pg 123
Times known. . . . . PR 7:4 | Pg 126
times of the Gentiles. . . . . . . PR 7:9 | Pg 131
Tithe of God's People. . . . . . PR 10:4 | Pg 150
Translations

    faulty. . . . . PR 5:1 | Pg 81
tree
    Daniel, of. . . . . PR 3:8 | Pg 68
Tree of Daniel. . . . . PR 3:8 | Pg 68
trumpet
    first. . . . . PR 5:25 | Pg 105
    fourth. . . . . PR 5:26 | Pg 106
    second.. . . . . PR 5:25 | Pg 105
    seventh. . . . . PR 5:30 | Pg 110
    sixth. . . . . PR 5:28 | Pg 108
    third. . . . . PR 5:26 | Pg 106
trumpets. . . . . PR 5:17 | Pg 97,
                                PR 5:24 | Pg 104
two olive trees
    two witnesses. . . . . PR 8:2 | Pg 136
Two Olive Trees / Two Witnesses
    . . . . PR 8:2 | Pg 136
Two Witnesses. . . . . PR 5:10 | Pg 90,
                                PR 8:1 | Pg 135
    1260 days. . . . . PR 5:10 | Pg 90
    Spirit of Moses and Elijah
    . . . . PR 8:5 | Pg 139
Two-thirds of Mankind Cut Off
    . . . . PR 10:5 | Pg 151
Unity Power. . . . . PR 2:13 | Pg 53
Ur of the Chaldeans. . . . . PR 1:22 | Pg 34
verbs
    aorist.. . . . . PR 5:1 | Pg 81
vials. PR 5:30 | Pg 110
vision
    Daniel's.. . . . . PR 7:4 | Pg 126
war
    last. . . . . PR 5:12 | Pg 92
War Last
    how long.. . . . . PR 5:13 | Pg 93
Watch
    all must watch.. . . . . PR 7:8 | Pg 130
    Why. . . . . PR 7:6 | Pg 128
whore. . . . . PR 5:6 | Pg 86
Wicked Servant. . . . . PR 7:7 | Pg 129
wine
    Spiritual meaning. . . . . . . PR 4:6 | Pg 76
    wrath.. . . . . PR 4:6 | Pg 76
wine cup. . . . . PR 5:7 | Pg 87
woman. . . . . PR 5:6 | Pg 86
wonders
    lying wonder of Satan
    . . . . PR 11:2 | Pg 156
world
    end of. . . . . PR 7:1 | Pg 123
wound
    deadly. . . . . PR 11:3 | Pg 157
Wrath All at Once. . . . . PR 5:18 | Pg 98
Wrath: All At Once. . . . . PR 5:14 | Pg 94

Appendix

Beast of Revelation and Daniel

Characteristics of the Individual Beast

Christ's Prediction about the End Time

Details of Tentative Dates

Beast of Revelation and Daniel

By reading the Beast Papers (PP2 & PP3) and by studying the following table/chart/graphic, you will be helped in understanding the great Beast of the Book of Revelation.

Please print this document in "Landscape" mode for better results.

[The following table and chart was taken from charts (15x22 inches) that I created in 1970-71. I pasted clipped verses from the Bible into columns so as to better understand the scriptures pertaining to the Beast of Revelation.]

Seven Headed and Ten Horned Beast Four Great Beasts						
DBY Daniel 2:31 Thou, O king, sawest, and behold, a **great image**. This image was mighty and its brightness excellent; it stood before thee, and its appearance was terrible. 32 This image's head was of fine **gold**, its breast and its arms of silver, its belly and its thighs of **brass**, 33 its legs of **iron**, its feet part of iron and part of clay.	DBY Revelation 13:1 And I stood upon the sand of the sea; and I saw a beast rising out of the sea, having **ten horns and seven heads**, and upon its horns **ten diadems**, and upon its heads names of blasphemy. [*Notice* this system has ten crowns or diadems on its heads; one for each nation.]	DBY Revelation 13:2 And the beast which I saw was like to a **leopardess**, and its feet as of a **bear**, and its mouth as a **lion's mouth**; and the dragon gave to it his power, and his throne, and great authority;	DBY Daniel 7:1 In the first year of Belshazzar king of Babylon, Daniel saw a dream and visions of his head upon his bed: then he wrote the dream; he told the sum of the matters. 2 Daniel spoke and said, I saw in my vision by night, and behold, the four winds of the heavens broke forth upon the great sea. 3 And **four great beasts** came up from the sea, different one from another.	DBY Daniel 7:17 These **great beasts, which are four, are four kings**, {that} shall arise out of the earth.	
First Kingdom; First Head Babylonian Empire						
DBY Daniel 2:32 This image's head was of fine **gold**, its breast and its arms of silver, its belly and its thighs of brass, DBY Daniel 2:37 Thou, O king [Nebuchadnezzar of Babylon, v.1], art a **king of kings**, unto whom the God of the heavens hath given the kingdom, the power, and the strength, and the glory;	DBY Daniel 7:4 The first was like a **lion**, and had **eagle's** wings: I beheld till its wings were plucked; and it was lifted up from the earth, and made to stand upon two feet as a man, and a man's heart was given to it. [see Dan 4:33]	DBY Revelation 13:2 And the beast which I saw was like to a leopardess, and its feet as of a bear, and its mouth as a **lion's mouth**;	DBY Daniel 4:33 The same hour was the word fulfilled upon **Nebuchadnezzar**; and he was driven from men, and ate grass as oxen; and his body was bathed with the dew of heaven, till his hair grew like **eagles'** {feathers}, and his nails like birds' {claws}. 34 And at the end of the days I Nebuchadnezzar lifted up mine eyes unto the heavens, and mine understanding returned unto me, and I blessed the Most High, and I praised and honoured him that liveth for olam, whose dominion is an olam dominion, and his kingdom is from generation to generation.		
Second Kingdom; Second Head Medo- Persia Empire						
DBY Daniel 2:32 This image's head was of fine gold, its breast and its arms of **silver**, its belly and its thighs of brass, DBY Daniel 2:39 And after thee shall arise **another kingdom inferior to thee** [silver]; then another third kingdom of brass, which shall bear rule over all the earth.	DBY Daniel 8:3 And I lifted up mine eyes and saw, and behold, there stood before the river a **ram** which had two horns [for Media & Persia, Dan. 8:20]; and the two horns were high; and one was higher than the other, and the higher came up last. DBY Daniel 8:20 The ram that thou sawest having the two horns: they are the kings of	DBY Daniel 7:5 And behold, another beast, a **second**, like unto a **bear**, and it raised up itself on one side; and {it had} three ribs in its mouth between its teeth; and they said thus unto it: Arise, devour much flesh.	DBY Revelation 13:2 And the beast which I saw was like to a leopardess, and its feet as of a **bear**, and its mouth as a lion's mouth;		

		Media and Persia.					
Third Kingdom with Four heads (3rd, 4th, 5th, 6th)							
Grecian Kingdom							
DBY Daniel 2:32 This image's head was of fine gold, its breast and its arms of silver, its belly and its thighs of **brass**, DBY Daniel 2:39 And after thee shall arise another kingdom inferior to thee; then another **third kingdom of brass**, which shall bear rule over all the earth.	DBY Daniel 8:5 And as I was considering, behold, a he-goat came from the west over the face of the whole earth, and touched not the ground: and the goat had a notable horn between his eyes DBY Daniel 8:8 And the he-goat became exceeding great; but when he was become strong, the great horn was broken; and in its stead came up **four notable ones** toward the four winds of the heavens.	DBY Daniel 8:21 And the rough goat is the king of **Greece**; and the great horn that was between his eyes is the first king. DBY Daniel 8:22 Now that being broken, whereas four stood up in its stead, **four kingdoms shall stand up** out of the nation, but not with his power.	DBY Revelation 13:2 And the beast which I saw was like to a **leopardess**, and its feet as of a bear, and its mouth as a lion's mouth;	DBY Daniel 7:6 After this I saw, and behold, another, like a **leopard**, and it had four wings of a bird upon its back; and the beast had **four heads**; and dominion was given to it.			
Fourth Kingdom with Ten Kingdoms							
DBY Daniel 2:33 its legs of **iron**, its **feet** [w/ ten toes] part of iron and part of clay. DBY Daniel 2:40 And the **fourth kingdom** shall be strong as iron: forasmuch as iron breaketh in pieces and subdueth everything, and as iron that breaketh all these, so **shall it break in pieces** and bruise. DBY Daniel 2:41 And whereas thou sawest the **feet and toes**,	DBY Daniel 8:9 And out of (the) one of them came forth a **little horn**, which became exceeding great,	DBY Revelation 13:1 And I stood upon the sand of the sea; and I saw a beast rising out of the sea, having **ten horns and seven heads**, and upon its **horns ten** [had] **diadems**, [*Notice* this system has **ten** crowns or diadems on its heads; one for each nation.]	DBY Daniel 7:7 After this I saw in the night visions, and behold, a **fourth beast**, dreadful and terrible, and exceeding strong; and it had great iron teeth: it devoured and broke in pieces, and **stamped the rest with its feet**; and it was different from all the beasts that were before it;	DBY Daniel 7:20 and concerning the **ten horns** that were in its head,	DBY Daniel 7:23 He said thus: The fourth beast shall be a **fourth kingdom** upon the earth, which shall be different from all the kingdoms,		
Ten Nations to Seven Nations							
[at the 1260th Day]							
DBY Daniel 2:41 And whereas thou sawest the feet and toes, part of potter's clay, and part of iron, the kingdom shall be divided; ... the kingdom shall be **partly strong and partly fragile** [broken].	DBY Daniel 8:9 And out of (the) one of them came forth a **little horn**, which became exceeding great, toward the south, and toward the east, and toward the beauty {of the earth}. 10 And it became great, even to the host of heaven; and it cast down {some} of the host and of the stars to the ground, and trampled upon them. 11 (And he magnified {himself} even to the prince of the host, and from him the	DBY Daniel 8:23 And at the latter time of their kingdom, when the transgressors shall have come to the full, a **king of bold countenance**, and understanding riddles, shall stand up. 24 And his power shall be mighty, but not by his own power; and he shall destroy marvellously, and shall prosper, and shall practise, and shall destroy the mighty ones, and the people of the saints. 25 And through his cunning shall he cause craft to prosper in his hand; and he will magnify {himself} in his heart, and by prosperity will corrupt many; and he will stand up against the Prince of princes: but	DBY Revelation 12:3 And another sign was seen in the heaven: and behold, a great **red dragon**, having seven heads and ten horns, and on **his heads seven diadems;** [*Notice* this system has **seven** crowns or diadems on its heads; one for each nation.] DBY Revelation 13:3 and one of his heads {was} as **slain to death, and his wound of death** had been healed: and the whole earth wondered after the beast. DBY Revelation 13:4 And they did homage to **the dragon**, because *he gave the authority to the beast;* and they did homage to the beast, saying, Who {is} like to the beast? and who can make war with it? 5 And	...and it had **ten horns**. DBY Daniel 7:8 I considered the [ten] **horns**, and behold, there came up among them another, a **little horn**, before which **three of the first horns were plucked up by the roots;** and behold, in this horn were eyes like the eyes of a man, and a mouth speaking great things.	DBY Daniel 7:20 and concerning the **ten horns** that were in its head, and **the other** [little horn] that came up, and before which **three fell**: even that horn that had eyes, and a mouth speaking great things, and whose look was more imposing than its fellows. 21 I beheld, and that horn made war with the saints, and prevailed over them;	DBY Daniel 7:24 And as to the ten horns, out of this kingdom shall arise **ten kings**; and **another** [kingdom] **shall arise after them**; and he shall be different from the former, and **he shall subdue three kings** [was 10, now 7].	

continual {sacrifice} was taken away, and the place of his sanctuary was cast down. 12 And a time of trial was appointed unto the continual {sacrifice} by reason of transgression.) And it cast down the truth to the ground; and it practised and prospered.	he shall be broken without hand.	there was given to it a mouth, speaking great things and blasphemies; and there was given to it authority to pursue its career forty-two months. 6 And it opened its mouth for blasphemies against God, to blaspheme his name and his tabernacle, and those who have their tabernacle in the heaven. 7 And there was given to it to make war with the saints, and to overcome them; and there was given to it authority over every tribe, and people, and tongue, and nation;			25 And he shall speak words against the Most High, and shall wear out the saints of the most high {places}, and think to change seasons and the law; and they shall be given into his hand until a time and times and a half time.

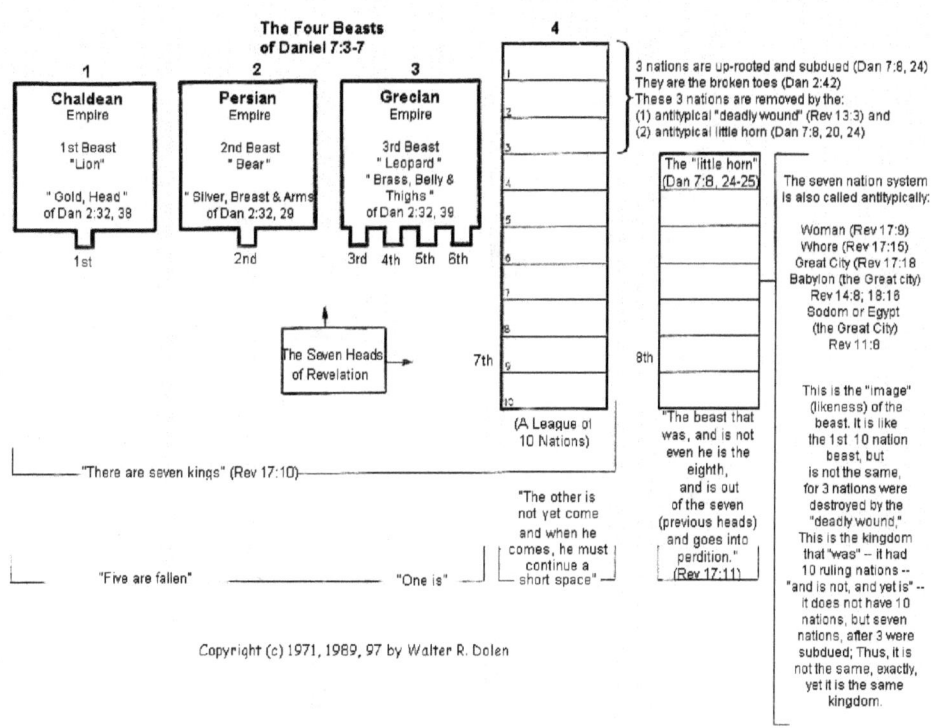

Kingdom of God

DBY Daniel 2:34 Thou sawest till a stone was cut out without hands; and it smote the image upon its feet of iron and clay, and broke them to pieces. 35 Then was the iron, the clay, the brass, the silver, and the gold broken in pieces together, and they became like the chaff of the summer threshing-floors; and the wind carried them away, and no place was found for them. And the stone that smote the image became a great mountain, and filled the whole earth. 36 This is the dream; and we will tell the interpretation of it before the king.

DBY Revelation 11:15 And the seventh angel sounded {his} trumpet: and there were great voices in the heaven, saying, **The kingdom of the world of our Lord and of his Christ is come,** and he shall reign to the ages of ages.

DBY Revelation 12:7 And there was war in the heaven: Michael and his angels went to war with the dragon. And the dragon fought, and his angels; 8

DBY Daniel 2:44 And in the days of these kings shall the **God of the heavens set up a kingdom** which shall never be destroyed; and the sovereignty thereof shall not be left to another people: it shall break in pieces and consume all these kingdoms, but itself shall stand for olam. 45 Forasmuch as thou sawest that a stone was cut out of the mountain without hands, and that it broke in pieces the iron, the brass, the clay, the silver, and the gold, --the great God hath made known to the king what shall come to pass hereafter. And the dream is certain, and the interpretation of it sure.

DBY Daniel 7:9 I beheld till thrones were set, and the **Ancient of days did sit:** his raiment was white as snow, and the hair of his head like pure wool; his throne was flames of fire, {and} its wheels burning fire. 10 A stream of fire issued and came forth from before him; thousand thousands ministered unto him, and ten thousand times ten thousand stood before him: the judgment was set, and the books were opened. 11 I beheld therefore, because of the voice of the great words that the horn spoke; I beheld till the beast was slain, and its body destroyed, and it was given up to be burned with fire.

DBY Daniel 7:14 And there was given him [Christ] dominion, and glory, and a kingdom, that all peoples, nations, and languages should serve him: his dominion is an olam dominion, which shall not pass away, and **his kingdom {that} which shall not be destroyed.**

DBY Daniel 7:27 But the kingdom and the dominion, and the greatness of **the kingdoms under the whole heavens, shall be given to the people of the saints of the most high** {places}. His kingdom is an olam kingdom, and all dominions shall serve and obey him.

and he prevailed not, nor was their place found any more in the heaven. 9 And the great dragon was cast out, the ancient serpent, he who is called Devil and Satan, he who deceives the whole habitable world, he was cast out into the earth, and his angels were cast out with him. 10 And I heard a great voice in the heaven saying, **Now is come the salvation and the power and the kingdom of our God, and the authority of his Christ**; for the accuser of our brethren has been cast out, who accused them before our God day and night:

DBY Revelation 20:6 Blessed and holy he who has part in the first resurrection: over these the second death has no power; but they shall be priests of God and of the Christ, and shall reign with him a thousand years.

DBY Revelation 21:4 And he shall wipe away every tear from their eyes; and death shall not exist any more, nor grief, nor cry, nor distress shall exist any more, for the former things have passed away. 5 And he that sat on the throne said, Behold, I make all things new. And he says {to me}, Write, for these words are true and faithful. 6 And he said to me, It is done. I am the Alpha and the Omega, the beginning and the end. I will give to him that thirsts of the fountain of the water of life freely.

Please print this document in "Landscape" mode for better results.

Copyright (c) 1970-71, 1997 by WRD

BeComingOne Church

[*Page Name*: Beast's Character]

Characteristics of the Individual Beast (1)

Individual Beast: Coming with the power of Satan

A Deceiver - A Liar - with Cunningness

1. Whose coming is according to the working of Satan in all [Satan's] power, signs, and wonders of **falsehood** and in all **deceit** of unrighteousness (2 Thessalonians 2:9, 10; Rev 13:2; Dan 8:24a)

2. He [Devil] was a murderer from the beginning, not holding to the truth, for there is no truth in him. **When he lies, he speaks his native language**, for he is a liar and the father of lies." (John 8:44)

3. And in the end of their kingdom, when the rebellion are come to the full, a king of strong presence, and skilled in **double-dealing** shall stand up.... And through his **cunningness** also he shall cause deceit to prosper in his hand (Daniel 8:23, 25)

4. And it **cast the truth to the ground**; and it practiced, and prospered (Dan 8:12)

5. And after the league made with him he shall work **deceitfully** (Dan 11:23)

6. He shall corrupt by **flatteries** (Dan 11:32) But he shall come in peaceably and obtain the kingdom by **flatteries** (Dan 11:21)

7. And the Beast... he **deceived** them (Rev 19:20) Who **deceived** them (Rev 20;10; 12:9)

8. And there was given to it a mouth, speaking great things and blasphemies [**lies about God**] (Rev 13:5)

9. It **deceives** them that dwell on the earth (Rev13:14)

World Deceived: How, Why

10. His lying wonders appeal to those destroying themselves, because they have not received the love of the truth that they may be saved, and for this reason God sends to them a working of error, that they should believe what is false, that all might be judged who have not believed the truth, but have found pleasure in unrighteousness (2 Thes 2:10-12)

11. For he shall come up, and shall become strong with a diminished people [the 7-nation Beast that came from the 10-nation Beast; diminished from 10 to 7 nations] (Dan 11:23)

12. The deceived are those that received the mark of the beast, and those that worship his image (Rev 19:20)

Egotistical: Will Place Himself as God
[As Christ fulfilled scriptures on his last day, so too will the Beast-man fulfill many of the following verses on his last day]

13. Who opposes and exalts himself on high against all called God or worshiped, so that he himself sits down in the temple of the God, **showing himself that he is God** (2 Thes 2:4) "**I am God**." (Ezek 28:2, see Hebrew text; the prince of Tyrus was a type of the Beast-man)

14. A mouth speaking great things (Dan 7:8) whose **look is greater than his fellows** (Dan 7:20)

15. He shall speak **great words against the most High** (Dan 7:25)

16. He **magnified himself** even to the prince of the host (Dan 8:11; 11:36, 37)

17. And he shall **magnify himself** in his heart (Dan 8:25)

18. He shall **stand up against the Prince of princes** (Dan 8:25)

19. And the king shall do according to his will; and **he shall exalt himself**, and **magnify himself** above every god, and shall speak marvelous things against God of gods (Dan 11:36)	
20. Neither shall he regard God of his fathers (Dan 11:37)	
21. And there was given to him a mouth, speaking great things and blasphemies.... And it opened its mouth for **blasphemies against God**, to blaspheme his name and his tabernacle (Rev 13:5, 6)	
22. And it had **two horns like a lamb** [Christ], and spoke as a dragon [Satan] (Rev 13:11)	
23. False prophet (Rev 19:20; 20 10; 13:11)	

	World's Reaction [It is the Satan inside of him that most perfectly deceives the whole world and that the world worships; he is but a reflection of what is inside of him]
	24. And all that dwell on the earth shall do it homage ... And it deceives those that dwell upon the earth (Rev 13:8, 14)
	25. Deceives the whole world (Rev 19:20; 20:3; 12:9)

Beast gets Power and wonders from Satan
26. And the Dragon [Satan] gave it [Beast] his power (Rev 13:2)
27. And his power shall be mighty, but not by his own power [but the power of Satan], and he shall prosper, and practice (Dan 8:24)
28. Thus shall he do in the most strong holds with a strange god [Satan] (Dan 11:39)

	World's Reaction
	29. And the whole earth wondered after the Beast. And they did homage to the Dragon, because he gave authority to the Beast (Rev 13:3-4)

Other Characteristics and Actions

30. He has the **number of the Beast** which is **666** (Rev 13:18), which is the number of a person, not a title, state, language, or nation.

31. Man of lawlessness, Son of Destruction (2 Thes 2:3, 8) Because he is lawless he hopes to **change the holy set times and laws** (Dan 7:25) To a lawless person, morals mean nothing. The lawless have no shame.

32. In his estate shall he **honor the god of forces** (Dan 11:38)

33. And his **power shall be mighty** (Dan 8:24), and it practiced, and prospered (Dan 8:12)

34. In prosperity (or in careless security or peace), he shall destroy many (Dan 8:25; 11:24)

35. Grows great toward the south, and toward the east, and toward the pleasant land (Dan 8:9) except the land of Edom, Moab, the chief of the children of Ammon (Dan 11:41) Remember Jerusalem, especially in the Old Testament, is the geographical center of the Bible.

36. He will stretch forth his hand also upon the countries, and the land of Egypt shall not escape. (Dan 11:42)

37. He shall enter peaceably or with ease upon the fat places of the province and he shall scatter among them the prey, and spoil, and riches (Dan 11:24) shall return into his land with great riches (Dan 11:28)

38. Shall divide the land for gain (Dan 11:39)

39. He shall enter into the glorious land [Jerusalem and surrounding area], and many [countries] shall be overthrown (Dan 11:41)

40. And he shall plant the **tabernacles of his palace** between the seas in the glorious holy mountain. (Dan 11:45)

41. He shall have **power over the treasures of gold**

and of silver (Dan 11:43) and **no one should be able to buy or sell except** he that had the mark, the name of the beast, or the number of its name. (Rev 13:17)

42. By reason of the Last War **he will take away the daily sacrifices** of the whole world, for it is with this war that the **old age will end** and the new age without suffering will begin, and it is by him that the living sacrifices of the saints will end. (See *Last War* paper; Dan 8:11, 12; 11:31)

43. And causes that those who don't worship the image [7 nations or Satan] to be killed (Rev 13:15)

Time of the Beast's Power with Satan -- 3 1/2 Years

44. There was given to him authority to pursue his career **forty-two months**. (Rev 13:5)

45. And he shall speak great things against the Most High ... and they shall be given into his hand until a **time and times and dividing of time** [3 ½ years: "time" = one year] (Dan 7:25, 8, 20, 24)

46. The **abomination that makes desolate** (the Abomination of Desolation) is set up 1290 days before the daily sacrifice is taken away (Dan 12:11); the abomination is the Beast system and individual who leads the system which is set up at first with ten nations [horns] (Dan 7:8, 20, 24; Rev 13:1; PP2#pp180), but three nations [horns] are subdued or destroyed leaving seven nations [horns] (Dan 7:8, 20, 24; Rev 13:5 "deadly wound" leaving the second beast w/ seven nations); and it was this second beast who had the deadly wound yet lived (Rev 13:3, 17:8) that had the "mouth speaking great things and blasphemies" (Rev 13:5; Dan 7:8, 20, 25) for forty two months or a time and times and dividing of time [3 ½ years]. (Rev 13:5; Dan 7:25)

So 30 days after the system of the Beast is set up, three nations are destroyed, and then the seven nation beast with the individual Beast who blasphemies God will rule for 3 ½ years or 1260 days.

47. This 1260 days or 42 months rulership of the Beast System and Individual is just before Christ and his Saints take control of the whole world. (Dan 7:25-27, 9-11; see *Beast Papers* PP2 and PP3)

Church During the 3 1/2 Years

48. Holy city shall they tread under foot **forty-two months** (Rev 11:2)

49. Holy people's power scattered for **a time, times, and a half** [3 ½ years] (Dan 12:7); woman or Church nourished for **a time, and times, and half a time** [3 ½ years] from the face of the serpent (Rev 12:14)

50. The woman or Church is fed [Spiritual food] for **1260 days** (Rev 12:7); the two witnesses teach in their **1260 days** (Rev 11:3)

At the very end, Beast fights against Christ and his Saints

51. Make war against the saints (Dan 7:21; 8:24; Rev 13:7)

52. Stand up and try to make war against the returning Christ (Dan 8:25; Rev 17:14; 19:19)

53. Sits in the temple and **calls himself God** (2 Thes 2:4; Ezek 28:2)

But

54. The **saints will prevail** (Dan 7:22, 27; Rev 11:18)

55. The Lamb or **Christ will overcome** (Dan 7:14; Rev 11:17; 17:14; 2 Thes 2:8)

---

1. Read our *Prophecy Papers* for more information not provided here; read the Greek and Hebrew scriptures if possible; Since the Beast-man is in the shadow of Satan, most scriptures that describe Satan will also describe the Beast-man.

© 1998 by Walter R. Dolen

Christ's Prediction About the End Time

- A. Sign of the End Time
- B. Last War and wars
- C. Church Persecution
- D. Great Tribulation
- E. Abomination of Desolation
- F. About the Beast & Abomination of Desolation
- G. Great Tribulation (continued)
- H. Immediately After Tribulation
- I. As in the Day of Noah

A. Sign of the End Time

DBY Mark 13:3	DBY Matthew 24:3	DBY Luke 21:7
And as he sat on the mount of Olives opposite the temple, Peter and James and John and Andrew asked him privately, 4 Tell us, when shall these things be, and what is the sign **when all these things are going to be fulfilled**? 5 And Jesus answering them began to say,	And as he was sitting upon the mount of Olives the disciples came to him privately, saying, **Tell us, when shall these things be, and what is the sign of thy coming and {the} completion of the age?** 4 And Jesus answering said to them, See that no one mislead you. 5 For many shall come in my name,	And they asked him saying, **Teacher, when then shall these things be; and what {is} the sign when these things are going to take place?** 8 And he said, See that ye be not led astray, for many shall come in my name, saying, I am {he},

Take heed lest any one mislead you. 6 For many shall come in my name, saying, It is I, and shall mislead many. 7 But when ye shall hear of wars and rumours of wars, be not disturbed, for {this} must happen, but the end is not yet.	saying, I am the Christ, and they shall mislead many. 6 But ye will hear of wars and rumours of wars. See that ye be not disturbed; for all {these things} must take place, but it is not yet the end.	and the time is drawn nigh: go ye not {therefore} after them. 9 And when ye shall hear of wars and tumults, be not terrified, for these things must first take place, but the end is not immediately.

B. The Last War / the last wars
[see PP5 & PP6]

DBY Mark 13:8	**DBY Matthew 24:7**	**DBY Luke 21:10**
For **nation shall rise up against nation**, and kingdom against kingdom; and there shall be earthquakes in {different} places, and there shall be famines and troubles: these things {are the} **beginnings of throes.**	For **nation shall rise up against nation**, and kingdom against kingdom; and there shall be famines and pestilences, and earthquakes in divers places. 8 But all these {are the} **beginning of throes.**	Then he said to them, **Nation shall rise up against nation**, and kingdom against kingdom; 11 there shall be both great earthquakes in different places, and famines and pestilences; and there shall be fearful sights and great signs from heaven.

C. Church Persecution
Before the 3 1/2 years, *during* the 3 1/2 years, and *at the End* (Rev 3:14-22; Dan 11:33-35; 12:10; Mal 3:3)
Scriptural prophecy about physical Israel in the antitype = Spiritual Israel (PP1)

DBY Mark 13:9	**DBY Matthew 24:9**	**DBY Luke 21:12**
But ye, take heed to yourselves, for they shall deliver you up to sanhedrims and to	Then shall they deliver you up to tribulation, and shall kill you; and ye will be hated of all	But before all these things they shall lay their hands upon you

synagogues: ye shall be beaten and brought before rulers and kings for my sake, for a testimony to them; 10 and the gospel must first be preached to all the nations. 11 But when they shall lead you away to deliver you up, be not careful beforehand as to what ye shall say, {nor prepare your discourse}: but whatsoever shall be given you in that hour, that speak; for ye are not the speakers, but the Holy Spirit. 12 But brother shall deliver up brother to death, and father child; and children shall rise up against parents, and cause them to be put to death. 13 And ye will be hated of all on account of my name; but he that has endured to the end, he shall be saved. the nations for my name's sake. 10 And then will many be offended, and will deliver one another up, and hate one another; 11 and many false prophets shall arise and shall mislead many; 12 and because lawlessness shall prevail, the love of the most shall grow cold; 13 but he that has endured to the end, he shall be saved. 14 And these glad tidings of the kingdom shall be preached in the whole habitable earth, for a witness to all the nations, and then shall come the end. and persecute you, delivering {you} up to synagogues and prisons, bringing {you} before kings and governors on account of my name; 13 but it shall turn out to you for a testimony. 14 Settle therefore in your hearts not to meditate beforehand {your} defence, 15 for I will give you a mouth and wisdom which all your opposers shall not be able to reply to or resist. 16 But ye will be delivered up even by parents and brethren and relations and friends, and they shall put to death {some} from among you, 17 and ye will be hated of all for my name's sake. 18 And a hair of your head shall in no wise perish. 19 By your patient endurance gain your souls.

D. Great Tribulation

There is tribulation before the end but the end is the greatest of all tribulations--**the Great Tribulation**
Abomination of Desolation / Beast -- the last 1/2 week of years of the 70 weeks of Dan 9:24-27
(Dan 9:27; 11:31; Rev 13:5; Dan 7:25; 12:7)

DBY Luke 21:20 But when ye see **Jerusalem encompassed with armies**, then know that its desolation is drawn nigh.

> [DBY Ezekiel 38:16-18] And thou shalt come up against my people Israel as a cloud to cover the land--it shall be at the end of days--and I will bring thee against my land, that the nations may know me, when I shall be hallowed in thee, O Gog, before their eyes. 17 Thus saith the Lord Jehovah: Art thou not he of whom I have spoken in old time through my servants the prophets of Israel, who prophesied in those days, for {many} years, that I would bring thee against them? 18 And it shall come to pass in that day, in the day when Gog shall come against the land of Israel, saith the Lord Jehovah, {that} my fury shall come up in my face....
>
> [DBY Revelation 16:14,16] for they are {the} spirits of demons, doing signs; which go out to the kings of the whole habitable world to gather them together to the war of {that} great day of God the Almighty.... 16 And he gathered them together to the place called in Hebrew, Armagedon.
>
> [Revelation 19:19] And I saw the beast and the kings of the earth and their armies gathered together to make war against him that sat upon the horse, and against his army. [Revelation 20:9] And they went up on the breadth of the earth, and surrounded the camp of the saints and the beloved city: and fire came down {from God} out of the heaven and devoured them.]

These armies are some of the armies coming against Jerusalem (see PP5 & PP6)

E. Abomination of Desolation
[see PP2]

DBY Mark 13:14	DBY Matthew 24:15	DBY 2 Thessalonians 2:3
But when ye shall see the **abomination**	When therefore ye shall see the	Let not any one

of desolation standing where it should not, (he that reads let him consider {it},)	**abomination of desolation**, which is spoken of through Daniel the prophet, **standing in holy place**, (he that reads let him understand,)	deceive you in any manner, because {it will not be} unless the apostasy have first come, and **the man of sin** have been revealed, the son of perdition; 4 who opposes and exalts himself on high against all called God, or object of veneration; so that **he himself sits down in the temple of God, showing himself that he is God**.

DBY Daniel 12:11 And from the time that the continual {sacrifice} is taken away, and the **abomination that makes desolate** set up,[(1)] {there shall be} a thousand, two hundred, and ninety days.

DBY Daniel 11:31 And forces shall stand on his part, and they shall profane the sanctuary, the fortress, and shall take away the continual {sacrifice}, and they shall place [(2)] the **abomination that makes desolate**.

F. About Beast and the Abomination of Desolation

[As we see in the Prophecy Papers 2 (PP2), there is a system of the Beast and there is a Beast-man, who is the anti-Christ. You may need to study PP2 first to understand the following.]

This system of the Beast is actually the system of the abomination of desolation, because it is through this system's power (given to the Beast-man) that the world will be destroyed. (Dan 7:11, 24-25; Rev 19:20; see PP5)

This abomination is given to the world on the 1290th day before Christ returns. (Dan 12:11; PP2)

The **abomination of desolation is also the abominable**

person, who is the little horn that will speak for the system of the Beast. He is the horn/king/leader with eyes and mouth speaking great things and blasphemy against the most high and his saints. (Dan 8:9-10; 7:8, 11a, 20-21-, 24-25; Rev 13:5-7; pp171ff) He is the man with the number six-hundred and sixty six (666) that can be calculated for his name ("number of his name").

Beast-man shares power with the ten nations: He is the Beast-man who is connected and has power with the **ten horns/kings (toes) or nations** (PP2; Rev 17:12; 13:1; Dan 2:41-43; 7:7-8, 20, 24) He has power **with** them only for a short period of time. (Rev 17:10, 12)

30 Days is the short time: The short time or the "one hour" that the ten nations have power **with** the Beast-man is for 30 days or 1290 days minus 1260 days. (Rev 17:10, 12)

After this short time the Beast-man is given the full power of the system to speak for the whole group of nations. (Rev 17:13, 17; 13:12, 15, 5; Dan 7:8, 20, 24-25) Since the power of the Beast-system is given to the Beast-man (the little horn) for 1260 days or 42 months (Rev 13:5; Dan 7:8, 25), he thus speaks for the system; he is the eyes and mouth of the Beast-system for 1260 days. (Rev 13:5; Dan 7:25)

Beast-man given this power of the nations after three of the ten are "subdued": But the Beast-man is only given this power after three of the ten nations are "plucked up" or after three "fell" or after "he shall subdue three kings." (Dan 7:8, 20, 24)

Three "subdued" by a deadly wound of war: The removal of these three nations is the "deadly wound" to the seventh head. (Rev 13:3; 17:9-10) This deadly wound is a wound of war ("sword," Rev 13:14), with nuclear weapons and missiles (Rev 13:13).

Beast-man "subdues" the three: The one who will subdue three kings (Dan 7:24),

- is the "little horn" of Daniel 7:8,11, 20, 24; 8:9,
- is the king of Daniel 8:23-25,
- is the king of Daniel 11:36-45,
- is the abomination of Daniel 11:31; 12:11 and Matthew

24:15,
- is the "man of sin" or the "son of perdition" of 2 Thessalonians 2:3-12,
- is the mouth or spokesman or leader of the Beast system (Rev 13:5-6; Dan 7:8, 20; 24-25),
- and is the false prophet or lamb or anti-Christ of Revelation who speaks for Satan the Dragon (Rev 13:11-18, 4; 16:13; 20:2), who has the power to kill and destroy, and who has the number of his name that calculates to six-hundred and sixty-six (666).

During this Beast-man's 1260 day sole rule he will magnify himself in his mind until he, at the end, will actually think he is God, and will say he is God. (Dan 8:25; 7:8, 11 25; 11:37; 2 Thes 2:4) At that time, at the end of the 1260 days, he will be destroyed, and the Kingdom of God will take over the kingdoms of men. (Dan 2:44; 7:11, 25-27; 8:25; PP5, PP6) It is about that time (at the end of the 1260 days, when the Beast-man says he himself is God) that Jesus spoke about when he said in Matthew 24:15:

> "When therefore ye shall see the abomination of desolation, which is spoken of through Daniel the prophet, standing in (the) holy place, (he that reads let him understand,)"

G. Great Tribulation (Continued)

DBY Mark 13:14b	DBY Matthew 24:16	DBY Luke 21:21
then let those in Judaea flee to the mountains; 15 and him that is upon the housetop not come down into the house, nor enter {into it} to take away anything out of his house; 16 and him that is in the field not return back to take his garment. 17 But woe to those that are with child and to those that give suck in those	then let those who are in Judaea flee to the mountains; 17 let not him that is on the house come down to take the things out of his house; 18 and let not him that is in the field turn back to take his garment. 19 But woe to those that are with child, and those that give suck in those days. 20 But pray that your flight may not be in winter time nor on sabbath: 21 for then	Then let those who are in Judaea flee to the mountains, and those who are in the midst of it depart out, and those who are in the country not enter into it; 22 for these are days of avenging, that all the things that are written may be accomplished. 23 But woe to them that are with child

days! 18 And pray that it may not be in winter time; 19 **for those days shall be distress such as there has not been the like since {the} beginning of creation** which God created, until now, and never shall be; 20 *and if {the} Lord had not cut short those days, no flesh should have been saved*; but on account of the elect whom he has chosen, he has cut short those days. 21 And then if any one say to you, Lo, here {is} the Christ, or Lo, there, believe {it} not. 22 For false Christs and false prophets will arise, and give signs and wonders to deceive, if possible, even the elect.	shall there be **great tribulation**, such as has not been from {the} beginning of {the} world until now, nor ever shall be; 22 *and if those days had not been cut short, no flesh had been saved*; but on account of the elect those days shall be cut short. 23 Then if any one say to you, Behold, here is the Christ, or here, believe {it} not. 24 For there shall arise false Christs, and false prophets, and shall give great signs and wonders, so as to mislead, if possible, even the elect. 25 Behold, I have told you beforehand. 26 If therefore they say to you, Behold, he is in the desert, go not forth; behold, {he is} in the inner chambers, do not believe {it}.	and to them who give suck in those days, for there shall be **great distress** upon the land and wrath upon this people. 24 And they shall fall by the edge of the sword, and be led captive into all the nations; and Jerusalem shall be trodden down of {the} nations until {the} times of {the} nations be fulfilled.

H. Immediately *After* the Great Tribulation, then Christ comes

DBY Mark 13:24 But in those days, *after* that distress, the sun shall be darkened and the moon shall not give its light; 25 and the	**DBY Matthew 24:29** But **immediately *after*** the tribulation of those days the sun shall be darkened, and the moon not give her light, and the stars shall	**DBY Luke 21:25** And there shall be signs in sun and moon and stars, and upon the earth distress of nations in perplexity {at}

stars of heaven shall be falling down, and the powers which are in the heavens shall be shaken; 26 and **then shall they see the Son of man coming** in clouds with great power and glory; 27 and then shall he send **his angels and shall gather together his elect** from the four winds, from end of earth to end of heaven.	fall from heaven, and the powers of the heavens shall be shaken. 30 And **then shall appear the sign of the Son of man in heaven**; and then shall all the tribes of the land lament, and they shall see the Son of man coming on the clouds of heaven with power and great glory. 31 And he shall send **his angels** with a great sound of trumpet, and they **shall gather together his elect from the four winds**, from {the one} extremity of {the} heavens to {the other} extremity of them.	the roar of the sea and rolling waves, 26 men ready to die through fear and expectation of what is coming on the habitable earth, for the powers of the heavens shall be shaken. 27 And then shall they see the Son of man coming in a cloud with power and great glory. 28 But when these things begin to come to pass, look up and lift up your heads, because your redemption draws nigh.
DBY Mark 13:28 But learn the parable from the **fig-tree**: when its branch already becomes tender and puts forth the leaves, ye know that the summer is near. 29 Thus also ye, when ye see these things happening, know that it is near, at the doors.	**DBY Matthew 24:32** But learn the parable from the **fig-tree**: When already its branch becomes tender and produces leaves, ye know that the summer is near. 33 Thus also ye, when ye see all these things, know that it is near, at the doors.	
	DBY Matthew 24:27 For **as the lightning** goes forth from the east and shines to the west, **so shall be the coming of the Son of man**. 28 {For} wherever the carcase is, there will be gathered the eagles.	**DBY Luke 17:24** For as **the lightning** shines which lightens from {one end} under heaven to {the other end} under heaven, thus **shall the Son of**

	Note: As quickly as lightning strikes, will be how quickly Christ will come. He doesn't come in stages, but all at once, as quick as lightning. **Note:** See the study about the fire that comes at the same time Christ returns.>>	**man be in his day**. 25 But first he must suffer many things and be rejected of this generation. 26 And as it took place in the days of Noah, thus also shall it be in the days of the Son of man: 27 they ate, they drank, they married, they were given in marriage, until the day that Noah entered into the ark, and the flood came and destroyed all {of them}; 28 and in like manner as took place in the days of Lot: they ate, they drank, they bought, they sold, they planted, they built; 29 but **on the day that Lot went out from Sodom, it rained fire and sulphur from heaven, and destroyed all {of them}: 30 after this {manner} shall it be in the day that the Son of man is revealed**.
		DBY Luke 17:31 In that day, he who shall be on the housetop, and his

		stuff in the house, let him not go down to take it away; and he that is in the field, let him likewise not return back. 32 Remember the wife of Lot. 33 Whosoever shall seek to save his life shall lose it, and whosoever shall lose it shall preserve it. 34 I say to you, In that night there shall be two {men} upon one bed; one shall be seized and the other shall be let go. 35 Two {women} shall be grinding together; the one shall be seized and the other shall be let go. 36 {Two men shall be in the field; the one shall be seized and the other let go.}
	>>> **Note:** Christ comes so quickly that no one has time to even get down from the roof, or to come back in from the field.	
	DBY Matthew 24:28 {For} wherever the carcase is, there will be gathered the eagles.	**DBY Luke 17:37** And answering they say to him, Where, Lord? And he said to them, Where the body {is}, there the eagles will be gathered together.

I. As in the Day of Noah

The End will come at once, as the flood in Noah's day and the destruction of Sodom:

As an overrunning flood (Nah 1:8); speedy riddance (Zeph 1:18); a moment (Ps 73:18);

one day (Isa 10:17); in an instant, suddenly (Isa 29:5); destroy and devour at once (Isa 42:14); avenge them speedily (Lk 18:8; Eccl 9:12); one day (rev 18:8); as a whirlwind (Ps 58:9-10); one hour (Rev 18:10, 19); as a flood (Dan 9:26); one day (Isa 47:9); suddenly (1 Thes 5:3); swiftly, speedily (Joel 3:4; Mal 3:5)

The transgressors destroyed together:

(ps 37:38; Isa 1:28; Jer 51:48-49)

Evil shall not raise again; perpetual peace after the instant destruction:

they shall not learn war anymore (Isa 2:4; Mic 4:3); violence no more (Isa 60:18); affliction not to rise a second time (Nah 1:9); shall not see evil anymore (Zeph 3:15); hail will sweep away the lies (Isa 28:17); they shall not hurt nor destroy in all God's holy mountain or kingdom (Isa 11:9); in all God's holy mountain or kingdom, no oppressor shall pass through them anymore (Zech 9:8); God's kingdom and peace will not depart or be removed (Isa 54:10)

At Christ's coming all the kingdoms will be his (Rev 11:15), and there will be no more war as the above scriptures prove.

Complied in 1970 by Walter R. Dolen, posted to the Net in 1997

with additional material on the abomination added on April 11, 1999

BeComingOne Church

---

1. "To give" Strong's # 5414

2. "To give" Strong's # 5414

Year Dates	Details of <u>Tentative</u> Dates See the *Chronology Papers,* Part 4 (CP4) for more details.	Events
0028 AD 0031 AD	**14th of Nisan (Aviv),** on Wednesday **Crucifixion of JC** was near the end of the 4th day of the week (Wed.), within the 4th millennium, near the very end of the 4th millennium. (Re: Gen. 1:14-19 [separating light from darkness]; Psa 90:4; 2 Pet 3:8; Rev 20:6,4) [**Date sources**: Using "SkySafari 4 Plus" and "AstroPixels - Moon Phases- 0001 to 0100"]	**Crucifixion of JC**
	17th of Nisan (Aviv), Saturday, shortly before sunset on this day.	**Resurrection of JC**
	Sept-Oct Last day of the 6th month of Moses' calendar	**End of 4th millennium**
	Sept-Oct First day of the 7th month of Moses' calendar	**Beginning of 5th millennium**
		1335th Day
		1290th Day
		1260th Day
		1150th Day

Year Dates	Details of <u>Tentative</u> Dates See the *Chronology Papers,* Part 4 (CP4) for more details.	Events
2028 AD 2031 AD	**May or June** **Pentecost** within the 6th millennium, near the very end of the millennium the time of the **1st Resurrection** (Rev 20:5-6; NM16) **Note:** Pentecost date is a Sunday, which according to the biblical calendar begins on Saturday at sunset to Sunday at sunset; Pentecost date depends on the dating of Nisan — the first month of Moses' calendar in Exodus, which is dependent upon when the first crop was ready to be harvested.	**1st Resurrection of the Church** After Christ's Resurrection, which was the first of the total of three resurrections
	Sept-Oct [Last day for the 6th month]	**End of 6th millennium**
	Sept-Oct [first day of the 7th month of Moses' religious/agriculture calendar] **Rosh Hashanah**	**Beginning of 7th millennium** The 1000 years mentioned in the book of Revelation

Why tentative dates?

Days start at sunset on the Jewish calendar initiated by Moses; The above dates are based on the year Christ died, which we figure is 28 or 31 AD. We add 2000 years to find His return date. More info for this count is found in our *Chronology Papers* book. All dates are based on the time of the day in Jerusalem. **Dates herein can only be confirmed on the 1260th day before Christ returns: this day is when the 10 nation Beast system is turned into 7 nation Beast system.**

See also CP4 = *Chronology Papers,* chap 4 I NM16= *New Mind Papers,* chap 16

Notes